NEWS VALUES

JACK FULLER

NEWS VALUES

IDEAS FOR AN INFORMATION AGE

UNIVERSITY OF CHICAGO PRESS
Chicago & London

The University of Chicago Press, Chicago 60637
The University of Chicago Press, Ltd., London
© 1996 by The University of Chicago
All rights reserved. Published 1996
Paperback edition 1997
Printed in the United States of America
05 04 03 02 01 00 99 98 97   2 3 4 5

ISBN: 0-226-26879-9 (cloth)
ISBN: 0-226-26880-2 (paperback)

Library of Congress Cataloging-in-Publication Data

Fuller, Jack.
    News values : ideas for an information age / Jack Fuller.
        p.   cm.
    Includes bibliographical references and index.
    1. Press—Objectivity.   2. Journalism—Moral and ethical
aspects.   I. Title.
    PN4784.O24F85   1996
    070.4—dc20   95-33951
                                                           CIP

FOR SUSIE PHILIPSON

CONTENTS

ACKNOWLEDGMENTS

THIS BOOK CAME INTO BEING BECAUSE SUSAN PHILIPSON persuaded me that I could and should write it. I want to thank Morris Philipson, John Tryneski, and all the others at the University of Chicago Press for their advice and encouragement. Thanks also to Wayne Booth, Michael Janeway, Norval Morris, Howard Tyner, Doug Kneeland, John Crewdson, Robert McLean, David Hiller, Joseph Thornton, Sanford Ungar, and Bryce Nelson for their helpful suggestions. I am also deeply grateful to my wife, Alyce, and children, Tim and Kate, for many things. Their patience is only one of them.

INTRODUCTION

FOR SEVERAL DECADES NEWSPAPERS HAVE SUFFERED the erosion of their audience by faster and flashier electronic media. Once the mass medium of urban America, metropolitan daily newspapers today face the deterioration of the cities they serve and the fragmentation of their markets through media such as suburban newspapers and direct-mail firms that can deliver more tightly targeted messages. The emerging new information delivery system that came to be known as the "information superhighway" offers great opportunities, but only at the risk of breakneck speed.

In light of all this, some people predict the death of newspapers as we know them. Others say a new age of newspapers is dawning. What we can be sure of is that the audience will develop new habits in response to the new choices offered it. Naturally, this unsettles the stewards of the existing order, who may see nothing but a slow, grinding process of decline, not only in the commercial value placed on the work they do but also in the larger values it serves.

In times of rapid and dramatic change it is important to be clear about the basics. The essays in this book represent my effort to understand the underlying public values a newspaper serves and the implications of those values for journalists' behavior. I aim to examine basic questions: What claim of truth do we make in our news columns? What disciplines should we follow in order to live up to this truth claim? How much should newspapers reflect the beliefs of the communities they serve? How much should they provide moral leadership? What is the proper relationship between journalism and marketing? Journalism and profit-making?

For the most part I have tried to locate the news values in the desires and interests of the American audience. I don't mean to suggest that they have no foundation in moral and political theory. But I am certain that the only way technological change can threaten the moral basis of what we do is if it undermines newspapers' commercial position. So the news values will be most durable if we find support for them in the people they are supposed to serve.

It is often said that a society gets the press it deserves. I am not sure about that. But I know that in the end it gets a press no better than it wants. Though I am optimistic that people want us to act in accord with our better angels,[1] they can be tempted. There are always snakes ready to do the job. If the public is led to accept shoddy or dangerous goods, the public will prevail. So it is up to the newspapers to make news values compelling enough that people will see in them their deeper interests.

The essays in this book fall into three parts. Part One examines the nature of the truth claim newspapers make and the disciplines journalists must follow to have credibility. Then it discusses the use of deception and other practices that also raise ethical concerns and affect credibility. Finally, it analyzes the newspaper's relationship with the community and what this has to do with the truth disciplines.

Part Two discusses matters of expression. It begins with the relationship between the journalist and the reader, examining how the study of rhetoric and marketing can help the journalist. Then it discusses the tension between the truth disciplines and certain literary techniques that have come into increasing use by journalists.

Part Three looks into the future of journalism. It first discusses the increasing complexity of the issues newspapers cover and the challenge this presents to reporters and editors.

It examines the relationship between the public's lack of interest in public affairs and the decline in interest in newspapers, suggesting some things newspapers can do to help reverse the trend. It then discusses the relationship between the news values and the commercial values of newspapers run by modern corporations. Finally, it attempts to identify the key issues that will shape the future of newspapers and the new interactive electronic medium that is now just beginning to develop.

Before becoming a publisher, I worked as a writer and editor for nearly thirty years. This exposed me to the sloppy, self-satisfied way journalists often talk about what they do. It also put me into intimate contact with the way readers respond to a newspaper's behavior. The unscientific observations I have made over the years give rise to the thoughts that follow. I have tried to fit what I have seen and heard into a coherent framework that relates to the larger world of social thought.

This book does not attempt to deal with the value issues raised by all news media. It deals with newspapers. This is because I have only recently begun to gain any experience with television journalism. I've never walked in the shoes of a TV or radio correspondent or news director, so I can't presume to explain the distinctive strengths and problems of their medium. Some may be quite similar to newspapers', but others are probably very different.

I do not deal, except in passing, with the economic structure of the new interactive medium. Today the audience pays only part of the cost of the news it purchases; advertisers pay the rest. How advertisers will use the new medium and what role newspapers can play in that relationship will determine a great deal about the future of news delivery. The economic model is still in the earliest stage of development, but one thing is clear: getting an audience will be the *sine qua non* of success. So it makes sense to take the question of readership first.

For ease of reference I have used examples that are readily available in books whenever possible. Footnotes are for attribution only, and I have tried to keep them to a minimum. At various places in the text I have made up examples of certain kinds of writing. These appear in italics to indicate to the reader not to take them literally or expect attribution. Some personal anecdotes relate to matters about which I cannot decently give all the details—for example, references to things I learned serving as a lawyer in the U.S. Justice Department. Hence, some people to whom I refer must remain anonymous. But I have tried to live by the rules I have prescribed and do not rely on the veracity of any source of information to whom I do not make attribution by name.

(PART ONE)

THE FUNDAMENTAL
DISCIPLINES

(*one*)
THE TRUTH OF THE NEWS

THE THOUGHT THAT NEWS REPORTS SHOULD BE TRUE
dawned on journalists only recently. Until well into the twentieth century, most American newspapers propagandized on
nearly every page. This sometimes meant strict adherence to a
political party line. Sometimes it meant reflecting the personal
and often eccentric views of a single owner. People selected
their newspaper or newspapers in full knowledge of what they
would find there. In fact, most readers probably chose papers *for*
the slant.

During the first decades of this century, the Progressive
Era ideal of disinterested judgment in the public interest took
hold of important figures in journalism. Later, university training of journalists became more commonplace, as did the idea
that news was a profession rather than a trade. The number of
newspapers serving individual communities began to decline.
Surviving papers passed out of the control of the founders and
their families and into the hands of the professional managers
of publicly held corporations. All this led to the sense that journalism should aspire to some higher standard of veracity. Publishers had always claimed to be printing the truth, the whole
truth, and nothing but the truth, but suddenly journalists began
taking this literally. It was an important step, and a salutary one

for the quality of public discussion. But to this day many of its implications remain inadequately examined.

This is not surprising, since most news people talk as if they think the examined life is hardly worth living. They consider themselves skeptics, but this is not so much a matter of philosophy as of style. Even among themselves, they rarely discuss the nature of the claims of truth they make in their work or the basis of the disciplines they follow in furtherance of these claims. And when they do think about the underpinning of their reports, they usually get no further than debating a two-source rule for unattributed statements or repeating the catechism of Chicago's legendary institute of street wisdom, the City News Bureau: "If your mother says she loves you, check it out."

The considerations that determine when journalists feel free to print a statement as fact typically do not take the form of written rules. They vary from news organization to news organization, passing down the generations by the process of example. And they are sometimes utterly self-contradictory. The same editor may reject one story for want of neutrality and another for insufficient authority of judgment.

The issues of fact journalists have to decide cover an enormous range. Often a newspaper must act in the face of quivering uncertainty, as when it announces which candidate has won an election before the vote has been tallied. (A mistake can leave a lasting mark, as the "Dewey Defeats Truman" headline marked the *Chicago Tribune* for decades. To this day the *Tribune* has an unwritten policy that it is better to be last than wrong.) A newspaper sometimes must even decide when to call a man dead, for example in the chaotic aftermath of an assassination attempt or when a totalitarian society hides its leader's demise. It has to attempt to state fact through the smoke and thunder of war and recognize the error that often hides in what Clausewitz called the "vividness of transient impressions."[1]

At the other end of the scale, a newspaper must decide when to believe the representation of a letter writer that he has given his real name, or of a person calling in from a community arts group that a concert will take place on a given day at a given time, or of a police officer that a burglary took place at a particular address. Even these decisions can involve great uncertainty. When I was about to take my turn at City News Bureau as a lad of eighteen, my father (a City News veteran) gave me this bit of advice: "When a fire is burning, you're going to be the only one who cares how the dead spelled their names." (Or at least he said words to that effect, if my memory serves me correctly.)

At another level of complexity, journalists make judgments about when to report the statements of authorities. We commonly rely blindly on scientists, economists, engineers, and other experts, all the while purporting to be ruthlessly skeptical. And the judgment journalists make concerning which government statements to pass on to the public as fact—which to report as debatable and which simply to disregard—stands near the very center of the press's social purpose in a self-governing society.

WHAT IS NEWS?

What is the proper standard of truth for the news? To answer that, one must first come to some clear understanding of what news is. Even at its most presumptuous, the news does not claim to be timeless or universal. It represents at most a provisional kind of truth, the best that can be said quickly. Its ascription is modest, so modest that some of the most restless and interesting journalists have had trouble making any claim of truth at all.

In *Let Us Now Praise Famous Men*, James Agee, then a writer for *Fortune* Magazine, savaged the whole idea of journalistic truth:[2]

Who, what, where, when and why (or how) is the primal cliche and complacency of journalism: but I do not wish to appear to speak favorably of journalism. I have never yet seen a piece of journalism which conveyed more than the slightest fraction of what any even moderately reflective and sensitive person would mean and intend by those inachievable words, and that fraction itself I have never seen clean of one or another degree of patent, to say nothing of essential falsehood. Journalism is true in the sense that everything is true to the state of being and to what conditioned and produced it (which is also, but less so perhaps, a limitation of art and science): but that is about as far as its value goes. . . . [J]ournalism is not to be blamed for this; no more than a cow is to be blamed for not being a horse.

Even accepting that news is not the kind of truth that would meet the rigors of science or the clarity of revealed religious insight, there is still too little agreement on how to define it. Though journalists might agree the beast is a cow, they will debate what breed and how much milk it can produce. Look at one day's newspapers from a dozen cities and you will find, even correcting for local factors, no consensus.

One might be tempted to say that news is anything that news organizations report. In fact, this definition has adherents among a few journalists whose fascination with power leads them to overestimate their own. It also appeals to certain outsiders, such as those who encourage the media to do more uplifting stories in the expectation that they might revise grim reality as easily as they revise a sentence.

But the definition of news does not have to be so empty in order to explain most variations in coverage. Most respectable journalists on American newspapers would, I think, roughly agree with this statement: News is a report of what a news organization has recently learned about matters of some significance or interest to the specific community that news organization serves.

This narrows the debate over the news value of any particular item but does not lead to unanimity. The *New York Times* may consider a vote in Congress on free trade to be the most important story of the day while the *New York Daily News* leads with a deadly fire in the Bronx. This is because of each newspaper's understanding of the community of readers it serves and, perhaps, because of differing judgments about what is significant.

There are some papers, to be sure, that do not seem to be concerned with the element of significance at all. Such a paper would always go with a sex scandal over a coup attempt in the Soviet Union. Most contemporary journalists would scoff at this as pandering, but the honest ones have to say that they, too, take account of the pull of basic (even base) human curiosity; the difference is whether any consideration of larger interests comes into play.

What is significant will always be a matter of debate, but in general the evaluation should turn on the foreseeable consequences. Significance and interest provide separate bases for calling an event or piece of information news, and either may be sufficient. No matter how few people were interested in reading about strategic arms limitation talks, the enormous importance of these negotiations to the future of the planet made them extremely newsworthy. And no matter how insignificant Michael Jordan's performance in minor-league baseball may have been to the history of the United States, the deep popular interest in it justified extensive coverage.

The Fundamental Biases

My proposed definition of news includes several elements that are not wholly subjective (though this does not mean they are unambiguous): timeliness, interest for a given community, significance. These look beyond the journalists' personal preferences outward to phenomena in the world that can be discussed, if not measured.

The elements of the definition also suggest some ways in which the journalist's report of reality is likely to be fundamentally biased.

First, journalism emphasizes the recent event or the recently discovered fact at the expense of that which occurred before or had already been known Journalists recognize this bias and talk about the need to put "background" information into their pieces. But commonly the internal logic of reporting puts "background" information very much in the background and tolerates little more of it than is absolutely necessary to permit the reader to make some sense of the new material. From time to time a newspaper may go back and attempt to tell about an event or issue comprehensively, but this is very special treatment. The bias of immediacy is the rule.

Second, the journalist has a bias in favor of information

that interests his audience. This helps explain the favorite complaint about news—that it accentuates the negative. People's curiosity shows a tropism for misfortune. Disaster always becomes the talk of a community in a way that good fortune less commonly does. Trouble touches some people's empathy and others' sense of doom. Fear and anger operate strongly at greater distances than love, so bad news travels farther. One might delight to hear that the daughter of someone he knew had just received a prestigious scholarship, but he would shudder at the brutal murder of a stranger's child a continent away.

The bias of interest also means that the audience's blind spots will tend to be blind spots in the news. If people are generally indifferent about a particular subject—say international trade talks such as GATT—the journalist knows that it will be very difficult to make them pay attention to it, regardless of how important it may be in their lives. Whole areas of inquiry go years, decades without attention in the news until they become involved in an event that captures people's imagination. The engineering of bridges receives scant notice until a large span collapses. Human retrovirology meant nothing to the general population until the scourge of AIDS. Even disciplines that find themselves more commonly in the news—economics, law, medicine—are lit up piecemeal, depending on the fascination of the day. The Phillips curve in economics reaches public print when in defiance of it inflation and unemployment both begin to run high. Even an obscure field of law such as admiralty might get an examination in the news when something of sufficient drama happens upon the high seas. We learn everything we never wanted to know about the human colon when a president has part of his removed.

Walter Lippmann described the press as a searchlight that restlessly prowls across the expanses, never staying on any feature for very long.[3] Actually, human curiosity is the searchlight. We journalists just go where it points.

Finally, there is a bias toward what occurs close to the audience's community. Often this manifests itself as a simple matter of geography. A *National Lampoon* parody of a hometown newspaper called the *Dacron Republican-Democrat* some years back had a page one headline that read: "Two Dacron Women Feared Missing in Volcanic Disaster." The drop head read: "Japan Destroyed."[4]

Community is not always defined by physical proximity. Communities of interest have newspapers, too, and the list of publications includes more than the trade press. Consider, for example, the *Wall Street Journal* and the *New York Times*. Both have specialized audiences and are edited to satisfy their interests. *USA Today* also appeals to a distinct public—the business traveler away from home—and this explains many of the editing choices it makes, which would be foolish for a metropolitan daily newspaper with an audience that has a much different set of shared interests.

The bias of community provides an answer to a snobbish question one often hears: Why don't other newspapers pay as much attention to international affairs as the *New York Times* does? The *Times* recognizes that for much of its audience the world is the pertinent community of interest. A disproportionate part of its readership engages directly in international business and public policy. Since it is circulated nationally, the *Times* becomes a kind of local newspaper for this community (and can be as provincial about matters outside its territory as any other paper; just try to get guidance from the *Times* about the best easy-listening CDs or religious TV shows). There are not enough people in most cities who are deeply engaged in international affairs to command strong international coverage in their metropolitan dailies, though in certain centers such as Los Angeles, Washington, D.C., and Chicago the audience is large enough to support a substantial foreign-news commitment by the local papers, and in others such as Miami there is enough interest in one part of the world to require the newspaper to make a large commitment of space and attention to it.

The element of significance in the definition of news does not necessarily introduce a bias. Rather it might be said to be the heading under which to group all other biases. These may arise out of the social circumstances of journalists, the imperatives of the economic market on their news organizations, the culture from which a journalist comes, or the larger intellectual currents of the times: interesting issues, but I do not mean to pursue them here, as they do not distinguish observational bias among journalists from the bias of any other observer.

Later chapters will discuss in much greater depth the relationships between news and the audience and between news and the interests of a self-governing community as well as the reasons journalists define news the way they do. For the moment, though, suffice it to note that the biases that arise out of the definition of news sharply restrict whatever truth claim journalism makes, narrowing its angle of vision and establishing the qualities of the lens.

What is the standard of truth to which the news ought to aspire? A report that meets the criteria of timeliness, interest to a community, and significance may be more truthful or less so. It may reflect reality or show it on a skew. Once again, journalists tend to look at this practically rather than philosophically. And they have suggested over the years several ways of describing the disciplines to which they adhere in order to correct against bias and maintain a proper relationship with the truth.

ACCURACY, ACCURACY, ACCURACY

When nineteenth-century New York publisher Joseph Pulitzer made "Accuracy! Accuracy!! Accuracy!!!" his motto,[5] he meant the small things: names, ages, and addresses. Like other press barons of his day, he committed his share of sins against the larger truths. Nonetheless, his emphatic insistence upon the smaller ones demonstrated a great deal of practical wisdom: Get the little things wrong and readers will not trust you to get the big things right.

And so before going into more subtle issues, it is worth spending some time in a realm of knowledge where there isn't much question about what truth means. Not that everything is perfectly transparent even at this level. Writers sometimes face ambiguity about how to express facts that are easily verifiable. Does one call a married woman Ms. if she prefers it that way, or does the newspaper have a general style on married names? Should the cause of a person's death be described as AIDS or the opportunistic condition that was the more immediate cause of his demise? When a building carries a vanity address—One First National Plaza, One Magnificent Mile—should it be assigned a number on the street that passes by it? In most instances a convention of some kind designates proper usage, and it is possible to verify the simplest facts through sources virtually anybody would agree are authoritative—telephone records, county files, Dun & Bradstreet.

Journalism's unacknowledged shame is how often it fails to live up to Pulitzer's standard even with respect to the most commonplace details. Nearly everyone who has ever been close to a news event has had the experience of finding the report flawed in the simple things. Susan Jones is an associate professor, not an assistant professor. John Smith is the chief operating officer and not chief executive officer of Widget Company. It is Widget Company, not Widget Corporation; Lincoln Street, not Lincoln Avenue. The burglar got in by the back window, not through the basement door. It's Diane, not Dianne.

There are as many reasons for these errors as there are occasions: sloppiness, mishearing, misstatement, mischief. But the reader of the news does not care about reasons any more than the driver of a new automobile cares why his door handle came loose. Error is the journalist's responsibility, regardless of the cause.

The rate of error is a long-term problem of the first magnitude for news organizations. Author Michael Crichton makes the comparison between the media's failures and the quality problem American industry has had to face under the stimulus of increased foreign competition. In the case of the American media, Crichton argues, the reckoning will come not from abroad but as a result of new technology that will vastly increase the reader's choices of what to read. When anybody can have any information source he wants at the touch of a keypad, the reader will not settle for shoddy goods:[6]

More and more, people understand that they pay for information. Online databases charge by the minute. As the link between payment and information becomes more explicit, consumers will naturally want better information. They'll demand it, and they'll be willing to pay for it. There is going to be—I would argue there already is—a market for extremely high-quality information, what quality experts would call "six-sigma information." (The trendsetter for benchmarking American quality was always Motorola, and until 1989 Motorola was talking about three-sigma quality—three bad parts in a thousand. Six-sigma quality is three bad parts per *million*.) [Emphasis in original]

Among journalists the resistance to this warning is as great as the resistance among electronics company executives to the warning about the inadequate quality of American TVs in the 1960s or among automakers to the warning about American cars in the 1970s. Journalists have just as much trouble admitting error as anybody else—including the public officials whose "coverups" reporters delight in uncovering. Judging from the small number of corrections published in most American newspapers, journalists may have even more difficulty. Surely nobody thinks newspapers run so few corrections because they all operate at the six-sigma level. Most editors do not give an accounting of all a paper's daily errors (or even of its factual errors, disregarding the spelling and punctuation mistakes, garbled type, dropped lines, transposed captions, and so on) because doing so would be too embarrassing.

Properly understood, though, a lack of corrections ought to be much more embarrassing, for it discloses a shocking lack of concern about the basic quality of the goods. Aggressive correction of factual errors, while initially provoking amusement in the public and consternation in the staff, ultimately builds both credibility and pride. It makes Pulitzer's point emphatically. It says: We do not tolerate error here. And when we discover it, we cannot rest without repairing the record. It says: While we recognize that exigencies of time and circumstance make perfection impossible in the immediate rush of the news, we are committed to making sure that anything less than perfection at the level of the readily verifiable will not stand.

The whole culture of journalism must change before simple accuracy becomes once again one of its signal virtues. In an informal survey of upper-level editors at newspapers in other cities taken by a staff committee at the *Tribune* most of the editors thought little of trying to obtain a rigorous understanding of a paper's rate of error:[7]

> Editors at most of the larger papers contacted . . . said such a system [of checking with people close to news events after a story runs to see how accurate they perceived it to be] opens the door to disaster, and they would never consider using it at their paper.

Typical was the remark of one editor who called the idea insane and said it would invite lawsuits. That kind of defensiveness shows how far journalism has to go.

Newspapers need to get back to the basics before changes in telecommunications force them to a public accounting. Reporters who do not meet the simple standard of accuracy should not be taken seriously, however stunning their work may appear to be in other respects. Newspapers should overcome their reluctance to use quantified performance measures and begin rigorously counting up their accuracy score. Goals should be established. Incentives should be provided to reward improvement. The quality techniques used in other industries should be applied in the newsroom, beginning with the elegant ideas that obsession with quality saves time and effort and that excellence comes most reliably as people first do the work, not through elaborate fail-safe mechanisms. (This is because one of the most facile and common excuses given for declining quality is that financial pressure has eliminated redundancy in editing, which means fewer chances to catch errors.) If we are clever enough, we can get our computers to help us by standardizing certain error-prone material (prep sports box scores, for example, or routine listings) so that once we get a name or address or telephone number right, it stays right. We might also build in spelling- and style-checking routines tailored to identify the errors our measurement system discloses are most common. Journalists will find no thrill in this project. It is as dull as making sure the doors on automobiles open and shut properly. And just as vital to the continued success of the enterprise.

When the idea of accuracy has really taken hold of a news organization, we don't hear it respond to a challenge with a "we stand by our story" statement before it has even had a chance to examine the complaint thoroughly. News organizations rightly hold up this kind of behavior to criticism when other enterprises engage in it—petrochemical companies denying responsibility for oil spills, auto manufacturers blaming drivers for safety defects in their cars, government protecting its own. A quality-driven news organization examines each serious complaint of error, open to the possibility that it may have been wrong, and takes the time to be sure before either correcting itself or reaffirming the truth of what it said. Of course, even a quality-driven newspaper will make errors, because eliminating all possibility of error would bog everything down. But when it errs, such a newspaper quickly and without defensiveness acknowledges its mistake and corrects it.

The commitment to an exacting standard of truth is essential at the level where it is easy to agree what the truth is, because the disciplines at the next level become far more difficult to apply.

Objectivity

Almost nobody talks about objective reporting anymore. What philosophical analysis had not already undermined, radical multiculturalism did. But for many years the ideal of objectivity prevailed in the schools, and you still hear it from people who haven't spent their lives thinking about the press but simply don't like some of the things it does. So the concept of objectivity provides as good a starting place as any for the inquiry into the meaning and limitations of the words journalists have used to describe the truth discipline.

The idea of objectivity came naturally to a group of people seeking legitimacy in an era of scientific discovery. In its purest usage, the term suggested that journalism meant to be so utterly disinterested as to be transparent. The report was to be virtually the thing itself, unrefracted by the mind of the reporter. This, of course, involved a hopelessly naive notion from the beginning. And surely every reporter who has ever laid his fingers on the typewriter keys has known it.[8]

No one has ever achieved objective journalism, and no one

ever could. The bias of the observer always enters the picture, if not coloring the details at least guiding the choice of them. I don't use bias here as a term of opprobrium. One might have an optimistic bias or a bias toward virtue. It is the inevitable consequence of the combination of one's experience and inbred nature. An observer may be able to recognize his biases and attempt to correct for them, but even when this difficult psychological effort occurs, the resulting depiction is still subjective, doubly so. The process of correction requires a self-conscious mental intervention that is at odds with the concept of objectivity.

Trying to think objectively while recognizing the universality of bias becomes a bit like trying not to think of a purple cow. An example of how difficult it is to free the mind in this way occurs whenever a news organization attempts to deal with reports concerning its own people or interests. Say WGN-Television, a subsidiary of Tribune Company, which also owns the *Chicago Tribune*, becomes embroiled in a public controversy concerning one of its programs. Ideally, the story should be handled just as though it involved any other TV station. But quickly this equivalence becomes complicated. WGN is not like any other station. It is, for example, a superstation seen on cable television all over North America. It is a sibling of a newspaper with a long and colorful tradition and a certain position in the local and national communities. Its behavior reflects upon the family. And this gives its acts more significance than they might have had if done by a station owned by a faceless entity.

Bad publicity concerning the station could adversely affect its ratings and advertising revenues, which could hurt the price of Tribune Company stock, in which every *Chicago Tribune* reporter and editor has a stake through the company retirement plan. Moreover, the fact that the newspaper has a financial interest in the performance of the TV station is no secret. Most readers know this and will, presumably, be looking for evidence that the conflict of interest has led the paper to deal too favorably with the story. And so the editors will worry about the effect their handling of the story will have on the newspaper's credibility. Though the hierarchy of Tribune Company has, through long experience, developed a thick skin in these matters, everyone involved in the news decision still knows that all people have similar wiring when it comes to bad publicity: Whether they say so or not, they do not like it. And so there is a certain nervousness in the situation, coupled with a summoning up of courage, which may cause an overreaction against the source of the anxiety and an exaggeration of the play of the story. So it is impossible to handle the story disinterestedly, just as though it involved some other station, let alone objectively, as though no mind got in between the event and the depiction.

Despite the difficulty, good journalists always discipline themselves to correct against bias. And good newspapers try not to shade the facts, even when the facts are detrimental to their interests. They try to play it straight. There are many examples. *New York Times* labor writer A. H. Raskin was assigned in 1962 to cover a strike against the paper. His report, critical of some *Times* negotiators, appeared in the paper immediately after the strike ended and publication resumed; the paper's chief negotiator later resigned.[9] The *Tribune,* in a matter close to the circumstances of the hypothetical situation I just posed, played a controversy between the TV station and the Roman Catholic archdiocese on its front page. WGN-TV returned the favor by giving similarly prominent coverage to a later dispute between the newspaper and Chicago's Roman Catholic archbishop.

I need to make a distinction here between discipline and style. Objectivity as a discipline defeats itself. But as a style of expression marked by affectless recitation of fact, it can have considerable force. The book *Friendly Fire*[10] by C. D. B. Bryan provides an excellent example. Originally a series of articles in *The New Yorker,* which once specialized in reporting of this sort, *Friendly Fire* tells the story of the attempts by two parents to determine how and why their son died in Vietnam. The narrative describes in detail how the mother and father became frustrated with the way the Army bureaucracy responded to their inquiries. Without facts to moor it, the family's imagination began to race.

The first time through this book, a reader cannot help thinking the author shares the family's ideas about conspiracies and elaborate official coverups. The objective style helps build this expectation. Here is an example. In it Bryan describes the boy's mother's feelings after receiving a form letter from the commanding general of U.S. forces in Vietnam:[11]

Peg was still disturbed that with the exception of Culpepper none of Michael's friends had written. She was now certain that at least half the casualties in Vietnam were due to mysterious circumstances, "accidents," because maps were wrong, because someone high on drugs was shooting off his gun or because men were being killed by their own artillery. That was why no communication was permitted. What was it that Waverly mother said, the one whose son was missing in the burned-out tank? "We've been told by the Army that we can't discuss this with anyone because it might 'aid and abet' the enemy."

The enemy, it had begun to appear, was anybody who opposed the war.

Bryan effectively plays upon the reader's preconceptions of journalists' biases—particularly the biases that operated at the end of that distressing war. We assume the author thinks, along with the family, that there was official misconduct, because journalists usually do. Why else tell the story?

Bryan acknowledges his own presence in the narrative by reporting his interactions with the family. He becomes so intimate with his subjects that when he reports their thoughts (a technique discussed in a later chapter) he does not seem to overreach. Coupled with his withholding of judgment, these elements of his style only heighten the sense that he must believe what he is being told, since he does not try to set the family straight. But as the family's ideas about what happened to their son become more and more extreme, a deep discomfort comes over the reader, at least a reader who has enough acquaintance with the reality of that war to see the flaws in what the family imagined. To such a reader, both the characters and the author seem increasingly unmoored.

If the story went no further, the plain-style rendering of the "objective" facts of the family's statements and behavior might demonstrate another difficulty of objectivity as a standard for journalism, namely that it begs the question: Whose perception of reality is the journalist attempting to be objective about? The objectivity of a mystic is different from that of a scientist, unless perhaps he is a particle physicist. How can a writer be "objective" about a reality he can only discern as it is refracted through the consciousness of others, who may disagree among themselves? But in the end C. D. B. Bryan resolves this tension by permitting the reader to understand that all along his story has been about the family's growing distance from reality. He does this, not by changing his voice, but by letting the factual details pile up until the reader has a fair idea that the young man died as the result of a tragic but not uncommon accident of war.

By the close of the book it becomes clear that Bryan's "objective" stance is a writerly technique, an effective one at that. It serves to tell this story most vividly. It permits the reader to sympathize with the family without sharing the family's view. It creates intellectual suspense as the reader wonders whether these people (Bryan included) are ever going to get a purchase on the truth. And it depicts memorably the corrosive emotional effects of public doubt and official silence.

But it is not "objective." The author does not in the end withhold his view of the events he narrates. Because Bryan knows exactly the meaning he wants to convey, he can make *Friendly Fire* appear objective, though in fact it represents a marvelous act of intellectual intervention.

As she often does, Janet Malcolm put the point provocatively. "The ideal of unmediated reporting," she wrote, also in *The New Yorker*, "is regularly achieved only in fiction, where the writer faithfully reports on what is going on in his imagination."[12] She may be simplistic in her understanding of fiction, in which irony and the complex use of point of view (including unreliable narrators) sometimes make it difficult to determine what the writer really thinks. But she certainly has a point about objective journalism.

OBSERVER AND OBSERVED

Objectivity, along with certain other concepts journalists have used to describe their truth discipline, assumes an independence between the observer and the phenomenon observed that simply does not exist. Whether at the level of skittering sub-atomic particles or the clash of nations, the object may be trans-formed by the attention paid to it.

Good reporters know how to make themselves unobtru-sive so that life will go on around them close to the way it would if they were not there. Some of the best share the shuffling, stuttering, down-at-the-heel genius of the *New York Times*'s late, legendary Homer Bigart, who had a great gift for making his intelligence seem harmless. Bad reporters try to dominate the room.

One of the most serious difficulties of contemporary re-porting grows directly out of the effect of observation on the phenomena observed. The most common objects of coverage—beginning with government and politicians—have become ex-traordinarily sophisticated about the imperatives that drive journalism. Consequently, events are planned and public policy decisions are made merely to play well on TV and in the press. In one sense this development simply represents democracy at work in an era of immediacy. The need for consent of the gov-erned, after all, should put a burden on public officials to try to determine how people will respond to what government has done or is planning to do in their name and then to change course, if necessary, to achieve support. The problem is not the immediacy or the continuous seeking of consent. The problem is the means, which have placed an unhealthy emphasis on appearances.

This is not a new phenomenon. Daniel Boorstin caught the leading edge of it with his 1961 book, *The Image: A Guide to Pseudo-Events in America*.[13] But the intervening years have seen politicians take Boorstin's complaint as an instruction manual; what he decried has become the very basis of American political life.

The White House is an extreme but useful example of what has happened to the process of decision-making as the day-to-day grooming of public image has grown in importance. Michael Kelly has described in the *New York Times* the extent to which image has become a political creed:[14]

In this new faith, it has come to be held that what sort of person a politician actually is and what he actually does are not important. What is important is the perceived image of what he is and what he does. Politics is not about objective reality, but virtual reality. . . . It exists for only the fleeting historical moment, in a magical movie of sorts. . . .

By the time Bill Clinton was elected the 42d President of the United States the culture of Washington (and therefore of governance and politics) had become dominated by people professionally involved in creating the public images of elected officials. They hold various jobs—they are pollsters, news-media consultants, campaign strategists, advertising producers, political scientists, reporters, columnists, commentators—but the making of the movie is their shared concern. They are parts of a product-based cultural whole, just like the citizens of Beverly Hills. Some are actors, some are directors, some are scriptwriters and some are critics, but they are all in the same line of work and life. They go to the same parties, send their children to the same schools, live in the same neighborhoods. They interview each other, argue with each other, sleep with each other, marry each other, live and die by each other's judgment. They joust and josh on television together explaining Washington to conventions of doctors and lawyers and corporate executives.

Not surprisingly, they tend to believe the same things at the same time. They believe in polls. They believe in television; they believe in talk; they believe, most profoundly, in talk television. They believe in irony. They believe that nothing a politician does in public can be taken at face value, but that everything he does is a metaphor for something he is hiding. They believe in the extraordinary! disastrous! magnificent! scandalous! truth of whatever it is they believe at the moment. Above all, they believe in the power of what they have created, in the subjectivity of reality and the reality of perceptions, in image.

Note Kelly's assertion that Washington correspondents share the political spin doctors' belief in the subjectivity of truth. Nothing could be more subversive of the journalist's traditional role, especially since this belief links up in an ominous way with radically skeptical social and intellectual currents in our culture (discussed in Chapter Four) which threaten the very idea of truth.

Kelly is certainly right that the media and politicians are in the game together. In the conventional understanding of journalism's truth discipline, the separation of observer and observed must be maintained. Even if a reporter does not pretend to be objective or neutral (and Kelly makes no such pretense in this piece), he still can insist upon operating at a distance from the event. But in the new order, the journalist may think of himself as being as much a part of the event as the President. He just has a smaller part, and so he has to work harder to be noticed.

The paradox is similar to what happens to journalists dealing with stories that involve their organizations and other direct elements of self-interest. Reflexivity reigns. It becomes impossible to separate the dancer from the dance. The political writer finds himself in the odd position of analyzing how a particular message or action will play with the public when what he says affects how it plays. To complicate matters further, the central purpose of the message or action in the first place may have been to influence what political reporters say.

This may seem an enviable position for a journalist to be in, since the reporter cannot be all wrong: The very existence of the article he writes provides evidence of the political success or failure it describes. But at the same time, if he is at all thoughtful, he will recognize that whirl is king and he is dealing only with spin. He will yearn for some truth referent beyond the small, closed loop of which he is a part. (It is interesting that the "spin" metaphor is so close to the language of particle physics in which the Heisenberg Uncertainty Principle arose.)

Dealing with this reflexivity is not simply an abstract problem for decision makers in news organizations. It has real and immediate bite. I recall the night the story broke that a nominee for the U.S. Supreme Court had admitted smoking marijuana some years before when he was teaching at a prestigious law school. I got into a heated debate with colleagues, especially those in the *Tribune*'s Washington Bureau, over my decision not to run the story on page one. I reasoned that it was not terribly significant that a person this man's age had smoked marijuana in the past, that the experience was common enough that it probably reflected no more about his character than having had an occasional drink during Prohibition would.

The counterargument was that the professor's admission was going to be political dynamite. Opponents of the President were on a tear after defeating the confirmation of Judge Robert Bork. They would be able to use this to make things embarrassing, perhaps even to stop this nomination, too. I argued that this might not be true if everyone treated the information as having little genuine significance to the merits of the appointment. As it turned out, the *Tribune* was alone among major papers in playing the story inside. And the nominee went on to his political doom. The information *was* dynamite, of course. But should it have been? And would it have been if the story had been generally played for its real rather than its symbolic importance? (Since this episode we have elected a vice president who admitted having smoked marijuana and a president who deepened an image problem for himself, not by saying he had smoked, but by saying that he had not inhaled.)

The self-imposed constraints journalists try to follow affect the general methods of politics. For example, if journalists were to universally disdain the use of unnamed sources, it might appreciably increase the power of the presidency. (It would also dramatically decrease the amount and timeliness of information available to the public, which may be a way of saying the same thing.) This is because the use of unnamed sources permits anyone with inside information to use it against the position of those in authority and take minimal risk of punishment in doing so. The leak is an equalizer.

THE PROBLEM OF AUTHORITY

This is one of authority's problems with journalism, but journalism also has problems with authority, even in a culture that offers remarkable leeway to free expression. One vexing aspect is how to deal with authoritative untruths.

Journalism's goal is to depict significant things learned about reality since the last report. When a scientific journal publishes a paper warning of a frightening new environmental health hazard, or the junior senator from Wisconsin says he has in his hand the names of fifty-seven members of the Communist Party who work in the federal government, what should a disciplined newspaper report? The facile answer is that both are verbal events in the world and, as such, are true. But this narrow conception of truth disregards whether the authoritative assertion is accurate.

When the man next door says something to a reporter over the back fence and the reporter has serious reason to doubt it, he does not publish a word unless he concludes on independent scrutiny that the neighbor's assertion has met the general standard of proof. But when someone makes a statement from the position of the authority either of rank or of expertise, the situation becomes more difficult.

If the reporter has evidence refuting or clearly casting doubt on such an authoritative statement, the proper approach is to publish both assertion and rebuttal. It may even be appropriate for the journalist to present a factual judgment of his own. But often the contrary evidence does not emerge in time for simultaneous rebuttal. If the journalist still does not believe the statement, should he print it anyway? Or should he cast doubt upon it even without articulable facts tending to refute it? Are there ever circumstances in which the journalist should withhold a statement by an authoritative figure simply because he disbelieves it?

For analytical purposes let's put the issue in its starkest form: Should a journalist ever decide not to report what the President has said because the reporter strongly believes, but has no way to prove, that the President is dead wrong? The same, of course, could be asked of statements by the Pope or a member of the Senate or House of Representatives, the chairman of General Motors, and so on all the way down to a policeman at a homicide scene. Any general approach to this question should deal with the difference between such cases.

At a minimum, the truth discipline requires that if a journalist publishes anything that might mislead, he must take steps to correct the misimpression. This basic rule helps parse out problems that will occur in an electronic, interactive news-paper, in which news space is virtually unconstrained and large amounts of textual material can be published (speeches, press releases, statements, and so forth) that bear on the news. The journalist presiding over such an environment has a responsi-bility to assure that the texts that he publishes are what they purport to be (that the XYZ Corporation and not an imposter posted the press release on fourth-quarter earnings, for ex-ample). But beyond that, the journalist also should generally provide readers a context in which to understand these mate-rials and, if he has reason to disbelieve what they say, the evidence supporting his disbelief. This is not to suggest that the electronic newspaper should exclude original source texts (which are valuable in giving readers a full picture and the means for making their own judgments). It only suggests that journalists have a responsibility to shed light on the ones that are dubious.

Getting back to the initial question, if the President says insurgents in the tiny country of Xenobia have systematically massacred hundreds of women and children and the journalist suspects this is bloody-shirt propaganda, he has a duty to try to determine whether these massacres have taken place. But that takes time. What should he do the first night?

It seems clear to me that if the President made such a statement, a journalist must report it, even in the face of his own serious doubts about its veracity. He might write his report in such a way as to put the remarks in the context of the Presi-dent's efforts to create the political conditions for military in-tervention in Xenobia, but he probably should not (in the ab-sence of anything more than a hunch) transform his doubts into a clear statement of skepticism about the President's claim. (If a reasonable reader[15] would take the account as indicating the journalist's disbelief, the journalist has gone too far.)

The reason for permitting a journalist to violate the ordi-nary truth discipline and publish something he thinks is false is that the significance of the statement, accurate or inaccurate, far outweighs the risk that it will mislead people. It is impos-sible to avoid this kind of balancing test. Onto one side of the

balance goes the significance of the utterance and the level of
the public's interest in knowing of it (whether or not it is true);
onto the other goes the likelihood that temporary belief by
others in the statement will have irreversible consequences,
the severity of those consequences, and the degree of doubt the
journalist has concerning the truth of the statement.

In some circumstances perhaps even a president's statements might be withheld on the basis of no more than a hunch.
But trying to imagine them forces one to such fantastic ex-
tremes that they do not represent any important qualification
of the general rule in favor of straightforward publication. If on
the first night of the Gulf War President Bush had stated that
U.S. planes had destroyed the Iraqi Air Force on the ground or
decimated the Republican Guard in their bunkers, I would have
published it without hesitation, because all we had was a gut
feeling that this assertion could not be so. The hunch was good
enough for us to withhold rumors reported on TV, but it would
not have justified withholding the President's words.

Few journalists would be tempted to withhold in these circumstances. But the itch of doubt is epidemic. Journalists today
have persuaded themselves that they have a duty to show their
universal skepticism of authority. In the White House pressroom it operates as a kind of collective gag reflex. And it becomes most acute when the political environment turns mean
and personal, as it too often does these days. Thus we have to
be very clear about the rare circumstances in which subjective
disbelief of authoritative statements may be permitted to in-
trude into news reports.

In cases involving authority less exalted than the President, the statement itself is generally less newsworthy in its
own right, so the threshold for withholding publication is lower.
For example, a passing remark by a police officer at a murder
scene that the husband of the dead woman must have killed her
can easily go unpublished. The level of doubt is high, the consequences of publication severe to the person involved, and the
significance of the statement (even the public's curiosity about
it) low.

One unavoidable consequence of this analytic framework

is that it permits reporters to treat differently cases that are alike from the point of view of the potential victims of the utterance. A false and disparaging statement by a highly placed public official in a supercharged political contest might be published while a similar statement in a more tranquil situation by someone of less prominence would not be. Likewise, an official pronouncement—like a grand jury indictment or congressional report—would be publishable even in the face of doubts about its validity. But so long as the journalist accepts the obligation to follow up on his doubts and correct misimpressions, the temporary inequity of this approach is acceptable, given the alternatives.

The Adversarial Approach

Moral revulsion at publishing doubted information and the fear of being deceived by skilled image specialists have led some journalists to adopt an adversarial stance in their relationship with public officials and others they cover. The adversarial model comes from the conflict resolution methods of American law. The journalist postures himself as a relentless cross-examiner, hostile to every assertion by those he faces. He begins with the supposition that everyone in authority is a liar. Both his questioning and, inevitably, his reports may reflect this supposition. The adversarial journalist has no trouble figuring out what to do about a presidential statement he doubts. He simply lets his doubts show.

Though the law protects the journalist who strikes such a posture, neither the nature of the system of free expression nor the reasons underlying the Anglo-American adversarial system of law should be taken as intellectual support for using the adversarial model in journalism. Both systems were designed to achieve some degree of truth from a competition among people with no necessary commitment to accuracy, but both recognize at least tacitly that there may be better ways of arriving at the truth.

The adversarial model in law puts a duty on the advocate to state the best possible case for his client. He has no general obligation to reveal the weaknesses in his position, to discover the falsehoods in his client's assertions or to put his opponent's case (though he is theoretically bound by minimal requirements that he reveal certain things that may conflict with his client's interest). After both advocates speak single-mindedly on their clients' behalf in a highly stylized debate constrained by elaborate rules of evidence, a third party (judge or jury) decides what is the legal truth. Some rules of evidence frustrate the objective of reaching truth in the interest of advancing other objectives. For example, the rule against introduction of illegally seized evidence withholds facts from juries in order to deter wrongdoing by the police. The point of the adversarial process is in the first instance to resolve conflicts by providing the means of reaching some approximation of truth from participants who may dissemble or speak with less than perfect candor.

The free expression model embodied in the First Amendment to the U.S. Constitution has a similar rationale. The system of free expression permits almost any message to be sent, recognizing that some messages will gravely need refutation. But it assumes that this is best entrusted to a large, decentralized network of participants in the system. It does not impose a general, legally enforceable duty of truth because it does not trust any authority officially to establish the truth. It permits speakers to make false statements even when they know them to be false, but it does not encourage people to speak falsely. Nobody denies that the system would work more efficiently as a generator of truth if everyone felt an obligation to speak candidly despite their right to do otherwise. (The classic form taken by debates within the academic world, for example, assumes disagreement but presupposes a shared morality of truth-telling. It recognizes that when everyone accepts this obligation the cause of knowledge is most efficiently advanced.) If nothing else, with the range of disagreement narrowed, the audience (as the ultimate finder of fact) can focus on the areas of genuine conflict.

The cause of knowledge is also better served by journalists who accept a duty to tell the truth rather than to take an adversarial posture toward those in authority. The adversarial model encourages less than candor, which is why it is so subversive of good journalism. Furthermore, though journalists certainly participate in the marketplace of ideas, their role is not an advocate's. They review the debate and try to come to some form of judgment. They act as surrogates who help the public discover and weigh the evidence. Their role should be more like the judge's than the lawyer's, more like the scholar's than the partisan's.

NEUTRALITY

Since objectivity and the adversarial model are inadequate descriptions of how journalists should do their duty to the truth, one might use a general standard of neutrality to describe the journalist's truth discipline. This accords with journalists' description of their duty to be "impartial" or to act "without fear or favor." As a description of the proper attitude in reporting a story, these oft-used descriptions have utility. They describe an aspiration, of course, an unattainable standard of perfection. Only an amnesiac could approach anything in a state of pure neutrality. But, even recognizing this, journalists can discipline themselves to correct against bias and deal with each new situation with an open mind.

What about situations that are not entirely new? Or situations in which a study of history provides some guidance? Preconception, after all, can be another word for experience or even wisdom. If editors had no preconceptions about the nature of warfare, they might have accepted early reports from the Persian Gulf about the level of destruction achieved by the allies' first air strikes. If they had relied on these preconceptions a little more, they might have been warier about the military's reports of how flawlessly "smart weapons" performed.

Some years before the Gulf War, not long after the bombing of Muammar al-Khadafy's headquarters in Tripoli, a senior defense official visited the *Tribune* editorial board. I asked him what he thought when he heard the Secretary of Defense say the night of the attack that since the bombs were precision-guided weapons he found it inconceivable that, despite reports of damage to the French Embassy, any had gone off track. The

Pentagon official, a combat veteran, replied something like this: "Each aircraft carried two young men in their twenties who flew half a day in uncomfortable seats to reach the Libyan coast. At that point they ran into heavy flak. It flew up at their aircraft from all directions, trying to kill them. They dropped down to low altitude and flew at a high rate of speed toward the target, then turned the plane upside down to make the final run. If they dropped a bomb one second early or late it would land miles off target. No, I did not think that missing was inconceivable."

His was a preconception, a very knowledgeable one.

The attitude of neutrality in reporting a story has to be tempered by experience, always recognizing that experience in turn must be tempered by the new insights provided through the gateway of an open mind. But that is just common sense. So why not simply declare a general standard of neutrality? The difficulty comes when neutrality is meant not only to describe a state of mind for reporting a story but also the way the story should be told.

Journalists often hear complaints that a news story showed bias because it openly stated the reporter's conclusions or because it had a clear point of view. This complaint assumes that neutral presentation of information is always a journalistic virtue. Often the people who make these arguments, sometimes with great intensity, have a strong point of view of their own. In fact, hearing enough complaints of this sort tempts an editor to treat them all as hopelessly partisan. What such people want is not the journalist's neutrality but his agreement. Still, an honest evaluation of the work that appears in newspapers today reveals that most of it would not begin to satisfy any meaningful standard of neutrality of expression.

Political writers regularly evaluate the efficacy of statements by politicians and government officials. Stories about the economy commonly put changes in the statistical indicators into perspective (saying that a drop in unemployment does not mean what it appears to mean, for example) even when economists show no unanimity on the point. Reports of foreign affairs include critical discussions of the government's policy or lack of one. Local news articles contrast antiseptic official statements with gritty recitations of the reality of the streets. Business writers look at companies' activities in light of theories of management that are by no means universally accepted. When great events occur—whether wars or disasters or triumphs such as the breaching of the Berlin Wall—news organizations try to write directly about the larger historical meanings and even to imagine the probable consequences some years down the line, again in circumstances in which there is no consensus among knowledgeable observers. Either journalism is regularly disregarding a basic discipline or else neutrality of expression should not be the standard.

There are many reasons to abandon the pretense: Journalism needs to help people understand increasingly complex issues that affect their political and social decisions, and this is impossible to do without making judgments of fact and value. People don't usually find perfectly neutral accounts interesting, because bare recitation of fact can be tedious and leaves too much unresolved. Busy people expect their newspapers to do much of the analytic work for them. Neutral writing may actually undermine the relationship between the newspaper and its community by making it difficult for people to find a personality in the paper, a unique voice to which they can relate.

The judicial analogy is far from perfect, but it offers a useful place to begin. Though we expect judges to be impartial and unbiased and to act without preconception about the case before them, we do not expect them to end in a state of indecision about the truth and its implications or to leave readers of their work in a state of confusion about what they have decided. The best judges recognize the limits of their knowledge and their duty to act in the face of factual uncertainty in accord with clear rules setting forth the burden of proof and other tie-deciders. They do make use of their experience—both as human beings and as lawyers—to try to make judgments that have some logical coherence with other judgments they have made. But they do not let partisanship or ideology (which could be thought of as an extreme case of coherence) prevent them from seeing the exception that might challenge the structure they helped to build. And when they write, they do not shy away from making judgments about the weight of evidence and logic. We only expect that they give due account of the advocates' positions and then reflect their own true reasoning so that it might be evaluated by others. They aim to be neutral in their inquiry but not in the expression of their findings.

INTELLECTUAL HONESTY AND THE GOLDEN RULE

The judicial analogy suggests a whole set of virtues—open-mindedness, impartiality, the duty to be candid about one's reasoning and about what one knows and does not know, the responsibility to put as forcefully as possible the positions of those with whom one disagrees. These virtues all come together in the concept of intellectual honesty, which links the truth discipline in journalism with the highest standards in scientific and academic debate. It is as good a statement of aspiration as any I can think of for journalists.

Intellectual honesty means that in presenting a news report a journalist may draw certain conclusions and make certain predictions about the consequences of a particular event, but it also imposes a duty to do justice to the areas of legitimate debate. This is what separates news from polemical writing. The former must attempt to represent a matter of public concern in its fullness. A polemic aims to persuade the audience that one view of the matter is undoubtedly correct.

The Golden Rule has endured through the centuries as an ethical proposition of enormous force because it offers a subjective method for determining the moral direction one's behavior should take. It asks that an individual treat others the way he would like to be treated, to turn the tables, to empathize. This is a useful way to look at the requirement of intellectual honesty. In reporting a matter of legitimate debate (How big should the Pentagon budget be? Did Alderman X take a bribe?), the journalist will surely reach some conclusions. And, with some constraints described later, he should feel free to share his conclusions with his readers. But in doing so, the Golden Rule sug-

gests that the reporter must try to put the case against his conclusions as forcefully as he would want an opponent to put the
reporter's own arguments.

This, like many moral propositions, sets an extraordi-
narily high aspiration. If you deeply believe your own position,
you will find it very difficult to express the opposite point of
view with the same enthusiasm and force. But the Golden Rule
is a corrective; it points the right direction. And, with discipline, it is not too much to expect reporters (freed of the
impossible requirement of objectivity and the nonfunctional
requirement of neutral expression) to play square with others'
arguments, stating them honestly and presenting the facts and
logic supporting them. The Golden Rule is a perfectionist goal,
toward which to stumble in our imperfect, human way.

Even the unalloyed gold standard does not require a journalist to report every view of a subject, only those that could be
held by informed, reasonable people. Of course, a journalist's
bias may unduly restrict what he considers the range of reasonable, informed opinion. And illegitimate claims may need to
be reported as important facts in their own right—such as the
racist, antisemitic, and xenophobic views that mar the political
landscape from time to time. A reporter also needs to operate
within the constraints of time, space, and reader attention span
that limit everything a newspaper does. But these must not
become excuses for lapsing into the one-sided, polemical approach in the news columns. A journalist's reputation should
turn in large part upon the quality of his judgment in wisely
sorting through these difficult issues so as to produce work of
genuine intellectual integrity.

Too much of what appears in newspapers today fails to
live up to the Golden Rule. Once journalists recognized the
philosophical impossibility of objectivity and the rhetorical
weakness of neutral expression, many of them threw off all traditional restraints against asserting opinion in news reports.
Today many TV correspondents' stand-ups end with a little
homily fit to conclude one of Aesop's fables. You can find plenty
of this in the newspapers, too, though there the moral of the
story usually comes at the beginning. In both media too often

arguments that would tend to undermine the journalist's judgments either remain unreported or else are put forth as straw men that the reporter easily knocks down. There are a hundred ways to do this. Common to all is the adversarial unwillingness to permit the audience to make its own assessment of the contrary position without the journalist's heavy-handed guidance.

FAIRNESS

Journalists often use the concept of fairness to describe their discipline. Unfortunately, the idea of fairness has a rich philosophical history. This gives it implications that may be inimical to the truth discipline. Even as journalistic cliche, the idea of fairness leads in odd directions.

"Journalism," one saying goes, "should comfort the afflicted and afflict the comfortable." Taken loosely as a call for journalists to concern themselves with the suffering of the weakest members of society and to have the courage to tell unpleasant truths about the powerful, the statement makes sense. But it also can be an invitation to bias, and journalists too often accept the call. Should journalists *always* afflict the comfortable, even when the comfortable are doing no harm? Should they afflict them simply *because* of their comfort? And what about the afflicted? What if telling the truth to and about them would cause them discomfort? Should the truth be shaded or withheld in order to give them comfort instead? What if truth were the painful antidote that in the long run would cure the affliction?

Any deep consideration of the idea of fairness leads eventually to questions of distributive justice of the very sort raised by these tidings of comfort and affliction. In its simplest terms, the issue is whether fairness means letting everyone compete on the same terms, regardless of the advantages and disadvantages they bring to the competition, or whether fairness requires that players carry a handicap. Is it fair to say that a poor child from the urban projects and the child of wealth and privilege should be judged by the same standard when evaluating them for admission to college? What about when trying to understand the moral quality of their behavior?

John Rawls's *Theory of Justice*[16] provides an excellent contemporary example of the idea of distributive justice. Rawls has the courage to face the whole range of social advantages and disadvantages, as well as natural abilities and disabilities (with which one may be born and for which one thus may be said to have no personal responsibility)—not only physical strength and intellectual acumen, but also creativity, ambition and indolence, beauty and ugliness. He boldly calls on people's sense of distributive fairness to compensate for them, as if to repair God's injustice. This leads him a long way from the idea of fairness as equality of opportunity.

What might fairness in its Rawlsian, distributive sense mean in journalism? Some participants in the public debate come better equipped for it than others. Distributive fairness would have to involve some form of compensation by the journalist for this disparity. He might, for example, call all close factual issues for the weaker party or shade the way he put both sides' arguments in order to give the weaker side a chance of persuading the audience. In more extreme cases, he might have to withhold information helpful to the advantaged side in order to keep the game even. All of these compensatory strategies sharply conflict with a journalist's primary duty of simple candor, and this is why fairness is a poor choice of words to describe a journalist's discipline.

The ideal of intellectual honesty, tested by the Golden Rule, offers a much surer guide. But this requires a degree of self-restraint that is not natural in people who become immersed in a subject and develop strong feelings about it. The Golden Rule must be taught, and that has been difficult in journalism because of the lack of clarity and consensus about just what the proper discipline should be.

One problem has been the shift in weight between fact and value in news reports. No journalist I know would favor lying to give the weaker party a more even chance of prevailing in the debate. Far more likely would a journalist shade his report of a valuative debate to favor an individual suffering under a disadvantage. Somebody, he might say, has to speak up for the flood victims, or the physically handicapped, or the urban underclass, or the Vietnam veteran, or the AIDS victim. And he might even overlook some strong counterarguments on the assumption that the secure, well-financed majority interests can look out for their side of the argument very well by themselves, thank you very much. This helps account, I think, for the populist streak in American journalism as well as for journalists' reputation for being more liberal than their audience. It also may be one reason journalists have seemed to many people to be getting more liberal over time. As self-restraint against expressing opinion in news reports has fallen, the compensatory impulse becomes more marked.

It is not always easy to distinguish between fact and value, of course. In pure narrative, value is expressed solely through the selection of fact. And it is easy, once one starts handicapping the argument, to start calling more and more disputes for the supposed underdog. Consider the balance of environmental reporting over the past few decades. Once journalists became persuaded that powerful interests were causing danger and using their strength to cover it up, the tilt set in. It was not easy to learn from news reports about the evidence suggesting that emissions from tall smokestacks do not cause widespread acid rain damage to forests or that Agent Orange's dioxin does not cause severe health problems in human beings or that the white spotted owl seems to be living happily in unendangered numbers in non–old growth forests.

Better than attempting to distinguish between fact and value and applying different standards to each, the discipline of intellectual honesty applies the same rule across all domains. And with the help of the Golden Rule it provides appropriate guidance and restraint over the expression of opinion in news stories without having to forbid the practice outright.

THE LIMIT OF OPINION

But this is not the end of the requirements of journalism's basic disciplines. Beyond intellectual honesty, journalists reporting the news need to restrain the expression of their opinions, showing modesty in their judgments about facts and always withholding ultimate judgment on matters of value. A political writer should not include in his report on a presidential campaign his view about whom people should vote for. Nor should he write his story in a way that would lead a reasonable reader to infer his preference. A reporter covering a trial should not reveal his conclusions about who is lying or whether the defendant is guilty or innocent. In an article about the abortion controversy, the writer should not come out for or against *Roe v. Wade.*

This departs from the judicial analogy and imposes a tighter constraint on journalists. But the stricter approach is necessary in order to uphold the traditional distinction between news reporting and editorializing. (Editorials are polemical. They make their opinion about ultimate issues plain. And they need not recite all contrary arguments, though taking them into account makes for more persuasive editorials.) Preserving this distinction makes good sense for a number of reasons. People have grown used to it. Withholding ultimate judgment communicates the reporter's commitment to neutrality in his approach to reporting a story even as he departs from strict neutrality of expression. (It is hard to read the comments of an explicit supporter of a candidate and avoid the thought that he will not give the candidate's opponent an even break.) Modesty of opinion and holding back ultimate judgments of value produce a report that invites the audience to weigh information for itself and at the same time offer the audience some help in getting through the ambiguities and complexities. These disciplines make it easier for journalists to put all reasonable positions forcefully. (It is one thing to give all arguments their due when one does not choose between them explicitly. It is another to take an ultimate position and then have to give everyone the benefit of the Golden Rule.) Finally, withholding ultimate judgments makes pluralism in the reporting staff easier to manage.

It is hard enough under the discipline of modesty of opinion to permit writers latitude and still produce a newspaper with a sense of coherence. This would be virtually impossible if reporters were freed to express ultimate judgments. To make all the judgments in the paper consistent, editors and publishers would have to impose a political view, story by story, or else choose only those reporters whose views were essentially consistent with the paper's editorial positions. The result would be a coherent publication, on the model of the European press, but not one that reflects a large, geographic community the way American audiences have come to expect their newspapers to do.

To illustrate the way intellectual honesty and withholding ultimate judgment work, contrast *Friendly Fire* with another book-length report, *America: What Went Wrong?* by Donald L. Barlett and James B. Steele,[17] originally published in the *Philadelphia Inquirer*.

In *Friendly Fire* the writer had an unmistakable point of view about the factual truth of the events he described and about their deeper meaning. He presented his efforts to come to some conclusion in a way that made his neutrality in approaching the story apparent, even when he became involved in the action. And he scrupulously permitted everyone in the story to have his say. There was never a sense that he had left an inconvenient argument out or shaded it in order to make it weaker. A compellingly readable piece of work, *Friendly Fire* went from magazine article to book to made-for-TV movie, helping those who came into contact with it to understand what the Vietnam War had done to us.

America: What Went Wrong? also created quite a stir. Readers of the *Philadelphia Inquirer* responded with an intensity rare in the newspaper business when it was published in 1991 during the recession that ended the Bush presidency. The articles and then the book touched something in the audience so powerfully that some journalists began talking about it as a model for how the news could be made relevant. It is not a model that fits with the disciplines for reporting I have been describing.

Barlett and Steele begin with this premise:[18]

You might think of what is happening in the economy—and thereby to you and your family—in terms of a professional hockey game, a sport renowned for its physical violence. Imagine how the game would be played if the old rules were repealed, if the referees were removed.

That, in essence, is what is happening to the American economy. Someone changed the rules. And there is no referee. Which means there is no one looking after the interests of the middle class.

They are the forgotten Americans.

From that point on the report marches steadily along, marshaling evidence and emotional anecdotes to drive home the message that the Reagan-Bush years in America laid waste to ordinary, middle-class America. The subjects include health care, pensions, corporate raiding, bankruptcy, foreign competition, lobbying. In each area the approach is the same. Here is just one example.

Barlett and Steele take the position that deregulation for the American taxpayer and consumer has meant "fewer airlines and higher air fares, more unsafe trucks on the highways, and more of your tax money diverted to pay for the savings and loan debacle."[19] They assert that today there is less competition in the airline industry than before regulation but never mention that airlines now can compete on price and do so with a vengeance. Nor do they report that economists' predictions that deregulation would mean lower prices and better service have proven correct in almost all industries where they have been tested.[20]

Competition did cause the shakeout in the airline industry that Barlett and Steele decry, complaining that small towns once served by airlines have lost service because of deregulation, but they do not report that under regulation the many consumers traveling on the higher volume routes had to subsidize the few flying from small towns. And on and on. Barlett and Steele give no quarter to arguments against their position.

My point is not that the *Inquirer* reporters' work was unworthy. *America: What Went Wrong?* is powerful polemical writing that understands its audience and speaks in a populist voice to the audience's deepest emotions. But it does not live up to the discipline of intellectual honesty in that it does not give voice to contrary facts and arguments. Nor does it withhold ultimate judgments. It begins and ends with them. To any moderately skeptical reader this approach leaves the distinct impression that the marshaling of evidence followed the conviction rather than the conviction arising from the proof. The lesson of *America: What Went Wrong?* is this: As newspapers encourage more analysis and conclusion-drawing, even some of the best reporters at the best newspapers can lose track of the line between news and polemics.[21]

DEGREES OF PROOF

It is not a simple matter to specify how much evidence a journalist should have before he publishes an assertion of fact. Certainty is generally self-deception. Even the testimony of one's own senses can mislead, as anyone who has watched instant replays in sports can verify. Most of the time, journalists do not have firsthand knowledge of the facts they report. They must rely on others to tell them, others with motives—sometimes pathological ones—for not telling the truth.

Nearly every journalist has at one time or another faced a consummate liar and taken what he said to be true. Likewise, nearly every journalist has experienced the education in skepticism that comes from being deceived by the government that acts in his and his readers' names.

Still, the basis of news reporting is a kind of trust. It begins with the trust between a journalist and his sources of information and from there builds to the trust he wants to establish with his audience. No rule of thumb can describe the complex factors that go into a judgment of trust. But it is worth singling out a few of them to establish a balancing test that can form a basis for evaluating issues of journalistic proof.

Experience is the most useful indicator; a source (either human or institutional) who has been regularly right in the past generally deserves to be believed, unless there are specific reasons not to. Experience with particular kinds of situations also plays a role. If someone tells you that a man got injured by falling down to the ground, there is no particular reason on the face of it to doubt the account. But if he tells you the man hurt himself falling up to the ceiling, it is probably worth doing some more checking.

There is a fine line, of course, between experience and closed-mindedness. The unprecedented event is more likely to be news than the commonplace, and conventional wisdom is often wrong. So a good journalist must not discount everything that conflicts with what he has previously known. Nonetheless, experience can send up a warning, that little nervous feeling in the pit of the stomach that says, "Watch out." Every careful journalist always heeds that warning.

Verifiability helps establish credibility. Reports that anyone might check against public sources deserve more trust than accounts that nobody accessible to the journalist other than the source could refute. Checking against public sources, of course, always makes sense when there is reason to doubt. But it is not always necessary. For example, when a reputable economist recites the unemployment rates for the last twelve months in the course of making an argument about the prospects for a recession, a time-pressed reporter ordinarily feels comfortable relying on them.

The advantage of using public record materials as authenticators of information is that their wide and ready availability permits a record over time to be corrected (which is another reason newspapers as an important part of this public record need to be aggressive about correcting their errors).

In the absence of public records, private documents should generally be given more weight than oral accounts. Though documents can be forged, the embodiment of information in this form creates more ways to discover a lie. As more and more communication takes place electronically, sophistication in determining authenticity needs to grow apace or else we will find ourselves in a state of increased uncertainty as a result of the change. For example, it is possible now to trick up moving video images to insert or remove people or objects in a way the eye would never notice. Now more than before, documentary evidence is highly persuasive but inconclusive.

When a journalist finds no public record or documentary

evidence to support an assertion, he must decide whether he can rely on human sources alone. It is not rare that he decides to do so. There is no rule that can tell him when to do it and when not to. Credibility turns on a subtle blend of factors that includes demeanor and even hunch, which is why law gives the decision of judges and juries about witnesses' credibility such enormous weight on appeal. Nonetheless, there are a few obvious guides.

Journalists often say they do not care about the motives of those who give them information. By this they usually mean they are uninterested in considering whose cause they promote by disseminating accurate, significant information. But the statement is misleading, because journalists must take motive into account in weighing what sources tell them. Motive gives a clue to the source's biases and reasons for lying or telling the truth only selectively. The trouble is, news sources always have motives, even when they are passing on true information. Most leakers do not leak on themselves.

Corroboration by other sources can be helpful. The *Washington Post* "two source" practice during the Watergate investigations reflects this. Dealing almost entirely with anonymous sources on that story, *Post* editors asked reporters to confirm and reconfirm information through more than one source when none could be put on the record. I don't know how such a practice would protect against being deceived by a group of willful people acting in concert, though in the *Post*'s extraordinary Watergate investigation it generally worked. Though corroboration is helpful, when all sources are anonymous, the level of uncertainty in many instances is still too high.

Better to require attribution to a source willing to be identified by name. At least others will be able to assess the credibility of the source, and if it later turns out that he lied, he will have to face the consequences, which tends to deter lying in the first place.

Other reasons not to rely on anonymous sources will be discussed in a later chapter. But restrictions by news organizations upon their use always raise the issue of whether the Watergate scandal would have gone unrevealed under such rules. Almost any self-restraint on the part of journalists might make it impossible in a particular instance to get or publish valuable information, but the only way around that is to take the position (which one sometimes hears when journalists get into swashbuckling postures in public forums) that any means of getting and publishing a fact is justified. Short of that, it is possible to recognize that certain kinds of stories require less restrictive rules than others. This leads to a difficult balancing test in which journalists must weigh the magnitude of the consequences of publishing along with the level of confidence in the accuracy of the information and the effect publication will have on particular individuals, especially those who may be harmed.

When a report would have the effect of disparaging an identified or identifiable private individual unconnected with government or public affairs, the case is strong for requiring a very high degree of proof and forbidding the use of anonymous sources. The reporting of private activities, while important, is not as central to the role of the press as the reporting of government. Private individuals often have less protection against unfair attack and less ability to fight back. But when the report is about government and politics and does not single out any individual, anonymity is much more tolerable. (For example, the articles that so often appear quoting "senior government officials" on cabinet secretaries' airplanes during overseas missions generally do more good in letting the public in on the government line than harm in hiding the identity of the speaker, usually the cabinet secretary himself.)

Likewise, when the potential harm from not publishing vastly exceeds the harm that might occur if the information published turns out to be in error, there may be reasons for accepting the accounts of anonymous individuals or other sources of information that would not pass muster in less grave circumstances. Perhaps this analysis would have justified the use of sources in the Watergate reports, though that is still worth debating.

The social gravity factored into this balancing test cannot be measured on a scientific scale. Journalists will tend routinely to overestimate it and accept inadequate evidence in the excitement and immediacy of the pursuit of a fascinating story. So newspapers should establish a strict rule against publication of disparaging information about individuals based solely on anonymous sources. They may then permit rare exceptions to be made only by decision at the highest level of the news organization. This does not guarantee wisdom; it only reduces the number of occasions for error, since the cumbersome exception process dissuades reporters from trying and gives them an incentive to get proof that meets the higher standard. (In my experience reporters usually come up with attributable proof when they cannot get the story into the newspaper any other way. This always produces a better story, because it allows the reader to evaluate the sources.) When newspapers do permit attribution to anonymous sources, they should attempt to provide the reader as much information about the sources as they can. It helps to be told that a piece of information came from a CIA official rather than from a "knowledgeable source."

The question of how and when one knows enough to publish has infinite variations. It produces some intriguing newsroom debates. But it is time for journalists to codify their standards in explicit guidelines.

(*two*)
DECEPTION AND OTHER CONFIDENCE GAMES

WHEN I BEGAN MY JOURNALISM CAREER AS A POLICE reporter in Chicago, I worked with several people Ben Hecht and Charles MacArthur used as models for characters in their pressroom drama, *The Front Page.* One ran City News Bureau, the wire service where I worked. Another roamed the halls of Central Police Headquarters at night. And though nearly forty years had passed since the play opened on Broadway, some of the fast-and-loose practices it depicted continued in regular use.

I learned, for example, that it was easier to get information about someone who had just died under unpleasant circumstances by impersonating a deputy coroner on the telephone than by identifying myself as a reporter. The bereaved were often able to pull themselves together to talk to a county official when they would have simply hung up on an intrusive inquiry from the press.

Certain newspapermen had become legendary for dramatic performances of this sort. The most celebrated of these figures worked for the *Chicago American.* A story was widely told of the morning he called the scene of a grisly mass murder. No false modesty for him. He did not impersonate the deputy coroner. He identified himself as the chief coroner. Unfortunately, during the phone interview the real coroner arrived at the scene, to the profound surprise of the individual who thought he had the coroner on the line. When challenged, the man from the *American* identified himself as a reporter for the *Daily News* and rung off.

I wasn't that good. But I did become a passable liar in pursuit of the truth. Blame it on my youth. I was eighteen years old when I first hit the streets on the police beat. My father had worked at City News when he was a young man and had told me stories of identifying himself as Deputy Coroner O'Malley. So in an act of filial devotion I became O'Malley, too. Though I had been a member of the church choir and the captain of the crossing guards, I rarely questioned whether I was doing something wrong; I was just doing my job.

It seemed part of the game, and everybody around me was in on it. Everybody. One night I was hanging out at the Brighton Park detective station on the South Side. I had used a pay phone so as not to be overheard by the desk sergeant as I impersonated a police investigator to the victim of a theft of heavy equipment. We had a nice conversation, but he forgot to tell me a few things, so he called back—on the police line. "Detective O'Malley?" the desk sergeant said. "There's no Detective O'Malley. . . . Wait a minute." He put his hand over the receiver and looked at the very nervous teenager across the squad bay from him. "You aren't Detective O'Malley now, are you, kid?" he asked. I looked behind me. There was nobody there. The sergeant went back on the line. "Oh, you mean O'Malley," he said. "One of our best men, O'Malley. Here he is now."

Once in a while, though, I let my thoughts drift to the fresh, raw grief of the people to whom I misrepresented myself. I wondered what they thought when they saw a story in the paper the next day with the information they had given to someone they believed represented duly constituted authority. And I heard some things done in the name of news that made me wonder whether the truth was worth it.

One night in the pressroom of Central Police Headquarters, one of the old-timers began calling to get a story on a fatal auto accident that had just claimed the life of a young man about my age in the south suburbs not far from where I lived

with my parents. I was half listening to his end of the conversation as he identified himself as a police officer and started asking all the usual questions about the dead. It soon became obvious to me that he had the boy's mother on the phone. And
slowly I realized that she had not yet heard about the accident.
This was a moment I had always dreaded—having to break the
news. Whenever it happened, I tried to be as decent as I could,
giving as much information as I knew and staying on the line as
long as the grief-stricken parent or loved one wanted me to. But
this was not the old-time reporter's style. "Is he a good kid?" he
asked the mother. "I see. . . . No, we just stopped him in his car.
Driving around at 4:30 in the morning, you never know what a
kid that age might be up to. But since he was going to work,
we'll let him be on his way. Thank you, ma'am." With that, he
hung up the phone.

I knew that the next phone call that woman would receive
would announce her son's death. Would she ever be able to resolve whether he had, in fact, been stopped by police just before
he was killed? Or would that question haunt her? I could not
get it out of my mind—and cannot to this day.

By the time I returned to Chicago journalism after school
and military service, I no longer impersonated O'Malley or anyone else. Nobody told me not to. Times simply had changed,
and so had I. But I did occasionally forget to identify myself as a
newspaper reporter when to have done so would have prevented
me from learning what I wanted to learn. For example, in pursuit of a group of charlatans who offered people with deadly diseases trips to visit "psychic surgeons" in Asia, I represented
myself as the son of a terribly ill father. This happened to be
literally true. But finding a cure for my father's emphysema was
not the reason I was inquiring about the "psychic surgeons."

Whenever I acted undercover in this way, I felt a thrill. Deception carried a hint of danger that ordinary investigative techniques simply did not have. Perhaps I sensed something forbidden about it, the secrecy, the betrayal. Or perhaps it was
the recognition that deception invites rage and retribution. The
feeling was not entirely pleasant, but still when it was over, I
wanted to feel it again.

Eventually undercover investigation (for which the *Tribune* had won several Pulitzer Prizes) went out of fashion altogether. And it was a decision by the Pulitzer Prize Board that, more than anything else, caused the rules of the game to change.

The *Chicago Sun-Times* in 1977 had opened a tavern, staffed it with reporters and photographers, and waited for the city inspectors to come and shake them down. They sardonically called the bar the Mirage, and it drew petty crooks like drought victims to a vision of water. The articles that resulted, accompanied by photographs taken with hidden cameras, made it to the Pulitzer Prize finals. But after objections from the *Washington Post*'s former executive editor, Ben Bradlee, the Pulitzer Prize Board decided not to award the *Sun-Times* the prize because the series was based on deception. The board concluded that truth-telling enterprises should not engage in such tactics.[1]

And yet there is still deception in the work of journalists, and it is still rewarded. Only the most extreme practices have gone out of fashion, like the boaters the reporters wore in "The Front Page." The question remains timely: Under what circumstances, if ever, is a reporter justified in lying to get information?

The easiest case to dispose of is Deputy Coroner O'Malley. He was simply a way to cut corners. To be sure, some information a reporter can gain by impersonation might not otherwise be obtainable. A loved one of the deceased might not freely give a touching quote for publication. A witness might not be willing to describe what he saw at the scene of a crime. But the lie used to obtain such information shocks the conscience. The person lied to has reason to feel deeply betrayed when he sees in the press an account of the information he provided in good faith at a moment of extremity. Such a lie also can do palpable harm. What if after a deceptive phone call from a reporter a witness then refuses to give information to real investigators? Or takes action on the basis of something the liar has idly said? The illegality of impersonating certain public officials adds bite to the point.

Sissela Bok, in her book *Lying: Moral Choice in Public and Private Life,* identifies four basic moral excuses for intentional deception: the avoidance of harm, the production of benefit, the requirements of fairness, and the protection of the truth. All involve a utilitarian calculus, a balancing of good and harm, so Bok arrives at several general principles for adding up the moral gains and losses:[2]

As we consider different kinds of lies, we must ask, first, whether there are alternative forms of action which will resolve the difficulty without the use of a lie; second, what might be the moral reasons brought forward to excuse the lie, and what reasons can be raised as counter-arguments. Third, as a test of these two steps, we must ask what a public of reasonable persons might say about such lies.

She begins with a presumption against the deception because a lie always does moral damage. The experience of O'Malley demonstrates why. First, the victim feels violated, and the suffering of an innocent argues powerfully against the practice that inflicts it. If a reporter honestly tried to imagine how he would feel being lied to in similar circumstances, he would surely see the point. Second, lying is habit-forming. So even a justified lie might change the character of the liar's general conduct, leading him to deceive in circumstances that offer no justification. It is a commonplace to note that one lie leads to another. Think of the reporter who, having lied about his identity to the mother of an accident victim, found it a short step to lie about the reason for his call so as not to have to break the news of her son's death. What about lying in print? Or shading the truth to flatter someone who might in the future be useful or covering up the failings of someone who had been helpful in the past? Once the lie becomes a technique for getting the job done, it can spread so far it destroys the purpose it was supposed to serve. Third, the liar often assumes he will not be found out, and it is easier for him to understand his own needs than those of others. So he will often exaggerate the harm to be avoided, the benefit to be achieved, the fairness to be accomplished, or the significance of the truth to be advanced by the lie. And finally, deception creates a demoralizing climate in which it becomes easy for people thoughtlessly to fall into a pattern of lying. My experience on the police beat confirms this. I had been raised as a boy to tell the truth, but I learned on the job to lie. Take this as a warning. Remember the choirboy who became Deputy Coroner O'Malley deceiving the bereaved on the telephone.

Undercover Tactics

One could pose hypothetical situations in which impersonating a public official would forestall such an immediate and drastic harm or would create such an enormous and universal benefit that any reasonable person would declare it justified. But this exercise would be fanciful in comparison with the actual situations in which a reporter might pretend to be the law. Rarely can a reporter avoid imminent danger only by impersonating a cop; the device works better for beating the clock or the competition than for saving a life.

What about undercover techniques? They do not involve the same level of audacity and usually do not violate the law. The government's extensive use of undercover tactics to root out crime may appear to add a gloss of legitimacy to the practice. And in some instances the deception may be minor. When I was working on a story for the *Chicago Daily News* on the Chicago Park District, I set about trying to get a job as temporary employee. Practices were so lax that I never had to say a deceptive thing as I followed the system from personnel office to union headquarters (temporary employees were not unionized but had to get union cards anyway). All it took was keeping silent about my newspaper affiliation and giving a highly selective account of my education and work experience.

A reporter will often share his subterfuges with readers (and usually gleefully), and this introduces some element of restraint. Bok does not permit after-the-fact publicity to substitute for before-the-fact moral analysis, but she does recognize its usefulness. "Moral justification . . . ," she writes, "cannot be exclusive or hidden; it has to be capable of being made public. In going beyond the purely private, it attempts to transcend also what is merely subjective. Wittgenstein pointed to these elements of justification in observing that 'justification consists in appealing to something independent.' "[3] Though it is not sufficient to justify journalistic deceit, this element of public disclosure should be the ethical *sine qua non* of any deception in the course of reporting.

Honesty in the aftermath does not cure the betrayal inflicted on those who originally believed the lie. Disclosure of the trick can even make the hurt worse, since it usually comes in the context of a story hostile to the interests of the victims. (*The Acme Ambulance Co. routinely charges for services never performed. The Daily Blurb fooled Acme into hiring one of its reporters as an attendant, and he watched as the firm engaged in an open pattern of cheating.*) When the people victimized by the reporter's lie are malefactors of some sort, one might not sympathize with their pain. Disclosure in such circumstances runs little chance of provoking public criticism. But what of those on the periphery who might have been guilty of nothing? And how often will a newspaper reveal its deception when the objects turn out to be innocent?

It would be intriguing to have public opinion data showing whether newspaper readers have grown more hostile to impersonation and trickery over the very years during which the general journalistic mores began to shift against these techniques. My suspicion is that attitudes probably have changed as confidence in all institutions eroded, but that the public has not become more hostile to the specific practice of undercover reporting than it has to other aspects of newspaper journalism. Today on any number of very popular television newsmagazine shows like *60 Minutes* one can see the work of hidden cameras, undercover news operatives, and so on. Often the journalist eventually confronts the victims of the deception on camera with the fruits of the lie so the viewer can see their surprised, awkward reactions. I have not noticed any public outcry against these spectacles, though speaking for myself, the moment of truth is always difficult to watch. The widespread use of these techniques on television and the general lack of public criticism (in contrast to the complaints one hears about other tactics such as the ambush interview and the mass stakeout of private homes) suggest that people accept them.

So why should newspapers shy away from impersonation and undercover practices? First, because in most cases there are other ways to get the information: deception is just a shortcut. Second, because it creates an environment that tolerates lying, which is highly dangerous for a journalistic enterprise. And third, because a newspaper's strongest bond with its audience is the simple truth. Any departure from that, even when the audience seems to understand the reasons, can hardly help but erode the confidence that forms the very basis of the enterprise.

In an extreme situation a newspaper might make an exception to the general rule against deception. But this decision should only be made at the highest level, probably by the editor, after vigorous discussion. He should treat with great skepticism the justifications mustered on behalf of using the deceptive technique. A shrewd editor will initially refuse the request simply to force the reporting team to be as clever as possible about how to pursue the story by other means. Because group thinking can be morally blind, it would help to invite some informed outsider into the conversation or take other steps to make sure that the arguments against making an exception get full consideration. And then the newspaper should commit itself to disclosure of what it did, regardless of the outcome. It should explain why and how the decision was made, whether or not the deceptive practice resulted in a publishable story. These disciplines would go a long way to meeting the powerful general objections to undercover reporting techniques.

There are plenty of circumstances in which a reporter can get a look at a situation firsthand without lying about his identity or his reasons for being there. I do not believe that the journalistic obligation of truth-telling requires reporters to wear their press passes on their chests. When a reporter in the course of his ordinary human activity and without lying gets into a position to witness newsworthy events (when a building inspector solicits a bribe at the reporter's own home, for example, or a city work crew goes to sleep on the job along his route to the office), he does not need to interrupt the action with a disclosure of his affiliation. Newspaper reporters do not need to give Miranda warnings. Only if they have some reason to reveal their identities (on a job application, under questioning by authorities, or even perhaps when asked by another person) does the requirement of candor come in.

Still, respect for people's privacy ought to make a journalist think twice before reporting something to which he was, essentially, a voyeur. If he overheard a conversation in circumstances in which the participants had a reasonable expectation that they were free of uninvited ears, the reporter should balance the privacy interests against the news value of the information before going into print.

OTHER DECEPTIVE PRACTICES

Unfortunately, deceptive journalistic techniques other than impersonation and undercover work have not received much scrutiny inside the business. One common practice, at least among investigative reporters, involved Ben Bradlee's *Washington Post* in its finest hour. Carl Bernstein and Bob Woodward referred to it in their book about their Watergate investigation, *All the President's Men:*[4]

> Though it wasn't true, Woodward told Deep Throat that he and Bernstein had a story for the following week saying that Haldeman was the fifth person in control of disbursements from the secret fund.
>
> "You'll have to do it on your own," Deep Throat said. . . . Since he had not cautioned them on Haldeman, he was effectively confirming the story.

Sissela Bok takes issue forcefully with Bernstein and Woodward:[5]

> [I]t is certain that the reporters deserve great credit for exposing the misdeeds of the Watergate scandal. It can be argued that, in order for this exposure to be possible, deception was needed; but what is more troubling in the book than the lies themselves is the absence of any acknowledgment of moral dilemma. No one seems to have stopped to think that there was a problem in using deceptive means.

No one weighed the reasons for and against doing so. There was no reported effort to search for honest alternatives, or to distinguish among different forms and degrees of deception, or to consider whether some circumstances warranted it more than others.

The absence of such reflection may well result in countless young reporters unthinkingly adopting some of these methods.

Other reporters did not need the example of Bernstein and Woodward to lead them to try this kind of deception. Telling somebody that you already know what you are actually trying to learn is a trick as old as time. I recall a surrealistic interview a colleague and I had with a high-ranking military officer concerning a code-word classified military intelligence activity. The rules were that he would not tell us anything, only confirm or deny what we knew. It was an invitation to fish, and we did, with such remarkable success that I later learned the military service had asked the Justice Department to investigate how we got the information.

There are other variations. The reporter may threaten to make the subject of his questions the fall guy in a story unless he comes across with information. This bears a close resemblance to police threats to a potential defendant unless he informs on another potential defendant.

The time has come to condemn this kind of thing. If the threat is honest, it means the reporter would tell his story differently as a *quid pro quo* for a favor, which violates the basic truth discipline. But usually the threat is a lie, because the reporter and his editors take the truth discipline seriously. Such a lie should be subjected to the same analysis as any other journalistic deception.

A reporter will rarely disclose this variety of deceit to the reader or even to his editors, which makes it especially questionable, since the unexamined lie is often the one with the least justification. News organizations should start giving direction and training to their reporters and editors in order to bring under control these insidious deceits, just as they have reined in the bigger, more open, and prize-threatening ones.

Manipulating Relationships

Janet Malcolm touched an even more fundamental issue of deception in her book *The Journalist and the Murderer:*[6]

> Every journalist who is not too stupid or too full of himself to notice what is going on knows that what he does is morally indefensible. He is a kind of confidence man, preying on people's vanity, ignorance, or loneliness, gaining their trust and betraying them without remorse. Like the credulous widow who wakes up one day to find the charming young man and all her savings gone, so the consenting subject of a piece of nonfiction writing learns—when the article or book appears—his hard lesson.

This broadside attack, originally published in *The New Yorker*, earned Malcolm a lot of attention and, unsurprisingly, a good deal of hostility from journalists. Later, when she lost a trial in a libel suit accusing her of making up quotes, reporters gleefully noted that her attack on journalistic morality apparently resulted from introspection. (She won the case after a second trial.)[7] Still, her point deserves to be taken seriously.

Malcolm's comment about the moral indefensibility of journalism came at the opening of her report of the relationship between writer Joe McGinniss and Dr. Jeffrey MacDonald, a former Green Beret doctor accused of murdering his family. The way she tells the story, McGinniss led MacDonald to believe that McGinniss believed in MacDonald's innocence and used this pose to get extensive access to MacDonald's thoughts. Then he wrote a book that depicted MacDonald as a manipulative liar as well as a murderer.

For my purposes it is irrelevant whether her account is accurate or not. (Her depiction of a lawyer I know very well is so at odds with what I know of him that I deeply doubt everything else she says.) But assume that the reporter in fact led MacDonald to believe that he wanted to help exonerate him when all along he knew he was going to turn the story into a brief for the prosecution. What is one to make of such behavior?

The question deserves to be taken seriously because offering an apparently sympathetic ear—or at least an understanding one—is among the journalist's most effective techniques in getting people to talk freely. The reporter may be no more fascinated by the individual he is speaking with than the average salesman is by his average customer, but getting the job done requires the establishment of a bond.

A journalist with an open mind should always feel justified in presenting himself that way, regardless of what preconception he has. If he tells someone he wants simply to learn the truth, this should not be deceptive if he is doing his job properly. If in the end he turns the story against someone he has been dealing with, it is not a betrayal, because that possibility was always implicit in the way he described his approach.

When the exchange involves as wary and cunning an individual as MacDonald, it is hard to summon up any moral outrage at his being manipulated as he tries to manipulate the reporter. Expectations are the key here. Both individuals go into the relationship with eyes open. Each has reason to respect and suspect the other. And each has a reason to understand the nature of the game. You can no more accuse McGinniss of immoral behavior than you can accuse a linebacker of battery when he sacks the quarterback—even if he secretly harbors malign feelings toward the man.

It is a different matter when the reporter deals with somebody who is unsophisticated, immature, or otherwise vulnerable, or who does not understand the game. A reporter who strikes up a friendship with such a person for the purpose of betrayal would receive decent people's contempt. The more intimate the bond, the more appalling the violation of it. (When a journalist is already in a close relationship with someone who then tells him something of great news value, this creates a different kind of moral dilemma, which I will discuss a bit later.)

The crucial thing for journalists to recognize is that their trade does not exempt them from the basic moral imperatives that guide all other human relationships. If they depart from the general standard, they must have a good and precise reason to do so. Pursuit of truth is not a license to be a jerk.

SILENCE AND SECRECY

Secrecy about lies told by journalists in pursuit of information is insupportable. Truth in the aftermath is fundamental to preserve the trust of readers whenever deception has occurred. But are there any circumstances that would justify journalists keeping a secret?

Secrecy, like lying, rubs roughly against the basic purposes of journalism and thus deserves scrutiny. First, it is important to deal with a word that journalists commonly use in this connection—censorship. Too often journalists seem confused about this concept. Censorship carries a harsh connotation because it historically referred to official acts of government, not private decisions about what to publish or say. The idea of self-censorship is too imprecise to be of much use in understanding the news values. It could mean the silence of cowardice or the silence of perfect discretion.

Every day a newspaper makes countless decisions not to make information public. Newspapers often have written rules limiting when they will identify juveniles accused of crimes, victims of sex offenses, and so on. A newspaper may decide not to publish gruesome photos of dead people. It may decline to show nudity. It may hesitate to print ripe language of the sort commonly spoken in newsrooms.

Beyond these matters, there are subtler judgments that have to be made. For example, a fact whose public disclosure would cause someone a good deal of pain (reporting a person's embarrassing medical situation, for example, or the details of his financial troubles) may be so significant that it nonetheless should be published or so insignificant that the violation of privacy is far worse than any good that would come of it.

Occasionally, newspapers will acquiesce in official appeals to withhold information—during kidnappings, for example, or when national security is in danger. In wartime, correspondents often readily agree not to publish certain kinds of information—the extent of casualties to friendly forces, for example, or plans for troop movements—when this information might provide an immediate battlefield advantage to the enemy. In Vietnam I heard horror come into the voice of an uncompromising war correspondent as he realized he might have revealed over a nonsecure line precise casualty information about friendly forces. Likewise, when a community teeters on the knife-edge of hostility and unrest, decent news organizations try to be careful not to make the situation worse. This, like battlefield decision-making by reporters and editors, is much more difficult now that we have entered the era of real-time, live television reporting from anywhere on the planet, including the front lines of combat. But perhaps with maturity even this wild new force will come under more respectable internal constraints.

So news organizations "censor" what they report all the time—in the interests of decency, taste, avoidance of unnecessary harm, to keep from whipping up a violent situation, or even at the behest of government to protect secret operations. But what calculus should a reporter and editor use in such situations?

Though one sometimes hears journalists say they do not concern themselves with the consequences of what they publish—so long as it is true—they don't usually act that way. When they make a decision to withhold, it is pragmatic, weighing the probable results of publishing against the probable results of not publishing. The presumption is to publish unless there are strong reasons not to. This comes directly from the role of newspapers as truth-tellers, and it reflects a justified skepticism about the reasons advanced on behalf of pleas not to disclose (especially the reasons advanced by people whose personal interests would be harmed by disclosure).

Of course, journalists' inclination to feel free to publish whatever they learn serves their self-interest and therefore needs to be treated with some skepticism, too. But at least publishing is an open act, and the consequences are there for everyone to see and evaluate. When the decision to publish is controversial, it should be subjected to public discussion in the paper's columns. The general standards for disclosing and withholding should be openly discussed in the newspaper by the editor or ombudsman before an actual situation requiring a decision arises. It also may be worth bringing outsiders into the discussion with editors on close calls, the same way they might be brought in to debate the use of a deceptive tactic.

When editors do make a decision to withhold information, it forecloses the possibility of openness with the audience. All the more reason to discuss publicly in advance of a specific situation the factors involved in such decisions and to invite outside participants into the debate as a counterweight to the internal biases of the reporters and editors. Decisions to withhold potentially important information should be viewed as particularly dangerous. That includes the decision to use confidential sources. The public can never adequately review the judgment to withhold information of this sort, a judgment that on the surface at least is at odds with the purposes and disciplines of journalism.

Hiding Sources

Legal concerns have unfortunately come to dominate the debate over promises of confidentiality to news sources. But let's put the legal arguments aside and deal with what journalists should and should not do, based on their values and disciplines. Where moral and legal imperatives are the same, journalists can take comfort. Where legal and moral analysis conflict, journalists should consider accepting the legal risk and should work to change the law so that it will accord with the proper and responsible standards of journalistic conduct.

Journalists find it useful to promise confidentiality for many reasons: civility, friendship, to make conversation easier. The best reason, though, is the one that is most consistent with the basic definition of the journalistic enterprise: In certain circumstances confidentiality can increase the total amount of useful information available to the public. For example, a reporter might by promising confidentiality persuade a frightened person to describe a crime he has witnessed. This might lead a newspaper to identify a criminal who otherwise would have gone free. Less dramatically, insiders can often be persuaded to give details of an activity or decision if they can be sure that their colleagues will not know who revealed them.

Set against this is the difficulty that withholding the source causes for the reader who wants to assess the reliability of the information. A charge that an individual misused his government power means something different when it comes from his opponent in an election campaign than when it comes from his own trusted aide. The identity of the source is often the most important fact in a story. The anatomy of a Washington news leak often says more about the political situation of the moment than any bit of leaked information does. And finally, secrecy with respect to sources makes it difficult, when the information is erroneous, for the truth to catch up with the leak.

I vividly recall one such incident that occurred while I was working for the Department of Justice. A Washington reporter quoted an unnamed Justice Department source about a significant criminal inquiry into whether a politician, then running for office, had misused campaign funds. The information attributed to the source was all wrong, and I wondered the morning it was published who had been saying such foolish things. Much later I learned from an editor at the newspaper that the reporter's story purported to refer to a conversation he'd had with me. I had talked with the reporter but had never asked for confidentiality (speaking on the record being the best discipline I know of to control an unruly tongue), and I had never said anything like what the newspaper reported. Had I known it was supposed to be me who was saying those things, I might have gone public with what I had really said and perhaps mitigated an injustice to the politician, who was never formally accused of any wrongdoing.

Using confidential sources can also protect a liar or manipulator. If an anonymous source lies and a reporter publishes it, how can the reporter put the situation right when he learns the truth? If he has made an unequivocal promise of confidentiality, he is bound by his word not to reveal the source of the fabrication.

The dangers of relying on anonymous sources should lead newspapers to discourage strongly all unequivocal promises to keep a source of a published piece of information confidential. The most a reporter should ordinarily promise is that he will not publish the source's name in the story, not that he will never reveal the name. Reporters may converse with people discreetly, but they should generally try to find attributable corroboration of anything they publish. Likewise, receiving information in confidence for background purposes in editorial board meetings or other similar settings need not be discouraged, because in such circumstances the newspaper is only trying to get a sense of a situation to advance its general understanding. Anything it wants to publish as fact, it would need to verify through attributable sources.

As a practical matter journalists cannot eliminate the use of unnamed sources altogether. Speaking "on background" has addicted government officials and others whose organizations are often in the news. When Ben Bradlee attempted to establish the admirable rule that the *Washington Post* would not deal on this basis with government, he quickly and uncharacteristically had to retreat. Nonetheless, newspapers should train their reporters to resist efforts by government officials and others to hide behind various forms of confidentiality so that reporters do not become addicted to the convenient habit, too.

When a confidential source asserts something damaging to an individual, particularly a private individual, the rule against publishing without identifiable sources' corroboration must be all but absolute. Personally damaging, unattributed assertions deeply offend the public's sense of fairness. The legal right to confront one's accusers arises from this sense of fair play. Anyone who has ever been the object of a rumor can identify with the frustration felt by a person accused by phantoms. I think readers begin disbelieving the newspaper when it relies on unnamed sources to make accusations damaging to individuals. I know the courts do, which is why the law has not given much protection to confidentiality of sources when it comes to libel cases. Generally, a newspaper faces a choice of either identifying a source or having the court treat the source as nonexistent, which is a strong practical reason to avoid promises of confidentiality.

One related issue that often comes up and is rarely discussed: the confidentiality of information provided in a setting of friendship. Every reporter and editor at some point has a friend begin telling him something newsworthy that would be a personal betrayal to publish. I know journalists who say that to steer clear of such a conflict they simply refuse to get close to news sources. Few if any actually live this way. Journalists often end up in close relationships with people who make news. Now that some journalists themselves have become celebrities and newspapers are covering each other as a beat, even within the cloister it is not possible to avoid such situations.

The best approach to the problem of the conflict between friendship and craft combines sensitivity to the reasonable expectations of the person one is dealing with and openness about the conflicting loyalties in play. For example, if an editor is having dinner with a friend in a family setting and the friend tells the editor that he has been nervous lately because the prominent company of which he is an executive is in financial difficulty, the editor might explain at that point that he assumes his friend does not mean for this to be made public and that it would make the editor uncomfortable to learn any more about the matter because this is something his newspaper would print if it learned of it under other circumstances. This is not an elegant approach, and it is possible to come up with hypothetical cases in which the information is so compelling that the journalist might feel morally obligated to publish. But these are not the common circumstance, and they are not much different for the journalist than for anybody else who might be at strong cross-pressures between a moral imperative to disclose and the demand of personal loyalty to remain silent.

VIOLATION OF THE LAW

Journalists sometimes need to deal with a tension between the imperatives of their work and the requirements of the law. This, of course, occurs in repressive societies where the law is designed to protect the state against independent scrutiny by the press. But even in freer societies the issue can arise either because laws of general legitimacy have particularly troubling consequences for the practice of journalism or because lawmakers have failed to take their duty to freedom of expression seriously enough.

The law in the United States tends to accommodate the press, even when a newspaper violates a responsibility that other institutions are expected to accept. For example, the rule against prior restraint of publication gives room for the press to disobey laws aimed at inhibiting publication. This rule, first announced by the Supreme Court in 1931 in the case of *Near v. Minnesota*,[8] prevents the government from censoring the press except to avoid the most extreme and immediate threats to national security. It does not give news organizations any special exemption from the requirements of generally applicable laws, like espionage or obscenity statutes. It simply says the government may not stop a news organization from making a story public and must wait until after the fact to bring punitive action.

This rule, in effect, permits newspapers to go first to the court of public opinion with a story and hope it decides the case in their favor. This is what happened in the Pentagon Papers case.[9] The government sought to stop publication of a secret Defense Department study of the Vietnam War. The Supreme Court refused, several of its members noting that the government was free to prosecute. Once the study was revealed and people were able to read what all the shouting was about, the government turned its attention away from the newspapers and attempted instead to prosecute the former government official who first leaked the documents.

This, suggested Alexander Bickel, the constitutional scholar who argued the *New York Times* position in the Pentagon Papers case, is an example of "domesticated civil disobedience."[10] The rule against prior restraints permits a newspaper to disregard the government's demands and risk punishment for it. This is quite similar to the less dramatic and more common situations in which a newspaper chooses to violate a law in order to prove that it can be violated. Stories about reporters buying narcotics or illegal handguns on the street are common examples of this. In most instances a prosecutor would be a fool to bring a case against the journalist, though sometimes the story makes law enforcement officials look so bad that they succumb to the temptation to strike back. So long as the journalists have handled the story with care, there is little real risk of punishment. Still, the existence of a valid, justifiable law should make journalists use considerable caution in deciding to break it.

A newspaper may face a law that it feels is manifestly and universally unjust (as segregation laws were). In these circumstances, its moral decision-making is no different from any other citizen's. Civil disobedience is always an option, this time without the domestication of protective constitutional rulings.

RESISTING SUBPOENAS

Some legal restrictions having general applicability affect news organizations uniquely—laws designed to protect government secrecy, for example. Government insiders who break those laws may be aided and abetted by journalists who think that by doing so they will discover significant factual information the disclosure of which is in the public's interest. (The Pentagon Papers case is a fine example of this. There are many others.)

Compelling disclosure of information is the starkest example of a law of general applicability that has to be understood differently when it comes to the news media. When the law compels a journalist to testify in a judicial or legislative proceeding concerning things he believes he must keep confidential, the journalist often finds himself defending secrecy with arguments that he rejects when they are advanced by government on behalf of its own need for confidentiality. I once asked Attorney General Griffin Bell about the similarity of the situations. He smiled and said, "We're all in the same ditch together." This is not as paradoxical as it seems.

The journalist's arguments for secrecy and the government's both grow out of a recognition that public disclosure can have unfortunate consequences. It can discourage individuals (news sources, police informants) from coming forward with information. It can open an organization to unwanted scrutiny (through revelation of internal policy documents or a reporter's notes). It can even make an activity impossible to carry out (the disclosure of either a newspaper or a police undercover operation, for example).

Both confidentiality in government and in news organizations can be used for selfish and unprincipled purposes. Government secrecy is often used to hide embarrassing facts and avoid accountability to voters. Press confidentiality can cover up embarrassing errors. Arguments for confidentiality in either institution need to be judged on the basis of the balance between the public's interest in disclosure and its interest in the activity that disclosure imperils.

Generally, the best legal rule is to keep the two institutions, press and government, from being able to use the law to force the other to disclose information it chooses to withhold. Bickel calls this the "game theory" of the First Amendment,[11] and except in extreme cases it works well.

But this does not give journalists any guidance about when they should freely agree to testify and when they should refuse. In fact, journalists have fallen into the habit of thinking they have no obligation even to consider a government request for information. This is utterly unjustified.

When I worked as a special assistant to United States Attorney General Edward Levi, one of my assignments was to review requests by United States Attorneys for subpoenas of journalists under guidelines requiring attorney general approval. It surprised me that in many circumstances news organizations refused to testify even to the accuracy of what they had published. In these cases there was no issue of confidential sources, no attempt to get a news organization to disclose anything about its internal processes or about information it had decided not to print. These organizations simply decided not to cooperate. One case in particular infuriated me. At the same time that the newspaper's reporters were adamantly (and privately) refusing to testify, the paper was publicly pillorying the Justice Department for doing nothing to pursue the case. Despite my angry recommendation that he should issue the subpoena, the Attorney General wisely declined. Though the newspaper was not behaving in a thoughtful or consistent way, the value of the information it had was not worth creating a confrontation between law enforcement and press freedom in this case.

News organizations should look more kindly on requests for their reporters to testify to the truth of what they have published. In some instances this will help bring to justice individuals already identified by and in the newspaper as villains. I do not see how it makes a newspaper an agent of the state to disclose something about an individual, provoke the government into criminal proceedings against him, and then cooperate in the enterprise. It seems to me that in such circumstances the newspaper is acting completely in accord with the crusading tradition of the press.

Where does one find the moral justification for refusal to testify in these circumstances? It is perhaps a little more apparent when the request is for unpublished information, since to disclose this reveals the internal decision-making processes of the newspaper concerning which there may be some need for protection against the government's prying eye. Practically speaking, cooperating with such requests invites every attorney involved in litigation to make a ritual demand for any and all materials. Since most of what the newspaper reports is litigable in one way or another, this would impose a burden on the paper. But nothing prevents it from receiving adequate compensation for its services in such instances. And the best legal rule requires any litigant seeking to subpoena a journalist to show that he has no other way to get the information.

The moral basis for refusing to cooperate is strongest when the reporter has promised to keep something confidential—usually the source of information. In such circumstances, which as I have said should be kept to a minimum, the newspaper should resist disclosure in the interest of protecting the integrity of its promises. Extreme and special cases—where life is in the balance, for example, or where a newspaper has been tricked into the promise—justify a newspaper in disclosing despite a promise not to, but the choice should be up to the newspaper.

On its side, government should be permitted to discipline its employees against revealing secrets. Freedom of information acts, open meeting statutes, and similar provisions should attempt to accommodate the government's legitimate needs for confidentiality and should not be subject to First Amendment attack when they do so.

When a newspaper does pierce the secrecy of government and discover information that government has a legitimate interest in keeping secret, the reporter and editors should take those legitimate interests into account in deciding whether to publish. Again, an effort must be made to predict the consequences of disclosure and of nondisclosure. Finding a way to discuss the matter outside the tight circle of journalists is useful. Appeals by the government that the newspaper suppress the information should be listened to and not dismissed out of hand. Disclosing classified national security information or other legitimate secrets (like details of ongoing undercover criminal investigations or information about private individuals and organizations that government has a duty to protect) should be done only for strong, articulatable reasons. Stating those reasons in the newspaper and offering to publish opposing views help establish a climate in which such editorial judgments will be made thoughtfully and respected by the community.

PRIVACY AND OTHER MATTERS OF CIVILITY

The news media face increasing public skepticism in part because television has put on public display so much of what they do. On camera, reporters often seem to feel as though they have to show off their toughness and independence, and this generally comes across as surly. During the Persian Gulf War Americans were treated to live broadcasts of press briefings in Dhahran, Saudi Arabia, in which reporters new to war often asked ignorant questions and demanded information that almost anyone would know would help the enemy if released. This gave rise to a parody on the comedy show "Saturday Night Live" in which reporters asked the military briefer where the most vulnerable point in the allies' front lines would be, when the invasion of Kuwait would begin, and other such questions.

All news organizations pay the price for this behavior,

even when their own representatives behave more civilly. People do not make distinctions among the people asking the questions at a White House press conference. The thoughtful and the thuggish are all just "the media."

I have often been tempted to call for the abolition of the presidential press conference on the ground that it does the state of public knowledge more harm than good. I can think of few worse ways to try to learn something factual than through this strange institution. The President, of course, has prepared carefully to answer each question without revealing anything, so the reporters escalate the nastiness of their questions in hopes of at least provoking an intemperate response. It is worse at White House press briefings, which resemble question periods in Parliament. The trouble with the British system as a model for the press, of course, is that in Parliament the questioners quite often have no particular interest in or expectation of eliciting actual information. They are from the opposing parties and seek only the embarrassment of the government. Journalists should be interested only in getting useful information.

Newspapers also suffer vicarious responsibility for other things beyond their control. The spectacle of a gaggle of camera operators and correspondents pressing in on some poor individual who has just suffered a tragic loss must make people doubt our scruples. As disturbing is the ambush interview in which some pathetic, small-time crook gets trapped by an imitator of Mike Wallace. Tabloid television tarnishes the rest of the news media—print and electronic—with its fixation on the lurid and all the permutations and combinations of sexual congress. Do not tell me that these shows are popular. I know they are popular. But that does not mean that the people whose natural itch of curiosity leads them to watch the shows respect the people who make them. This is the secret of gossip. Part of the pleasure of tawdriness is in asserting moral superiority to it.

Public sensitivity about these matters will grow so long as the bonds of journalistic propriety continue to loosen. At the same time the ability of computers to handle vast databases in increasingly sophisticated ways may also begin to haunt people about how much information others have gathered and recorded about their most private habits and decisions. Despite the efforts of public interest lobby groups and some journalists to increase public awareness of what kind of information is being collected and maintained, the public has not yet responded with any intensity. But if it does, you can bet that the media—simply because their intrusions are so very public—will be implicated.

Because they depend so much on the public's belief in their rectitude, newspapers should distance themselves as much as possible from any intrusion upon individuals' privacy that would strike reasonable people as gratuitous, excessive, mean-spirited, or venal. As they develop powerful database marketing capacities of their own, they should take care never to let that information be used in such a way that would lead people to feel the newspaper has violated their trust.

In the future, concerns about privacy may provide newspapers an opportunity in an electronic environment to serve as a buffer between their privacy-conscious readers and the firms that want to sell to them. The newspaper could direct ads to customers who have shown an interest in them without revealing the individual identities of those customers, thus providing readers with commercial information in a way that protects the anonymity of users of the information. Who, after all, wants to reveal to the world that he is interested in getting some more life insurance? Or advice about prostate relief? To capitalize on the commercial opportunity privacy consciousness may offer, the press has to begin strengthening its reputation for trustworthiness in this regard today.

(*three*)
NEWS AND COMMUNITY

EVERY NEWSPAPER, FROM THE MOST COSMOPOLITAN national daily to the smallest rural weekly, is provincial. To survive, a newspaper must reflect a specific audience, usually by holding up a mirror to a particular place. It must share with its readers a sensibility and a set of interests, tastes, and values. Sometimes the interests range widely and the tastes are catholic, but even then the newspaper will have areas of emphasis. The *Chicago Tribune* writes more about grain farming than the *Boston Globe*. The *Los Angeles Times* writes more about the motion picture industry than does any other metropolitan daily. Nobody writes as much about the details of federal employee benefits and work rules as the *Washington Post*. Limitations of time, money, and sheer bulk require the setting of priorities, which journalism calls editing. Even if the space available to print news were infinite (which may in effect be the case in the future with broad-band electronic delivery), there would still be a need for editing—simply to give readers a way to indulge their curiosity in a manageable amount of time.

The community served by a newspaper need not be defined geographically. *USA Today*, for example, has an international market, but it does not aim at every reader. It takes as its prime audience business travelers away from home. Common interests define a newspaper's community, a set of widely shared premises. One of the most important of these is the nature of the political rules under which it operates.

The discussion of journalistic disciplines in the previous chapters, for example, built on a tacit assumption that the newspaper serves a fairly open society that holds government authority over expression sharply in check. In an authoritarian regime the analysis would be different. An absolute ethical rule against printing information known to be false, for example, might be fatal to a newspaper in a tyrannical situation. A newspaper in such circumstances might find itself having to report a good deal of official information that it had excellent reason not to believe. Cunning rather than candor might have to serve as its signal virtue. An honorable strategy might be to reveal as much truth and as little falsehood as possible without being shut down.

Nor would intellectual honesty necessarily serve well a newspaper in a severely repressive society. Its highest calling might be revolutionary, in which case it would want to be remembered for provocation rather than prudence. You don't get people to risk everything on the basis of modest, tentative assertions of what is right.

Even in open societies factions often try to summon the newspapers to the intellectual barricades. This can sometimes be tempting, especially when society's very claim to openness seems to hang in the balance. The Cold War communist threat, for example, at times proved sufficient to overcome some journalists' scruples, and during the Vietnam War the might of the military-industrial complex seemed to some journalists so dangerous to the open society that they set out, in defiance of the moderating disciplines, to defeat it. Today populist attacks on the evils of entrenched power sometimes get the better of journalists' commitment to the full rendering of reality.

To avoid being led into error by such temptations, a journalist must be clear about what constitutes free expression so he can recognize when it is truly threatened. Such clarity also will deepen the meaning of the truth discipline, for a newspaper needs to reflect its community in no aspect more than in the way it seeks knowledge. The truth discipline grows out of assumptions underlying the system of free expression, which is the fundamental social guide to the search for truth. These assumptions concern not only epistemological issues but also fundamental conceptions about human nature. When journalism roots its practices in this firm ground, it reinforces the very ideas that give it protection. It reaches beyond the shifting directions of public opinion to a deeper and steadier consensus about value that over the course of American history has not only endured but grown stronger.

THE BASIS OF CLOSED SOCIETIES

The surest sign of a closed society is when the state makes a claim of absolute truth. The assertion may be as cynical as a tyrant's will. Or it may spring from profound, genuine, and widely shared beliefs, such as in the revealed word of God. As Karl Popper suggested in his study *The Open Society and Its Enemies*,[1] common to the ideologies of closed societies is a sense of historical necessity. This sometimes manifests itself in a doctrine of utopian inevitability (as in religious fundamentalism, as well as in Hegel and Marx), sometimes in the myth of perfection corrupted by historical decay (as in Plato's *Republic*[2]). Whether one views this as a philosophical or political matter, the consequence is the same: truth finds its sources of legitimacy outside public debate and cannot be altered by it. In a closed society the purpose of expression is to persuade people of the predetermined truth.

For Plato this justifies the idea that philosophers should rule as king, since they are in touch with the eternal. But philosophy is a lonely trade, and Plato's choice of monarchs never had much support among people in other walks of life. Still, other elements in the *Republic* have commonly found their way into the rationale for closed social arrangements.

Much of his argument for restraining expression concerns the conditions under which children should be raised—specifically the children who will grow up to guard the state—and this emphasis on the young echoes down to the present hour through the literature of illiberality. Dealing with children offers the most attractive grounds for controlling the expressive environment because children's individuality and powers of judgment have not been fully formed. Though they might be thought of as a special case, calling for different rules, the Platonic argument does not proceed this way. After dealing with children, he and other philosophers hostile to free expression extend their skepticism to the powers of judgment of adults. In other words, having dealt with children, they then go on to see nearly everyone as childish. Plato's deep mistrust of democracy (which he equates with anarchy) and of individualism (which he equates with selfishness) follows directly from his lack of respect for people of most classes and types. Democracy is no system for one who condescends to the general run of mankind or believes privilege means privileged access to the truth.

The parable of the cave is perhaps the most memorable moment in all of Plato's work. By likening the knowledge available to man through his senses to shadows on a wall, Plato at first seems to show a decent respect for the limits of human understanding, but that is not the end of the parable. The philosopher can look past the shadows and see the light, though he will be misunderstood when he returns to the land of shadows to report what he has seen. This is a myth of intellectual arrogance.

The Socrates Plato depicts in the *Republic* is a different Socrates than the one who emerges in other dialogues. He is not the brilliant, self-effacing questioner whose wisdom arises from his assertion of his lack of knowledge. A much less appealing Socrates speaks in the *Republic*. Intellectual humility would ill befit Socrates here, for Plato's king gets his legitimacy from the light of his knowledge of absolute truth.

Paradoxically, Plato's earlier, more epistemologically modest Socrates was executed for expression deemed corrupting to the young. In the spectacle of Socrates's trial and punishment Plato provided the first great drama of free expression. It was the very kind of public theater the Socrates of the *Republic* might have wanted to repress.

But despite the haunting impact of the *Defense, Crito,* and *Phaedo,* the Platonic arguments against free expression come down to the present day wrapped in the stately cloth of courage and civic virtue. In 1978 in a commencement address at Harvard, Nobel laureate Alexander Solzhenitsyn stunned the West with an attack on its liberal values. The Russian exile had described in *The Gulag Archipelago* the awful tyranny of the Stalinist state and through this supreme act of individual witness against authority had come to be seen as an heroic opponent of repression. People in the West naturally expected him to savor the freedom of expression he found in his new home in the United States. But instead, Solzhenitsyn launched a broadside attack upon the open societies of the West for failing to recognize the dark nature of absolute evil (which, like a photographic negative, derives from the light of absolute truth).

Many of his accusations had a decidedly Platonic ring:

- "[M]ediocrity triumphs under the guise of democratic restraints."[3]
- "[I]n early democracies . . . all individual human rights were granted on the ground that man is God's creature. That is, freedom was given to the individual conditionally, in the assumption of his constant religious responsibility."[4]
- "Society has turned out to have scarce defense against the abyss of human decadence, for example against the misuse of liberty for moral violence against young people, such as motion pictures full of pornography, crime, and horror."[5]

Solzhenitsyn used the entire Platonic arsenal—the reference to children, the distrust of individualism, the disrespect for common opinion, and most tellingly, the belief that freedom has brought society into conflict with transcendent truth:[6]

[T]he fight for our planet, physical and spiritual, a fight of cosmic proportions, is not a vague matter of the future; it has already started. The forces of Evil have begun their decisive offensive. You can feel their pressure, yet your screens and publications are full of prescribed smiles and raised glasses. What is the joy about?

It is perhaps impolite to the great man to mention that since that speech some of the smiles and raised glasses have

been for the triumph of the tolerant values he decried as cow-
ardly. Solzhenitsyn's sense of historical doom turned out to be
vastly exaggerated.

History regularly fails to live up to fatalists' dismal predictions because all such claims are deeply flawed. The man
emerging from Plato's cave has seen a light nobody else can see.
The idea of absolute truth denies the witness of our own senses,
the ambiguities of human interaction that defy sweeping prediction, leaving us with the unsettling recognition that the
truth is something we can only make provisionally, a day at
a time.

But no matter how many times reality confounds men's
attempts to know it completely, the Platonic yearning for pure
light and the Platonic fear of decay again and again reassert
themselves. You can hear them today even in the arguments of
people who probably think they are defending a society of free
discussion. Here is a recent example from the work of Neil
Postman of New York University:[7]

Changes in the symbolic environment are like changes in the natural
environment; they are both gradual and additive at first, and then, all
at once, a critical mass is achieved, as the physicists say. A river that
has slowly been polluted suddenly becomes toxic; most of the fish per-
ish; swimming becomes a danger to health. But even then, the river
may look the same and one may still take a boat ride on it. In other
words, even when life has been taken from it, the river does not dis-
appear, nor do all of its uses, but its value has been seriously dimin-
ished and its degraded condition will have harmful effects throughout
the landscape. It is this way with our symbolic environment. We have
reached, I believe, a critical mass in that electronic media have deci-
sively and irreversibly changed the character of our symbolic environment. We are now a culture whose information, ideas and epistemology are given form by television, not the printed word. . . . Like the fish
who survive a toxic river and the boatmen who sail on it, there still
dwell among us those whose sense of things is largely influenced by
older and clearer waters.

Postman's metaphor touches the most evocative contemporary image of decay—not spiritual decline but the human

destruction of natural environmental purity. It suggests that expression can be a kind of pollution in which the offender will not bear the costs of his actions unless government steps in to redress the situation. Postman also plays brilliantly on the sense of nostalgia that breathed through Plato's argument in *The Republic*. Many critiques of openness grow out of the same fundamental resistance to change and its uncertainties that Popper identifies as the center of Plato's thought.[8]

OPENNESS AND UNCERTAINTY

The distractions of a free society can be troubling, of course, and moral debate is always in order. But the system of free expression operates on the theory that discussion rather than the explication of authoritative truth is the best way to guide a society through an uncertain future. The recognition of uncertainty is, in fact, essential to the theory of free expression. The commitment to individual autonomy against authority begins with epistemology.

If absolute truth were demonstrable, the principal reason for permitting open debate would vanish. It would not be necessary to go to the marketplace of ideas to find a conception of the Good. The Good would have a clarity for all to see, and only fools and sinners would deny it. Even respect for individual conscience would not permit latitude of expression, since in the presence of absolute truth, the most just way to treat conscience would be to protect it from error by making it hew to the one true line.

An open society based on a system of free expression does not deny the value of the pursuit of truth. That position falls to the radical skeptics who doubt the possibility of any knowledge. The theory of free expression assumes that the pursuit of truth is a worthy goal that can reward with increasing understanding and satisfaction those who engage in it. But it also understands that human assertions of truth must always be thought of as either provisional or too personal to treat as absolute. Revealed truth does not reveal itself the same way to all persons.

The concept of the open society owes a great deal to the

emergence of scientific method as a mechanism for the advancement of knowledge. Scientific method regards all hypotheses about the world as tentative. No proposition is scientific unless it can theoretically be falsified by evidence available to the senses (aided by equipment and other indirect techniques). Falsifying data, when they mount up, goad scientists to attempt a new hypothesis. A shift in the basic scientific model occurs when a new hypothesis explains the data more completely or more elegantly than the old one did. Thus does knowledge proceed. Lack of certainty does not inhibit this process or keep us from acting. We successfully sent humans to the moon even though some future discovery in astrophysics might eventually cause a reassessment of the theories on which the calculations were made charting the *Apollo*'s path. Uncertainty does not threaten scientific knowledge; it drives scientific inquiry, which requires a toleration for continuous challenge to authority.

One may either accept this epistemological approach or reject it (as a mystic would, whose evidence is unique to him and thus cannot be refuted or replicated). But the point of a system of free expression is not to impose one orthodoxy (even the orthodoxy of scientific method) above all other possible ways to the truth. The point of free expression is to prevent the state from making a choice of absolute truth and enforcing it through law to the exclusion of the discussion of other possibilities.

Just as the open society is based on humility with respect to claims of truth, it is also based on a sense of the flaws in human nature. The philosophy of free expression doubts whether anyone can safely be entrusted with power to determine truth for others. Popper put the point this way:[9]

(W)e must ask whether political thought . . . should not prepare for the worst leaders, and hope for the best. But this leads to a new approach to the problem of politics, for it forces us to replace the question: Who should rule? by the new question: *How can we so organize political institutions that bad or incompetent rulers can be prevented from doing too much damage?*

This sense of caution was earlier elaborated in Montesquieu's idea of separation of powers and then in the rationale for the system of check and countercheck written into the United States Constitution. But there was no unanimity about human nature among either philosophers or practical politicians at the time the Constitution was drafted.

Some of the Founding Fathers made their wariness explicit. George Washington, who as a warrior was no stranger to the things of which men were capable, complained in a letter to John Jay about the veering legislative policies of the Articles of Confederation period, dryly observing, "We have, probably, had too good an opinion of human nature in forming our confederation."[10]

James Madison, in Federalist LI, stated famously the case for mistrusting government leaders:[11]

Ambition must be made to counteract ambition. The interest of the man must be connected to the constitutional rights of the place [office]. It may be a reflection of human nature that such devices should be necessary to controul the abuses of government. But what is government itself but the greatest of all reflections on human nature? If men were angels, no government would be necessary. If angels were to govern men, neither external nor internal controuls on government would be necessary.

But Madison's view of man's fallen condition was not universally shared then any more than it is today. Jefferson and others eloquently argued for the perfectability of man and the self-evidence of certain natural-law propositions. These related ideas found their fullest flowering in the powerful rhetoric of the Declaration of Independence. In Jefferson's case, self-evident natural law included the idea that people should be free to express their contrary views. But the trouble with basing free expression on natural-law concepts is that what was self-evident to Jefferson has not been self-evident to others. (After Clarence Thomas was nominated to the Supreme Court, a good number of intellectual heirs of Jefferson were shocked by his natural-law approach, mainly because his natural laws conflicted with some of theirs.) Or another way of putting it: Self-evidence has a paradoxical relationship with freedom of expression, since the existence of absolute truth would justify the repression of all discussion at odds with it. (This argument has been put forward most explicitly in times of stress; for example, it was used to defend restrictions upon advocacy of communism during the period when that ideology seemed to threaten the liberal democracies of the West.)

The inspiration for the American Revolution may have come from Jefferson's self-evident propositions in the Declaration of Independence, but the practice of government in the Republic has drawn more on the pessimistic political engineering inherent in the separation of powers doctrine. Freedom of expression, as part of this structure, creates a potent source of power against the coercion of the state. It is a decentralized power, which makes it difficult for authority to control, and it seeks to insure nothing less than that the people may always have their voice.

THE TEMPTATION TO REGULATE

Within this diffuse system, the media represent a locus of countervailing power against government, and thus they offer government an attractive regulatory target. Of course, even in the absence of regulation their power is anything but unchecked. The economic marketplace exerts uncompromising control. To the tedious question so often asked of journalists, "Who elected you to tell us what to do?" there are two complete answers: First, the people who pay to read what we publish. And second, nobody needs to elect us at the ballot box because we do not have the authority to make anyone do or even read what we say.

But however constrained the media may feel, government officials feel constrained by them. So the authorities have every reason to want, one way or another, to gain the upper hand in the relationship.

One way is to court the media with attention, invite them into the inner circles, treat them as if they are as much a part of the political establishment as senators or members of Congress. This happens nowhere as grandly as it does in Washington, where the symbiotic relationship between government and the news media has gotten so intimate that the system seems at times like a closed feedback loop, with the prevailing view growing louder and louder until it is difficult for an outsider to discern what all the noise is about.

The other way government officials seek to control the media is to exercise the power of the state directly upon them. For a number of reasons, the danger of this is increasing.

From the beginning of the radio age, government has always had a selfless rationale for regulating broadcasting. Because the electromagnetic spectrum that carries radio and television signals is finite (there are only so many frequencies), government stepped in to allocate it and to protect against electromagnetic trespassers. Since the spectrum "belonged" to nobody, it was deemed to be owned by the public. Thus, when a broadcaster obtained a license to use part of it, the government required him to use it in the public interest, conveniently reserving unto itself the power to define what that interest is.

Today the whole idea of regulation based on physical limits on the number of broadcast frequencies is hopelessly outdated. One might just as readily justify an exception to the right against unreasonable search on the grounds that housing is always in limited supply. The means by which electromagnetic signals reach people have so proliferated that every automobile and pedestrian can be a mobile wireless sending and receiving station. Soon cable systems will be delivering programming in such profusion that a subscriber will dial it up the way he dials up a number on the telephone. The days when television meant channels 2, 5, 7, 9, and 11 are long past. Any area of significant population density already has scores of channels available at all hours of the day, not to mention the profuse information available by connecting a personal computer to a telephone line and dialing into vast database networks. Any individual in the United States can today have instantaneous access to a world of information that only a few years ago was not even available to the highest realms of government.

But the Federal Communications Commission still allocates broadcast frequencies. And politicians use a natural monopoly rationale of the sort applied to public utilities to justify cable television regulation. With the breakup of AT&T, the federal government (encouraged by the established media) stepped in to prevent the newly independent, local telephone monopolies from owning the information they distributed (thus keeping them from competing in the cable TV, classified advertisement, or news markets). Government has also hated to let go of elaborate, technical rules keeping companies from having outlets in markets that overlap, so that a company that owns a radio station with a strong signal in Cleveland cannot start a daily newspaper in Toledo. These rules may have made some rough sense in a competitive environment in which anyone who owned a newspaper and TV station could dominate the information flow in a city. But what sense do they make in places like Los Angeles, New York, Chicago, Miami, Dallas, or Houston where the greater challenge in the marketplace of ideas is getting heard over the crowd?

As government has become more and more deeply involved in the business of the news media (sometimes at the invitation of the media themselves), no matter how independent they may want to be, media companies find themselves lobbying like special-interest groups. Government decisions so profoundly shape their business that many media firms (including Tribune Co.) regularly employ full-time professionals in Washington to keep their positions before the administration and Congress. Their trade organizations engage in this as well, and delegations of publishers and broadcast executives often can be found in the offices of key legislators. This is not because they have an interest in general legislation (like tax rates or environmental standards), where their voices would only be a few among a chorus of different kinds of firms. It is because the government intervenes directly in the way their enterprises operate. If they are public companies, their duty to shareholders requires executives to take reasonable steps to encourage the government to act in ways that help or at least do not hurt. They are enmeshed in government interactions because they have no choice.

This positions the government to reward and punish news media separately from other enterprises. Once segregated this way for special treatment, whether protective or restrictive, the media become supplicants. This is the wrong relationship.

There should be a balance of power between the two estates. The media should have no authority to require government to do anything (even to compel it to reveal information it has not chosen through legislation or the exercise of official discretion to reveal), but the government should certainly have no authority to regulate the media other than through the extension of generally applicable laws (like the income tax).[12] This balance has tilted farther and farther toward the government side, especially in the regulation of electronic media. No matter how much you hear about deregulation, do not expect government officials to give up this power without a fight, even when all the old grounds for exercising it have slipped away. Already new reasons are being incubated.

The United States seems poised on the verge of creating an information distribution system so capacious that the mind reels at the profligacy of choices an individual will have. It has come to be known as the "information superhighway," and the way that metaphor has found its way into the common parlance should send a chill through proponents of free expression. Superhighways were built and managed by the government.

The new information network need not be. Private firms seem willing and able to put large amounts of capital to the task. One of the virtues of this "superhighway" is that by vastly increasing the number of channels through which people can communicate, it will shatter the government's rationale for regulation. Technological change and the inventiveness of enterprise have already outstripped government's cumbersome regulatory mechanisms.

The most likely argument the government will raise to defend clinging to its involvement will be the need to guarantee universal service. Suppose private enterprise were allowed to do the job of rewiring the country (itself a crude metaphor that suggests the government-regulated electric or telephone companies even though important elements of the new technology require no wires). The level of use in poor and rural areas would probably not justify the capital investment it would take to provide service. Therefore, it will be argued, the government must treat the purveyors of the new technology as it treats public utilities. Of course, government could impose a general tax and use the money to pay private firms to provide the service. Or it could subsidize individuals directly through vouchers and let them choose what services to buy, but either of those methods would significantly limit the government's power over the channel.

Look instead for something like a new Stamp Act, the colonial law that controlled expression by levying special taxes on the sale of blank paper. In illiberal nations, the control of the importation of newsprint is a key element of autocratic authority. Any significant government regulation of the "information superhighway," including setting prices or levying special tolls, will give government officials a high-tech version of one of the crudest weapons in the dictator's arsenal.

To get the greatest benefit from the new high-capacity, low-cost communications channels, all the government has to do is use ordinary antitrust standards to encourage competition and require that distribution channels be offered to everyone on equal terms (making them, in effect, common carriers as railroads have traditionally been). In this way anyone with something to say will be able to put out a message and attempt to reach an audience. He will not have to own the means of distribution any more than a manufacturer needs to own a rail line.

Unfortunately, the debate over the governance of the information superhighway takes place at a time when even those one would traditionally think would be most likely to defend the libertarian approach have suffered a crisis of confidence. When such eloquent defenders of expressive freedom as Wayne Booth argue for putting a "sin tax" on speech undertaken for financial gain in order to subsidize programs to compensate for the harm speech does,[13] it is a sign that the growth of an "information economy" has deeply eroded support for the traditional understanding of free expression.

The contemporary complaints about free expression have a familiar ring. Booth, for example, cites "the vicious images and distortions that flood our lives and corrupt our children's ideals. . . . The grunge pouring from TV, movies and videos—not to mention magazines and newspapers—will destroy us unless we do something about it." He also appeals to a populist feeling that prosperity among people who make a lot of money from expression renders them unworthy of the protection to which the penurious are due. "(A)ll who are paid excessively for their wares—best-selling novelists, movie actors, directors and producers, cartoonists, newspaper and magazine editors, top lawyers, advertisers, bond salesmen, professors at the top, would share their 'profit.' " I shouldn't think that we need any more financial burdens on people entering the field of expression, though that is what the proposed tax would do, providing another encouragement to people to become basketball players or bankers rather than novelists, painters, professors, and journalists. Even more curiously, speech that gains a big, paying audience gets discouragement, while speech far fewer people are willing to pay for goes free or gets financial encouragement. (Booth proposes a graduated tax on the income of people in the business of expression when that income exceeeds the salary of public school teachers. At four times teachers' salaries, the tax is confiscatory: 100 percent.)

I cite Booth's arguments for a "sin" tax on expression in full recognition that he is a master of irony and fully capable of speaking with his tongue planted firmly in his cheek. But whether he has offered a modest proposal or a sincere one, he does register a feeling that goes deep in society today. Though this often manifests itself as concern for the young, it really transcends the special vulnerabilities of tender age. There is a growing sense that speech becomes commercially successful only by pandering and that people in the business of purveying messages have little or no genuine concern about the quality or nature of what they sell.

The media, of course, have responsibility for the formation of public taste. Others share the responsibility. The education system, especially, has a duty to advance the level of public taste, and it seems to be failing. If we cannot in this country teach people to be more discriminating, even though a large portion of the population goes to high school and beyond, then perhaps we deserve to be inundated by the junk people demand.

Ultimately freedom means that the people shape their information environment, so serious-minded newspapers should see it in their long-term interests to lead them toward the light, even as they try to satisfy their immediate interests and appetites. Fail to encourage high standards and newspapers will decline; fail to satisfy people's curiosity and they will die a quicker death. The tension between these two approaches to the audience provides journalism one of its greatest challenges.

FOR A PRESS AS OPEN AS THE SOCIETY

Every day as I enter Tribune Tower, I pass through a stone lobby engraved with testimonials to the importance of free expression:

> Congress shall make no law respecting an establishment of religion or prohibiting the free exercise thereof, or abridging the freedom of speech or of the press . . . [1st Amendment to the U.S. Constitution]

> The mass of every people must be barbarous where there is no printing, and consequently knowledge is not generally diffused. Knowledge is diffused among our people by newspapers. [Samuel Johnson]

> Where there is a free press, the governors must live in constant awe of the opinions of the governed. [Thomas Babington Macaulay]

> The constitutional right of free speech has been declared to be the same in peace and in war. In peace, too, men may differ widely as to what loyalty to our country demands, and an intolerant majority, swayed by passion or by fear, may be prone in the future, as it has often been in the past, to stamp as disloyal, opinions with which it disagrees. [Louis Brandeis]

Nowhere in those celebrations of free speech will you find anything said about a duty owed *by* the press. Let there be no mistake about this: the system of free expression, except in certain narrow circumstances (such as the law of fraud and libel), does not impose any special obligation on anyone engaging in expression. In fact, in most areas of discourse, free speech affords people a license to lie. So the government of an open society generally has no business enforcing journalistic disciplines, even truth-telling.

What the law cannot impose, however, the press should voluntarily accept. It should do so out of pure self-interest, if for no other reason. And the best place to begin finding the basis and meaning of these voluntary commitments is the philosophical underpinning of the system of free expression.

Journalists sometimes try to justify the truth discipline on the theory that newspapers have become monopolies; ethical disciplines are put forward as a way of correcting against market failure in the marketplace of ideas. This is a dangerous line of argument because it invites government intervention (as all market failures do). But it also is factually incorrect. Nobody knows better than a publisher that newspapers do not have monopoly power in the information market. The days of the island-like town with one individual or institution monopolizing the conversation ended when television marched across the plains.

Most metropolitan papers have a surfeit of competition. Even if they have no downtown opponent, they have plenty of daily competition in the suburbs. The story of the metropolitan newspaper business in the last several decades has not been the death of downtown papers as much as the growth of full-service suburban newspapers and broadcast news alternatives. *Newsday* on Long Island is the most highly developed example. It built a franchise just past the boroughs and then marched back into Manhattan to challenge the *New York Times* and *New York Daily News*. Something similar has happened in the suburbs of Los Angeles. Supplementing newspapers are broadcast TV and cable (with its heavy component of political programming), not to mention all-news and talk radio, on which it sometimes seems that every extreme of opinion is spoken every day. Beyond these old-fashioned media stretches the Internet, a kind of talk radio in text, raised to whole new orders of magnitude (and subject to no truth discipline at all as far as I can tell).

Of course, newspapers do still have the power to put subjects into the conversation. After all, what are they talking about on talk radio? Television does not do the routine, ground-level reporting that is required to keep track of what is going on across a large metropolitan area. It does not have the staff to cover the complex jigsaw puzzle of political jurisdictions and social networks of the modern American metropolis. This gives the papers an ability to do what is often dully described as agenda-setting. It is actually much broader than that. It is the ability to get people to look here rather than there and perhaps see what they otherwise wouldn't. So while there is no monopoly, there is power. And the public has lost confidence in all powerful institutions, the media included.

The best way in a free society to overcome the natural skepticism about power is to exercise it wisely. This is where journalistic disciplines come in. By following them a newspaper embraces the richness of public debate and thus constitutes itself as a forum for the community. It replicates within its pages the kind of openness the system of free expression means to provide.

Letters to the editor columns or op-ed pages most clearly fulfill this function. They give voice to opinions that otherwise might have been left out. And so good newspapers today generally accept the idea that whenever they speak pointedly in their editorials, they should go out of their way to publish opposing views. (What truth discipline to apply to the authors of these pieces is an intriguing question.)

THE TRUTH DISCIPLINE

Editorials openly stating opinion on ultimate issues of public policy represent only a small part of what a newspaper presents every day. And offering a forum for opposing views is not the most important way that a newspaper can exemplify the philosophy of free expression.

Through its general reporting, too, a newspaper can clearly demonstrate its commitment to the open process of determining truth and its recognition of its own human fallibility. The discipline of intellectual honesty measured by the Golden Rule arises from the same discomfort with the idea of absolute truth and recognition of the human capacity for error that underpin the system of free expression. They permit a newspaper to speak with confidence but acknowledge that it might be wrong. Though a newspaper does not need to pretend to be objective or neutral in expression, it should always be open to disagreement, even about its most strongly held beliefs.

Now this is not always altogether satisfying to the audience. Recognizing that there may be more than one reasonable point of view on some issues will often be taken as weakness, or worse, as a betrayal of truth. For example, if a whole community believes in the guilt of an individual and the newspaper points out flaws in the evidence, the newspaper probably will not be immediately rewarded for this demonstration of its commitment to the truth discipline. But if it takes a principled approach consistently, it can persuade its audience over time that its values are not simply a trick. Intellectual honesty, like any form of honesty, can be misunderstood. But it still offers the surest way to gain and retain respect.

The discipline that requires news reports to withhold ultimate judgment on matters of value does not come directly out of the philosophy of free expression. It is a call to prudent self-restraint in the interest of credibility, and exceptions to it abound. The ambiguous nature of this discipline has always caused journalists problems. For example, it has been difficult to uphold it as a journalistic virtue and still permit, even honor, the great newspaper tradition of the crusade. So some newspapers have given up on the tradition. But with a proper understanding of the relationship between a newspaper and its community, journalists need not abandon the practice of crusading, though they do need to be careful.

Sometimes a crusade attacks subjects about which there can be little debate—for example the *Tribune*'s 1993 campaign against the unconscionable level of violence directed against children. But even on matters about which reasonable people might deeply differ, newspapers engage in campaigns on the news pages that make their opinion explicit. For example, newspapers do not usually show much modesty about the opinion that government corruption is bad (even though there may be situations in which eliminating it would leave a community worse off than letting it go on). Newspapers also commonly display a clear preference for that which is advantageous to their own communities, even at the expense of the interests of other communities.

Nothing in the idea of free expression as a truth-seeking venture prohibits free statement of conclusions about right and wrong. Withholding such judgments does not necessarily, like intellectual honesty, advance the cause of knowledge. In fact, in some circumstances it could be seen as a form of dishonesty—hiding the speaker's real motivation, for example, when motive would be pertinent to the assessment of what is said. Scientific method requires open statements of opinion, though scientific hypotheses are usually closer to the factual statements about which newspapers regularly make explicit judgments than to the value statements about which newspapers should be more restrained.

But there are still good reasons for generally withholding ultimate value judgments in news reporting. They have more to do with rhetoric than epistemology, though the two are clearly related. Modesty of opinion in news columns helps allay readers' skepticism. Boldness of opinion, on the other hand, can close the minds of those who do not share it. Since the first purpose of news reports is to convey useful knowledge on matters of public interest, and establishing moral principles comes a good deal lower down the list, prudence suggests that journalists should be very cautious about stating opinion on ultimate issues of value in news stories, lest they alienate segments of the audience.

This discipline is far more flexible than the discipline of intellectual honesty. What is an "ultimate" judgment? When is a crusade appropriate? There is no golden rule to resolve the ambiguities of dealing with opinion in news reporting. In fact, most newspapers have over the past few decades moved in the direction of permitting more expression of opinion.

Though there are good reasons for this trend, it also can undermine readers' trust. Partisanship is familiar to Americans, more familiar by the day. Even the scientists and academics on whom one used to think one could rely for a disinterested information, get large amounts of money from industry or government and often will not be heard to utter a remark that conflicts with the interests of those who pay them. This climate makes it all the more important that newspapers not let news reports take on the appearance of partiality. Being sparing about making exceptions to the rule against the expression of ultimate value judgments in news reports will help distinguish newspapers from the adversarial tenor of the times.

THE SENSIBILITY OF A COMMUNITY

How then should a newspaper choose the occasions on which it makes an exception to the general rule? One of the clearest ways a newspaper reflects the basic sensibilities of its community is in its selection of issues about whose outcome it is explicitly not indifferent. This is not a comfortable issue for journalists, because it draws them from behind the protective pose of disinterest.

Some years ago, at a televised seminar on the relationship between the media and the military, CBS correspondent Mike Wallace was asked what he would do if, covering an American war from the enemy side (which he had previously said he would do), he found himself in an ambush position as American GIs walked into the trap. Wallace said he would film the battle and put the story out and that he would not warn the American soldiers. Asked whether he had a higher duty as an American citizen than as a journalist in such a situation, Wallace said, "No, you don't have the higher duty to, no, no." Peter Jennings of ABC had difficulty with this position, but he also had difficulty (beyond the possible danger to which he would expose himself) saying he would take action to alter the course of events in favor of the Americans.[14]

Years later in a similar, non-televised seminar sponsored by the McCormick Tribune Foundation, CBS anchor Dan Rather struggled mightily with the same kind of issue:[15]

> Yes, I would like to go [on a mission accompanying a unit of soldiers fighting against an army supported and advised by the United States], provided you understand the following: that if we get in any

situation in which U.S. troops are even remotely in danger, I don't want any part of it, and that's not what I'm looking for. . . . It's important for me that you understand that while I would like to be, and on my best days believe I am, a world-class journalist of integrity, I'm an American. And if and when those two things come into conflict, my loyalty to my country would prevail over the first. I'm not sure I could defend that in a journalism school back home, but I want you to know, sir, going in, that that's how I feel.

Why all the difficulty? If he is duty-bound to report the news without favoritism, a journalist should find it easy to say that he is professionally indifferent to the outcome of the battle and, for that matter, the war. But no American news organization can sustain the conceit. The audience will not let it. War is the extreme case that reveals the real nature of the interests of organizations that report the news. Lives are at stake, if not the survival of the community, and in such circumstances no institution can be neutral and retain the intimacy with the community it needs in order to do its work.

The Vietnam War may have caused confusion about this, as it did about so many things. Outside the newsroom, there were accusations that journalists were unpatriotic. Meantime, on the inside, journalists questioned whether they *could* be patriotic and still be journalists. This only demonstrates that in some situations, public feelings toward a war can become so conflicted that journalists can openly challenge its legitimacy while still retaining their bond with the audience.

Even when the community strongly supports a war, of course, an honest newspaper will have to ask questions about it. In extreme cases, the government's war policies or practices might be repugnant, and a decent newspaper will have to attack the whole enterprise, even at the risk of losing its audience. Well short of this, the exercise of a newspaper's responsibility to the truth will not necessarily sit well with the audience. But the truth must always command journalists' first loyalty, even if it subjects them to hostility.

Why, by the way, do newspapers seem to concentrate on

bad news, whether about a war or about the local sewer commission? This inquiry confronts journalists with such numbing regularity that they usually learn to deal with it without ever lapsing into thought. It deserves better. A newspaper seems negative, even about activity whose purposes it shares, because its social value is in revealing hidden facts. One can be confident that the good news—about a war, about a social program, about a corporation—will get out. Government and private institutions will make sure of it—through advertising and sophisticated public relations. Since journalism's duty to the truth requires it to present a full depiction of reality—good and bad—it has to work at learning the bad, which others will often obscure. And then when journalists reveal these secrets, they look like common scolds.

Newspapers can take steps to mitigate this impression. The truth discipline itself helps, since its rigorous application requires that reports of negative information include full statement of the opposite view. Beyond this, newspapers need to get over their discomfort about having loyalties. It is one of the best kept secrets of journalism that reporters do believe in things—even in the things they criticize. They should be willing to acknowledge this with pride, and then do their duty as journalists by telling the truth.

The first loyalty is to country. Newspapers are nationalistic institutions. They must organize around a coherent set of interests—one of which is geographic—to create an audience, and this defines the basic choices of what to report and how to report it. There are a few cases in which a particular set of interests defines a newspaper without giving it a national identity. For example, the *International Herald Tribune* has an audience of diverse nationality that ranges well beyond the American expatriate community. The *Financial Times* and the weekly *Economist*, along with various narrower trade publications, similarly reach across national frontiers. Television has gone farther in this direction. CNN and Sky Television have spread across the international landscape, and in their reporting you can detect the careful effort to take no sides.

As economic life becomes more global, other papers and electronic news outlets may grow up to serve a borderless community. But for the foreseeable future most people will not live there. Unless something happens to dissolve the bonds of kinship, geography, and common heritage so that nationalism and tribalism decline as forces in the world, most people will still cluster in nation-states and other groupings that see themselves apart. It certainly does not seem as if the moment for this historical shift has come, with nationalism and tribalism resurgent in the former Soviet empire and xenophobia everywhere rising. Add to this the surge in religious fundamentalism (which, though it cuts across and even against national sovereignty, is itself a kind of nationalism), and the possibility of a seamless world seems as distant a dream as ever.

War demonstrates starkly the way the audience shapes newspaper behavior, but there are many other examples, for the character of most metropolitan newspapers grows from local soil. In everything from sweeping elements of its editorial policy to the character of its arts coverage, a successful newspaper must reflect its time and place. This is why there are clear differences in the critical approach to literature exemplified by the *Tribune* (strong emphasis on the classic narration and character development that have always marked the "Chicago school" of fiction), the *New York Times* (more European in attitude, more interested in experimentation and intellectual fashion), and the *Washington Post* (strong interest in historical, political literature). The dominant writers on newspapers also usually relate closely to their communities. Think of Mike Royko in Chicago, Jimmy Breslin in New York, Herb Caen in San Francisco. There is a reason Molly Ivins fit better in Dallas than in the *New York Times*, why Sally Quinn was perfect for the *Washington Post*. Ivins's delightfully irreverent wisecracking conflicted with the overall tone in the *Times*. Her wicked tongue worked better in Texas. Sally Quinn had a streak of the devil in her, too, but she never fundamentally attacked the importance of the capital society she covered, because that was the one thing Washington did not take to be open for discussion.

THE EDITORIAL VOICE

A newspaper's editorial positions (its frankly stated opinions on ultimate questions of value) play a central role in establishing the linkage between newspaper and community. But the relationship is not simple, for it starkly raises the question of whether a newspaper should tell people what is good for them or what they want to hear, whether it should lead or follow.

Papers serving small, coherent communities might have a hard time coming out at odds with the general values of the place. A community of religious fundamentalists would probably not sustain a newspaper with an atheistic, libertarian credo. In larger communities, the diversity of the population gives the paper more leeway to define itself. Newspapers that hold audiences over long periods of time have editorial positions that rest comfortably within the mainstream of the political spectrum of their communities. They also try to develop editorial philosophies that have coherence and intellectual integrity so that they do not appear to blow this way and that based on pressure or the fashion of the moment. This helps explain how the *Tribune* holds its rural agricultural readers while sustaining an editorial policy that has consistently opposed farm subsidies. The fact that it generally looks askance at government subsidies for any industry and has a long, strong commitment to free trade helps make this position more tolerable to those whose interests conflict with it than if the paper opposed subsidies of farms but favored subsidies of steel or newsprint. (This is one reason why newspapers' editorial positions on governmental regulation of their own business are so delicate. The position needs to be consistent with the newspaper's general approach, or credibility plunges.)

Though a newspaper must be attentive to the views of its readers, nothing subverts a community's respect for a paper's editorial position more than the sense that the paper's editors are basing it on opinion polls, telling the community only what it knows will be popular. One of the worst and most common accusations an editor gets from angry readers is that he has done something only to get circulation or avoid hostility from some powerful or vociferous group. This angle of attack comes naturally because it strikes at the very center of a paper's claim to respect. And it appeals to a general cynicism about whether any powerful institutions play it on the square. It is extremely important today to reestablish and reinforce the idea of an independent-minded, principled, and courageous press.

Simone de Beauvoir in *The Second Sex*[16] includes a delightful analysis of what people look for in their intimate relationships. They yearn for the other person, she argues, to reflect them the way they would like to be seen. But at the same time they need the other person to be independent of them, or else the flattering reflection will have no significance. If they suspect that the other person is simply a mirror ground to favor, they lose respect for his or her opinion altogether, and intimacy dies. The relationship between a newspaper and its community is like that. Unless people believe that the newspaper makes its judgments on the merits rather than by guessing what the community wants to hear about itself, their affection for it will eventually fade.

This begins to get into the realm of rhetoric, which I will discuss more fully in a later chapter, but it is a mistake to think of a newspaper as merely a conveyor of data. If it is vital, a newspaper has a personality, a spirit, a sensibility, and a voice, just as a human partner does. If in these ways it speaks the language of its audience, it will build a genuine human bond with them. If it does not, it will become irrelevant to their lives.

Here is the tension: A newspaper that fails to reflect its community deeply will not succeed. But a newspaper that does not challenge its community's values and preconceptions will lose respect for failing to provide the honesty and leadership that newspapers are expected to offer. Such a newspaper may even end up following its community into evil. One does not have to look to pure tyrannies like Nazi Germany for examples of newspapers that reflect community sensibilities straight to Hell. The behavior of many newspapers—including the *Tribune*—during the civil rights movement and the McCarthy era provides a lesson uncomfortably close to home.

But there are at least as many examples of moral heroism among journalists in those and other periods of American history. It is not a new observation that a newspaper should bring people news that challenges their beliefs. More than any other medium, newspapers in America have been instruments of leadership.

LEADERSHIP AND NEWSPAPER CRUSADES

As we have seen, for a variety of reasons and in a variety of ways a newspaper will not be neutral. The most extreme example is the newspaper crusade of the sort newspapers launched against the trusts during the Progressive Era at the beginning of the twentieth century or the *Providence Journal-Bulletin* directed against corruption at the highest level of Rhode Island's judicial system in the 1990s. But under what circumstances is crusading appropriate? And can it be done in an intellectually honest way?

In most communities, people expect the newspaper to be out in front of the parade. Part of the romanticism of newspapering arises out of this element of social commitment: the embattled editor, the courageous reporter taking on the corrupt powers that be. These have become part of the mythology of the trade, but it is a myth built on reality. Just as some newspapers in the South exemplified the danger of accepting community values concerning race, others demonstrated the extraordinary force newspapers can exert on behalf of an unpopular moral position. When the level of unpopularity is extreme, the commercial and even physical risks to the newspaper and its people can be grave.

A community may be divided on a moral issue, and the newspaper may have to take the minority side. Or the community may be blind to the issue, and the newspaper will have to assault its complacency over the breakfast cereal day after day. In such circumstances, a newspaper that has already established its courage and outspokenness should be able to count on a large number of readers tolerating its ornery position, even if they are uncomfortable with it, because they expect this newspaper to take a stand.

This is not the place to try to determine how newspapers should choose their causes. Ideological factors come into play along with other sources of fundamental values. The more ambiguous or complex the issue, the more problematic it becomes to mount a crusade. This is especially so if the community is either deeply divided or resistant to the newspaper's point. But these are tactical considerations. All I really want to argue is that there is a place for crusading, even in a newspaper that has a due regard for the way it should limit the use of its power. One thing is sure, a newspaper will be judged by history based on the wisdom of large choices of this kind.

When a paper does begin to crusade, temptations to violate its truth discipline abound. Ordinarily it launches the campaign having decided roughly what it wants to achieve, and this makes it terribly difficult to exercise the self-control to give opposing voices their due. A quality of Platonic certainty always wells up in a newspaper campaign, and this can cause great harm, especially when the newspaper directs its campaign against individual conduct. The risk is greatest when the newspaper feels it is speaking into the wind. This happens when it is up against either powerful and sophisticated forces or the strong majority sentiment in its own community. In either circumstance, there may be an element of fear: if we don't turn this place around, we're going to pay a terrible price. Reporters and editors can easily become like prosecutors intent on proving their case at all costs. Editors must control this natural impulse. Even when a newspaper is crusading, it must avoid stiffening into an adversarial stance.

Where a Newspaper Stands

How can a newspaper, dependent as it is on support from readers and advertisers, ever hope to find the point of leverage from which it can move its world? The answer is that it has to set about building the platform long before it has occasion to use it. This is the most fundamental aspect of the relationship between a newspaper and its community because it encompasses all the rest.

To have a treasury of good will on which to draw in a serious controversy, a newspaper has to have established a reputation for honesty and decency of purpose. A paper known for taking cheap shots is not going to be effective campaigning against entrenched power or against the grain of its audience, because it simply will not be taken seriously. To be effective in matters of high controversy, a newspaper must have established an intimate relationship with its community through careful reflection of the community's sensibilities, through scrupulous regard for its journalistic disciplines, through the development of a consistent and intellectually respectable editorial policy, and through the control of its overall voice.

Personal involvement by newspaper people in civic and charitable activities can help solidify the bond. Journalists probably should stay away from such involvements in order to preserve their distance from the things about which the paper writes. But others in the noneditorial parts of the organization, starting with the publisher, should be active. This is not an onerous duty, since people are attracted to work in newspapers in the first place because they find value in the large and direct civic role newspapers play.

It also helps if a newspaper does not feel shy about singing the praises of its community's real virtues. After all, the community's success will shape the newspaper's own. And by being unafraid to praise, a newspaper positions itself to be more credible in its criticism.

Finally, when it comes time to take a position or launch a crusade that a large part of the community resists, the newspaper must do so from an explicitly stated position within the community, not from a distance. To come back to the extreme case of war, a newspaper will be in the strongest position to deal honestly and critically with the ultimate test of the national community if it is willing to acknowledge its loyalties. When a newspaper criticizes a war, it should be on the explicit basis of the ill effects the war will have on the interests of its community. Not only will this provide the platform from which to move public opinion, but it also will reflect the deep kinship between those who report a war and those who fight it. When our country fights a war, we as a sovereign people are responsible for its horrors. The pain and sacrifice are not anything from which we can distance ourselves. As Michael Herr wrote in *Dispatches* of the infantrymen he went into combat with in Vietnam: "[O]f course we were intimate, I'll tell you how intimate: they were my guns, and I let them do it."[17]

(PART TWO)

MATTERS OF EXPRESSION

(*four*)
THE RHETORIC OF THE NEWS

RHETORIC HAS BEEN DESCRIBED VARIOUSLY AS "THE art of using language effectively,"[1] "the body of rules to be observed by a speaker or writer in order that he may express himself with eloquence,"[2] and "the art of persuasion."[3] It is not a word heard very often in the newsrooms of the United States except preceded by the word "empty." And yet there was never a more rhetorical enterprise than the news.

A poet or novelist might swear by the conceit that he is writing for an audience of one, but a journalist should know better. He is more an architect than a sculptor; he builds things meant to work. His purpose is to provide useful information, and his privileged position in law arises from its utility to the system of self-governance.

To fulfill this purpose, he has to know not only some information of value but also how to communicate it to others. If he is a reporter and thinks the art of persuasion is irrelevant to him because he deals in fact, he is wrong. He is in the business of changing minds, if only from a state of ignorance to a state of knowledge. And that means he must master the art of getting messages through to people, which is rhetoric.

The study of rhetoric ranges over questions as abstract as epistemology and as practical as the business of marketing. This chapter will deal with the whole spectrum, but a question raised in the previous chapter threads through this one: To what extent should the audience shape the message?

The most shocking answer comes from contemporary theorists who assert, in effect, that the audience creates the message no matter what the writer tries to do. This should send a chill through every journalist, because it amounts to an attack on the very purpose of his work. And it has a special edge in the new interactive media environment, which some people suggest will overthrow the authority of all texts and replace it with the meandering logic of a man commanding a TV remote control.

The underlying intellectual attack upon the ability of texts to communicate coherent meaning comes from the tradition of skepticism, which has always been able to find the flaws in claims of absolute knowledge (happily enough for the cause of human freedom and the sustenance of the open society). Journalists may dismiss what academic theorists say as insignificant to the realm of practical affairs, and in the narrow sense they are right. In the world the journalists generally live in and describe, the debates of the graduate school seminar or the Modern Language Association have no immediate impact. Newspaper readers, by and large, have other, more pressing matters to worry about than the meaning of meaning. And yet, ideas have force. However hidden they may be from passing view, they provide the foundation of what we see and believe, what we do. So even as empty an idea as radical skepticism can undermine our aspirations and dispirit us like a mood we feel but cannot understand.

The Possibility of Communication

The extreme form of skepticism challenges two ideas that sustain the enterprise of the news. First, it doubts that one individual can truly communicate a thought to another through language. Second, it doubts whether there is any way to call some assertions better than others.

If it is right about the impossibility of a reader understanding what a writer meant, the center of the journalistic enterprise collapses. Journalists are not in a private game in which they gratify themselves upon the page and then offer the results to others who get nothing from it but what they themselves put into it. Journalism must be useful communication or it is nothing.

The radical skeptic makes his living finding the ambiguities in all texts. Applying a highly rarefied approach that reflects no normal reader's thought process, he asserts that the critic and reader can do nothing but create their own, new work over what the writer has written, like a palimpsest. This turns the usual relationship between author and reader on its head, making the recipient of the message the true author, since only through his act of interpretation does meaning emerge upon the impenetrable surface of the text. Of course, this also serves neatly to elevate the critic over those he interprets, which must be a solace for a group of writers almost nobody reads.

Stanley Fish is a useful example of extreme skepticism, but not because he is representative of all the radical skeptics; he is not. For one thing, oddly enough he seems to try to communicate effectively, writing in a more accessible, straightforward style than most, which makes him more congenial to nonspecialists. For another, Fish's claims are much less radical than some others'. Still, he is outrageous enough to suggest the fallacy at the heart of this kind of reasoning.

The publication of Wayne Booth's *A Rhetoric of Irony*[4] provided the occasion for an article by Fish in *Daedalus* entitled, "Short People Got No Reason to Live: Reading Irony," and a reply by Booth.[5] Irony is a perfect field for the radical skeptic to do battle, since the challenge of understanding irony is to detect when an author means the opposite of what he says. Fish's essay took its title from a line from a Randy Newman song. The songwriter had claimed he meant to criticize the sentiment expressed. Fish was not so sure. His essay attacked the idea that any one reading of a given text—as ironic or straightforward, for example—is inherently better than any other reading. He did not minimize what is at stake:[6]

What Booth sees (although not always as clearly as he might wish) is that the shoring up of stable irony is the shoring up of meaning itself: "If the universe is ultimately an absurd multiverse, then all propositions about or portraits of any part of are ultimately absurd . . . [and] there is no such things [*sic* in Fish, correct in original] as a 'fundamental violation' of the text." This is a dark vision indeed, and one can only agree with Booth's desire to resist it.

But for Fish there is nowhere to go for the meaning of the text other than its reader. And if readers disagree, then the text is indeterminable. Literal meaning, he wrote, "rather than being independent of perspective, is a product of perspective . . . ; it is itself an interpretation."[7] Even when all readers unanimously reject a particular interpretation, Fish argued, it does not invalidate that reading because someday somebody might persuade somebody else of its validity.

When Booth made his rebuttal in the same issue of *Daedalus*, he did the most devilish thing one could do to somebody who takes the position Fish did: he deliberately misread him. Misread him with glee. Fish, he wrote, actually can be understood to agree with almost everything Booth wrote in *A Rhetoric of Irony*. To be consistent, Fish should, of course, bow to the notion that this warped interpretation is as valid as any other. But then why does Fish spend, in Booth's words, "a lot of energy correcting people who give reductive reports of his views?"[8]

The paradox Booth exposed is common to all radical skepticism, whether it challenges the epistemological basis of mathematics, the reliability of the senses, or the possibility of principled decision-making in law. The same technique that lays waste to the idea of truth turns back on itself and undermines the very grounds of the attack. This is so even at the most abstract, mathematical level of analysis. At the more discursive level of literary criticism the paradox is simple to express: If there is no possibility of communicating, then why should I listen to you when you say so?

At first glance, this may deepen one's despair of ever knowing anything. But in fact the paradox leads the way to a better and more comforting understanding of the human condition and people's aspiration to knowledge. Karl Popper put it this way:[9]

It must be admitted . . . that there is a kernel of truth in both scepticism and relativism. The kernel of truth is just that there exists no general criterion of truth. But this does not warrant the conclusion that the choice between competing theories is arbitrary. It merely means, quite simply, that we can always err in our choice—that we can always miss the truth, or fall short of the truth; that certainty is not for us . . . ; that we are fallible.

This insight helps explain why, despite the irrefutability of radical skeptics' arguments about the fundamental limitations of human reason, it has still been possible to accomplish so many leaps of understanding that have had irrefutable results. If reason and communication are so useless, how did we think and talk our way to the moon? The lovely aphorism attributed to Richard Feynman sums it up nicely: "A very great deal more truth can become known than can be proved." [10]

All that the skeptics really demonstrate is that we must never stop looking critically at what we think of as truth. All human knowledge is tentative, though some truths are more tentative than others. The radical skeptics do not prove that nobody can communicate with anyone or that it is futile to attempt to understand what an author meant to convey in a text. They only prove that it is always possible to miss the point, that words convey meaning imperfectly, just as Newton's law describes gravity imperfectly. We live in an intellectual world of ambiguity, not certainty. Mathematician Kurt Gödel demonstrated that even closed, tautological (mathematical) systems like the ones that helped guide us to the moon generate propositions that can neither be proven nor disproven. This welling up of metaphysical statements represents imperfection at the very level of abstract reason itself. And yet mathematics works. So does language.

The Attack on the Hierarchy of Values

Even though human reason is fallible, this does not prevent us from saying that some propositions are closer to the truth than others. But another avenue of academic attack upon the intellectual basis of journalism denies the existence of a hierarchy of

knowledge or values (the idea that some things are more important, better, more beautiful than others) or at least denies man's
ability to reason usefully about such issues. This sometimes
presents itself as anti-elitism. It has lately hidden under the be-
guiling patchwork cloak of multiculturalism. And its most notorious recent manifestation on campus has been the debate
about the validity of the canon of texts that might be thought to
form the foundation of the learning of any educated person.

Do not mistake this with the argument that the traditional canon has been built on a bias. That observation does not
deny the existence of a hierarchy of values; it simply asserts
that the traditional list of great works has been skewed toward
the products of western, male thought. It aims at opening up
the canon to include books by women and non-western thinkers (not only the obvious ones such as Confucius or *The Upan-
ishads*, but also less well-known products of cultures generally
overlooked, like those in Africa or the Pacific islands). The purpose is to represent better the rich and various intellectual heritage of humankind. This is the more modest and helpful, even
exhilarating form of multiculturalism.

One can argue endlessly about whether a nomadic myth
or a folktale from above the Arctic Circle should displace *The
Odyssey* among the world's Top Forty, just as people might
endlessly argue about whether Rabelais or Marcus Aurelius be-
longs on the list. This kind of debate is one of the great pleasures of having a hierarchy of values, and it is not too different
from the conversations that occur every day in newsrooms
about which event is the most important of the day. Few in
those editorial discussions believe they have the philosophers'
stone that will resolve all questions through the application of
a single principle. But this does not keep them from advancing
their views. In Popper's terminology, although there is no general criterion of truth to guide judgments about the relative importance of events in the world, some answers are better than
others, and the best way to approach the matter is through open
and intellectually honest debate.

How can we recognize the need to open up the discussion
to heretofore excluded voices and yet avoid the intellectual trap

of radical multiculturalism? This is one of the great challenges of the aspiration that has come to be known as diversity. The complaint that this judgment or that one reflects cultural or gender bias has gotten shopworn, especially in the news trade. One hears it again and again, and it loses meaning every time it is used. But, like many cliches, the reason it has become so commonplace is that it is so commonly true.

When I was a boy, during the early years of the civil rights movement, I believed that by the time people of my generation came into positions of authority racial justice would have established itself in this country. Since I am a member of the Baby Boom generation, I believed, of course, that my age cohorts would make this happen through the pure rightness of our souls.

Sadly, this has not happened. We have not yet even agreed upon a definition of racial justice, let alone made it manifest on earth. And helping move our society toward the elimination of racial bias now seems to me to be a lifework.

Recognizing prejudice—whether racial or otherwise—is the first step. We all suffer from bias, and we must always cross-examine ourselves about our behavior to make sure we are correcting against it properly. It helps in this effort to hear from others, who come at things from a different skew.

To enrich the discussion and make the internal cross-examination effective, newspapers need to include people from a rich variety of backgrounds at all levels of their organizations. But inclusion also can threaten the coherence of the newspaper's overall message unless everyone involved in developing it has a clear and confident sense of the objective.

As we have seen, to succeed, a newspaper must have a character, a personality. On the editorial page it must present an intellectually consistent set of opinions about public policy and other important matters. In the news pages, it must put facts into an analytic framework that helps readers make sense of them. This means consciously permitting a modest amount of opinion into news reports.

The analysis in a newspaper should come together to form a roughly coherent vision of the world. I do not mean a partisan vision or a stiffly ideological one. But if readers find a news analysis on the front page of the paper one day suggesting that American military intervention in Fredonia would be futile and another the next day saying that it is vital, they may not be able to understand what in the world the newspaper would have them believe. A newspaper should not be dueling banjos. Though the analysis by reporters in the news columns need not proceed in unison, there must be some direction. Editors must bring harmony to the chorus of voices that makes up the newspaper's daily report.

Diversity (all forms of diversity, not just diversity of gender, race, and nationality) makes this task more complicated. Just as the challenge of this country has from its inception been to make one nation from the many, the challenge of a newspaper is to make diverse voices come together in a single song.

The radical model of dealing with diversity simply disregards the need for coherence and says that all opinions have the same validity and thus are appropriate for inclusion in the news report randomly, depending on who gets a particular assignment on a particular day. Everybody sings his own tune, and the result is cacophony.

Another model encourages surface diversity—biological diversity, if you will—and not the deeper diversity of life experience, viewpoint, and voice. One might, for example, have a rainbow reporting staff whose members nonetheless all share a liberal Democratic political cast. This whole chorus sings the same note, and only those with a certain sound need apply.

Neither model appeals to me very much. The first, I think, would destroy the personality of a newspaper and turn it into a loose daily anthology. The second accepts for employment only partisans of a certain bent, and it thus limits the organization's ability to behave in an intellectually honest fashion (no one is there to challenge the underlying assumptions) as well as its capacity to change.

Better to have a diverse staff that takes part in a discussion that creates the character and personality of the paper. Through open discussion—with the editor ultimately responsible for the coherence and appropriateness of the result—the newspaper's diverse staff can create and re-create the paper's vision over time. But there are a few constraints that I think need to be applied. (They come, frankly, from our experience at the *Tribune* creating an editorial page policy out of a politically and socially diverse editorial board.)

First, everyone should understand that nobody comes to the table representing a constituency. A newspaper is not a legislature. Decisions are collegial, but not a matter of majority rule. The editor has the final word. But the editor, along with every other person on the editorial staff, has the same primary obligation—to the truth—and must meet it even when doing so challenges the deeply held beliefs of various groups of readers. Make no mistake about it, this is where the radical skeptic does his most subversive work, because he says that there is no coherent truth to which we have a duty, through our imperfect means, to aspire. Without confidence in the legitimacy of this aspiration, we are in grave trouble—and not just on newspaper editorial staffs.

Second, everyone should understand that it is not their job to impose their individual personality and worldview on the newspaper. It has had an identity before they arrived on the job, and it will have one after they leave. They are there to build the personality of an institution that has a history different from theirs and a position in the community greater than any individual's.

The key to success in this collegial enterprise is an environment in which people can freely discuss the most controversial issues of the day professionally in an atmosphere of mutual respect. Employees need not hew to any ideological line, but they must be selected and promoted for their ability to thrive in and enhance such an open environment.

A newspaper that uses this method to find its voice faces some particular dangers. It must beware not to reduce itself to a safe, drab middle ground on every issue. Unlike other businesses, which typically shy away from great and divisive public controversies whenever possible, a newspaper staff must come together and speak forcefully about them the day they first arise. It must not be meek. Yet in an open, collegial, and diverse process, it may succumb to the temptation to avoid internal conflict by compromising it away. Staff members may end up walking on eggs in discussions of loaded issues, everyone avoiding the blunt statements that usually mark and energize news debates.

It is not easy to counteract this normal human tendency, which has come to be known as "political correctness." But a newspaper cannot do its work if it is afraid of trouble or of giving offense. A politically correct newspaper would abdicate its responsibility and in the process become a crushing, pious bore.

One day while I was editor of the *Tribune* two particularly noteworthy people died: entertainer Sammy Davis Jr. and puppeteer Jim Henson.[11] The question that evening was whether either or both obituaries belonged on the front page of the paper, and the editors had the kind of spirited debate about this issue that should be a journalist's joy. Some argued that neither story belonged on the front page, reflecting a narrow view of the newsworthiness of obituaries that I was trying to change. There was some sentiment for putting Sammy Davis Jr. alone on page one and Jim Henson on the obit page in recognition that Davis was the first black entertainer to present himself publicly as the social equal of white entertainers (though the "Rat Pack" with which he ran—Dean Martin, Frank Sinatra, Peter Lawford—was of dubious stature). Others argued that Henson alone belonged on page one because by creating Sesame Street he fundamentally changed the most important educational force in contemporary life—television. This made him a figure of vast influence, it was argued, well beyond mere celebrity or symbolism.

I think the majority view among the editors was that both obituaries should be played equally on page one (side by side at the top of the page, for example). This certainly had the virtue of avoiding risk. It was hard to imagine anybody canceling their subscription in protest of that play of the stories. But after hearing all the discussions I decided to put the Henson obituary on page one along with a good-sized photo of Davis and a line indicating that the story of his death could be found on the obituary page.

You will probably not be surprised to learn that this judgment was not universally recognized as Solomonic. That evening and over the next several days I had quite a few intense and extremely useful conversations with members of the staff about my decision. The prevailing view seemed to be that the paper should have treated the two stories equally, that anything less showed that the newspaper lacked respect for African American culture.

I was ready to admit that I might have wrongly decided the issue for one reason or another (including, I suppose, a blindness owing to my race). At the time I indulged my passion for music by regularly reviewing jazz. It was possible that my strong sense that Davis was not a terribly significant musical figure had clouded my vision of his social importance. What I refused to concede, though, was that absolute equality of treatment of these two stories represented journalistic virtue.

Time and again I was told that my insistence on the need to pick one or the other as the most important was elitist. I agreed wholeheartedly. Though elitism can mean a snobbish disdain for the genuine achievements of people from backgrounds other than one's own, it can also mean the belief that some accomplishments are more grand, more valuable, more lasting than others. It was in the latter sense that the decision to put Henson on page one alone was elitist. So would a decision be to put only the Sammy Davis Jr. obituary on page one. In fact, to put both on page one would also have been elitist in that no other person who died that day was accorded the same treatment. Editors earn their living making elitist judgments.

The newspaper makes hundreds, even thousands, of such decisions in putting together every edition. Why should it lose its confidence simply because two well-known figures (one African American, one white) happened to die on the same day? Maybe Sammy Davis Jr. should have been given the most prominent treatment in that day's *Tribune*, maybe not. But this much I am sure of: The accomplishments of Sammy Davis Jr. and Jim Henson were not exactly even. Their lives did not end in a perfect tie. One of them meant more than the other.

I do not know that the conversations I had about this issue

changed anybody's mind about the adequacy of my decision on the play of the obits. But they did open my mind to the recognition that I had probably undervalued the impact Sammy Davis Jr.'s success in the white entertainment world had on the black community. At the same time, I hope I got my message across. As we embrace a greater variety of experiences and attempt to speak to people from more diverse backgrounds, we have an obligation to state clearly what we think is true and what we think is most important: This campaign issue is going to have more impact than that one. This movie is more entertaining than that one. This book is better written than that one. This jazz recording was the most exciting of the year.

It becomes more difficult to reach these conclusions as we become more diverse because we need to discuss assumptions we previously took for granted. And getting those discussions to work isn't simple, either. We have to create the conditions in which candid conversations can take place. But greater diversity should permit us to make the judgments better, once we work through the difficulties. It should permit us to be even more authoritative, coherent, and confident in the statements we make about matters of value.

The most extreme form of multiculturalism argues just the opposite, denying the very possibility of reasoned judgments about values. It asserts that the whole discussion is nothing more than a trick by those with power to keep down those without power. This attitude has reached well beyond the academy. You find it in the oddest places. Here is a recent editor's note from one of my favorite magazines, *Downbeat*: [12]

> If jazz education is to play a larger role in today's music world, it must trash notions of high and low . . .
>
> Not that certain parameters and guidelines shouldn't be used, but insisting on a strict canon, preaching from the top down to young, aspiring students is to insult and distance them.

By the way, the editorial did not explain why—given its dim view of the notion of high and low—*Downbeat* still rates recordings on a scale of one to five stars.

The arguments supporting radical multiculturalism have a familiar ring. They begin with the insight that individual experience strongly influences human judgments. Then they leap to the conclusion that therefore one position cannot be proven to be inherently better than another (just as Fish argued that one reading cannot be shown to be inherently better than another).

In a society that still suffers grave inequities and biases, radical multiculturalism may sound like a generous argument on behalf of the powerless outsider. But in fact if this kind of fundamental attack on reason were to prevail, it would leave the powerless much worse off.

Radical multiculturalism has become the last, dispirited refuge of many of those who once adhered to now discredited forms of historical determinism. These thinkers show a strong authoritarian impulse; they have a taste for mounting attacks upon the system of free expression, and this is no coincidence. An open society is the enemy of many of these people, and this suggests one more paradox, a practical one.

The radical skeptics see the world as governed, not by reason, but only by power relations. (This appears most clearly in the work of the critical legal theorists, who use deconstruction and similar techniques to demonstrate that law cannot be principled, let alone just.) And yet if power were freed of the tug of principle, if government were free to repress expression, these academics' viewpoint would be among the first the majority would choose to suppress.

That would be poetic justice, for the radical multiculturalists have turned the *ad hominem* attack into a whole philosophy. By denying that anything a person says can usefully be separated from his unique circumstances, they discourage all reasoned basis for human charity and moral restraint. If the radicals are right and everything I do will be shaped by my own self-interest, why listen to conscience?

It is vital, though, to recognize that the flaws in the arguments of the radical skeptics do not discredit doubt as a mechanism for the advancement of knowledge. Journalists need not become gullible to avoid the philosophical pitfalls. They should remain skeptics, secure in the knowledge that in so doing they are not necessarily undermining all reason and sense of values.

Not all levels of doubt are the same. Skepticism only becomes dangerous when it replaces the aspiration to know the truth. Philosopher David Hume put it this way: [13]

[S]kepticism, when more moderate, may be understood in a very reasonable sense, and is a necessary preparative to the study of philosophy by preserving a proper impartiality in our judgments and weaning our mind from all those prejudices which we may have imbibed from education and rash opinion.

Skepticism has the power of an explosive to propel humans beyond the limits of their reach into entirely new worlds. It also has the power to destroy mankind's finest works.

RHETORIC AND MARKETING

To say that communication is possible, of course, does not mean it is easy. Words do not mean the same thing to all people. Speech is full of maddening and delightful ambiguities. Against certain kinds of messages, people have a wide range of defenses—boredom, rage, distraction. Simply getting someone to pay attention to what you have to say can be a challenge, particularly when the subject is painful or technically difficult or runs counter to a deeply held belief.

Rhetoric is the study of getting and holding attention in order to change a mind. When the purpose is to sell a product, rhetoric is called marketing. Both words carry the burden of bad connotations in most editorial departments. But journalists have a lot to learn from these two closely related disciplines. And the rhetoricians and marketers have something to learn from the sense of purpose of the journalists.

At least since Aristotle, students of persuasion have recognized that effective communication begins with an understanding of the audience. "[O]f the three elements in speechmaking," Aristotle wrote, "—the speaker, subject, and person addressed—it is the last one, the hearer, that determines the speech's end and object."[14] Aristotle meant his *Rhetoric* as a guide to orators, but journalists should find most of its basic lessons directly pertinent.

Take the endless debate in the newspaper business over whether articles should be short or long. I have heard writers explain that without a lot of space, they cannot do beautiful work. They ought to read Shakespeare's sonnets. The limits of a fourteen-line form or of a newspaper column can force a writer to go to creative lengths he might never otherwise have thought to try. On the other hand, I have heard publishers (who pay the bills for newsprint) argue that no story ever needs to occupy more than about a column of type. To them I commend John Hershey's *Hiroshima,* a journalistic masterpiece of succinct and understated horror that still would have been very long as a newspaper story.

Here is Aristotle's opinion on the matter, which should have settled it forever 2300 years ago: [15]

Nowadays it is said, absurdly enough, that the narration should be rapid. Remember what the man said to the baker who asked whether he was to make the cake hard or soft: "What, can't you make it right?" . . . Here, again, rightness does not consist either in rapidity or in conciseness, but in the happy mean, that is, in saying just so much as will make the facts plain.

Strangely, when Aristotle's basic insight—the primacy of the audience—arises in a modern context, many journalists turn hostile. The study of the audience has become the province of the marketing department, where it has taken on a relentlessly empirical cast, complete with opinion research, charts and graphs, trend lines, and all the rest. Journalists have a number of reasons to be wary. The marketers threaten the journalists' autonomy. They come from an entirely different discipline and may not share the social mission into which journalists are acculturated.

The antagonism also reflects the traditional division in newspapers between the editorial and business operations. The very name "marketing" suggests filthy lucre, in which journalists have no interest, except of course when it comes to pay raises and book advances. The scientific methods of the marketers clash with the more intuitive and anecdotal approach usually taken in the newsroom.

Journalists have traditionally been hostile to any quantifiable measure of their success in part, perhaps, for fear that they might not pass the test. Of course, they can point to a lot of silly ideas that have come and gone, sometimes doing a good bit of damage along the way—ideas like the simpleminded system developed by Rudolf Flesch that rated readability on the basis of the length and complexity of words and sentences. They recognize that the art of expression cannot adequately be captured in a numerical score.

The hostility between journalists and marketers has increased with the growing pressure on newspapers to find ways to expand readership. Publishers often turn to the marketers for answers, and this stirs dark thoughts in the minds of the journalists. Typical is a comment by a respondent to a 1993 Associated Press Managing Editors survey of journalists' job satisfaction: "I understand the need for my newspaper to do a better job of serving our readers, but I feel too many decisions are based on short-term goals and market research results, not recognizing our responsibilities to our readers and communities."[16] I do not know of any similar report of marketers' attitudes toward journalists, but I'll bet it would go something like this: "I know they are dedicated to their profession, but reporters and editors can be self-righteous bullies at times. They are living in a dream world of their own devising and do not care to compare it rigorously with the real world outside the newsroom."

The conflict between the disciplines has helped sustain a wave of nostalgia about the great newspapers of yesteryear before the coming of the marketers. In those days giants strode across the landscape—Pulitzer, Hearst, Ochs. Why, they did not feel inhibited by somebody's opinion survey telling them what people want to see in their newspaper. They did what they pleased, what they thought was *right*.

But as Michael Janeway, dean of Northwestern University's School of Journalism, points out, the real historical record is somewhat more ambiguous:[17]

Were they [the press barons] merely marketers, cynical about their definitions of "public interest?" Well, yes and no, no and yes, even Hearst was genuine in his iconoclasm. Pulitzer was both a sensationalist, and someone who believed that journalism needed to be professionalized . . .

Like all great news businessmen, these entrepreneurs saw their businesses both as manufacturing and marketing operations, *and* as socially and politically significant forces. [Emphasis in original.]

Journalists and marketers represent the two sides of the "duality of newspapers" that Janeway says came together in the persons of the great news entrepreneurs.

It is time to bring the two sides of that duality into line with one another again. Reading Aristotle might be a starting point. It would remind the journalists of their responsibility to understand their audience. Then they might read a little Plato to the marketers: "[T]he art of speech displayed by one who has gone chasing after beliefs, instead of knowing the truth, will be a comical sort of art, in fact no art at all."[18] This might remind everyone that the choice of a message and its purpose must not come from studying what the audience wants to hear. Plato knew. There is a difference between effective communication and pandering.

Modern opinion survey methods can be of use to journalists committed to understanding the audience. And given the daunting challenge of inventing a whole new mode of expression to fit the new, interactive electronic medium, the need to understand the audience has never been greater. But the research needs to become a lot more sophisticated. Most newspaper marketing studies I have seen concentrate on general questions about the preferences of various segments of the readership: What do you think of the local news in the *Daily Tattler*? Is there too much of it? About the right amount? Too little? Sometimes the surveys test the response to specific features to see how many people are actually reading them. Comics and columnists have risen and fallen on the results of these elections.

Marketing research has not gone deeply enough into the real appetites that newspapers fill. It has not sufficiently examined, for example, whether the basic relationship between a newspaper and its readers has changed with the development of radio, television, and twenty-four-hour broadcast news channels. I have seen no adequate explanation why columnists like Mike Royko can attract huge and loyal audiences by repeatedly provoking the very people who read them. It has not explained why people usually react so adversely to significant changes in the format of newspapers. They might read and enjoy both the *Tribune* and the *Wall Street Journal*, but if the *Journal* suddenly changed its front page to look like the *Tribune*, they would probably feel poorly served. (Do not think of this as exaggeration. When the *Tribune* in 1993 made a change in its typeface, the editors chose a new font designed to be more readable but otherwise virtually indistinguishable from its predecessor. Readers accepted the change, but it provoked, among other things, a half-hour call-in show on public radio in which people spoke with some passion about their feelings about the new type.)

Journalists often accuse marketers of looking at newspapers the same way they look at breakfast cereal or soap. I wish marketers did understand the newspaper's customers as deeply as the breakfast cereal and soap manufacturers understand theirs. Unfortunately, most market research has taken little interest in the deeper needs a newspaper fills, the very things the journalists worry are undervalued in the marketers' analysis.

There is, for example, every reason to believe that readers expect newspapers to be courageous and bold, to challenge conventional wisdom and question authority. There is every reason to think that readers want their newspapers to know the difference between the significant and the trivial. It is no coincidence that the surviving or predominant newspaper in most large metropolitan areas—the *Washington Post, Los Angeles Times, Boston Globe, Philadelphia Inquirer*—has been the more serious newspaper.

Readers expect more from their newspaper than useful

data, just as there is more to a person's choice of an automobile than its gas mileage. In the case of a newspaper, I believe research that went deep enough would reveal that people find in a newspaper some of the same things they find in a human relationship. When a newspaper drastically changes its look, it is like a neighbor who has always dressed for work in a business suit suddenly appearing at the train station in a motorcycle jacket. Even if you had nothing against Harleys or leather, you would still wonder what in the world had come over him.

Like a human friendship, the relationship between newspaper and reader can persist through some changes if it is strong enough going in. It can survive divergence in the attitudes of both parties; it can survive disagreements, even fundamental ones. But abrupt violations of expectations will always cause problems, and betrayal of trust will surely kill it.

People find reassurance in the regularity of the newspaper's voice. In an increasingly stressed and confusing world, newspapers help relieve anxiety. This begins with the very format of the paper, the mosaic that puts each report, even the most disturbing, in its appropriate place. While at one time the newspaper may have served principally to excite—with extra editions, blaring headlines, and so on—I think that today it provides a means of coping with the ubiquitous, breathless, unexplained rush of information provided by broadcast media.

During the Gulf War the editors of the *Tribune* talked a lot about what role we were playing in that time of massive information overdose. CNN and the broadcast networks preempted other programming to go live to the front. Correspondents described rocket attacks as they were happening. We saw the American air strike on Baghdad in living color. And yet people were coming to the newspaper in enormous numbers, and after the first day, it couldn't only have been to get a souvenir.

One day a few of us were talking about the differences between the televised coverage of the Gulf War and Edward R. Murrow's live feeds from London during the Blitz. The contrast was striking. And the principal difference (apart from Murrow's sheer eloquence) seemed to be this: In those CBS radio reports the human voice dominated, rising up over the violence one could hear behind it. But on the live Gulf War broadcasts, the welter of events themselves dominated any voice. It was not so much watching a report of the news as it was watching the process of reporting the news. Sitting in front of the television during that time came very close to the experience of being a journalist preparing to write a story out of the confusing array of information and misinformation that has come his way. Though the amount of data washing over people was vast beyond precedent, though twenty-four-hour live coverage had made the speed of newsprint seem even slower than usual, an appetite remained for what the newspaper offered.

We had become the voice. Like Murrow on the radio, we gave reassurance, provided a sense of security even amid the intense and unsettling events of war. We helped people master the data they had already received, master it intellectually and emotionally by putting it in a context, a mosaic that helped make it seem somewhat less gratuitous and unpredictable, somewhat less frightening.

Marketing professionals may take all the foregoing as an example of the kind of sloppy, romantic anecdotalism they expect from journalists. When I talk to them about this, a vague and distant look sometimes comes over their faces as they wonder how they might actually test these magical mystery notions. I respect their concern. And yet I believe that unless they begin understanding newspaper readers deeply enough to confirm or refute my model, they will not be able to provide much help to journalists in producing newspapers that reach readers' true needs.

This may require the marketers to use methods a bit less precise than they like. Janeway quotes a helpful reminder attributed to Joe Patterson, founder of the *New York Daily News,* that "[t]he art of newspapering is not to give the lady what she wants. It's to be a step ahead of her in anticipating what she wants."[19] Or as my colleague Colleen Dishon puts it, referring to what hockey star Wayne Gretzky calls the key to his success: You have to skate to where the puck is going to go.

Timing is not the only reason to go beyond traditional research methods. Human behavior and motivation do not always yield their secrets in answers to straightforward questions. There will have to be leaps of intuition that may seem uncomfortably unscientific. As Janeway put it:[20]

To make your publishing and marketing and editorial decisions on the basis of somebody's supposedly scientific data about public taste and interest, without consideration of the kinds of hunch, and vision, and gamble factors that are at the heart of journalism, is not even good business in the long haul.

Not good business because it produces bland newspapers. Not good business because it smooths out all the interesting edges, the elements of personality and character, of voice. Because it leaves no room for boldness, eccentricity, and other distinctions. You can see bad business in city after city across the country, their newspapers as prefabricated as the fast food franchises along their shopping strips.

But even if the marketers do the kind of penetrating research we need, the immune reaction of the journalists will still set in unless both disciplines begin with a common sense of purpose. The journalist sees his role as informing people of what they need to know in order to be functioning citizens, whether they want to know it or not. He takes it as his primary duty to tell the truth about important things. But to the marketer, the journalist's sense of duty often seems to contradict the fundamental rule of the marketing discipline, which is to let the customer define what the business does.

A proper understanding of the lessons of rhetoric may help resolve the difference. "[R]hetoric," writes Wayne Booth,[21]

is the art of persuading, not the art of seeking to persuade by giving everything away at the start. It presupposes that one has a purpose concerning a subject which itself cannot be fundamentally modified by the desire to persuade.

In other words, for the journalist, understanding the audience is the way one decides *how* to say something, not *what* to say about something. Marketing helps journalists get the message across successfully; it does not determine what message to give. The marketers should not decide what political position an editorial page should take any more than political polls should tell newspapers whom to endorse. But opinion studies can provide extremely useful information about what a newspaper is up against in attempting to get something done in the community, whether that be electing a candidate, building a road, or throwing a rascal out.

We need much more research that builds on the kind of work done at the *St. Petersburg Times* by the American Society of Newspaper Editors Literacy Committee, the Poynter Institute, and the University of Wisconsin-Madison, which tested different writing styles on random samples of readers to see which approach seemed to get through most effectively.[22] This research did not go deeply into the subtle interplay between the kind of message, the kind of audience, and the optimal approach, but it is an excellent beginning that suggests how very much in this line needs to be done before we really have a clear picture of how best to make our point to our readers.

Marketing research might also indicate the subject areas readers are interested in that the newspaper does not deal with adequately. This is just another way of helping journalists avoid blind spots. Truly sophisticated market research also might show that readers expect and want a newspaper to publish certain articles they are not particularly interested in. When Congress passes a budget, I doubt that a substantial proportion of the *Tribune*'s readers plow through the stories about that event. But I bet they expect us to be comprehensive and would think less of us if we devoted the space instead to a rundown of the hottest new music videos. Properly and broadly understood, readers' interests should be a principal focus of editors, helping them make decisions even about what the newspaper should pay attention to, because satisfying people's curiosity is one of the cornerstones of our business, and the audience's interest is part of the definition of the news.

HAVING A POINT

The reader also should be the focus of the writer's attention. Here is a clear statement of the elements of effective writing. Again it comes from Wayne Booth:[23]

The common ingredient that I find in all of the writing I admire—excluding for now novels, plays and poems—is something that I shall reluctantly call the rhetorical stance, a stance which depends on discovering and maintaining a proper balance among three elements: the available arguments about the subject itself; the interests and peculiarities of the audience; and the voice, the implied character of the speaker.

Reporters might object that this speaks of arguments and therefore only applies to editorializing. That reminds me of a story told to me by a friend who had moved from a newsroom position at the *Wall Street Journal* to the editorial page. One of his colleagues back on the news side confronted him in the hallway, angry about some highly charged conservative blast issued by the editorial board that day. "What gives you guys the right," he said, "to trumpet your opinions every day on the editorial page?" My friend feigned confusion. "I don't know why you feel that way," he said. "I always enjoy reading your opinions on the front page."

Some degree of opinion is and should be a regular part of newswriting. Every news story argues something, if only that these simple facts about a burglary arrest are true. So the writer must make a judgment about what he is attempting to do before sitting down to the keyboard to do it. This means sorting out the basic purpose of the piece and then deciding what arguments work best in advancing it.

Failing to decide what one wants to accomplish produces more second-rate newspaper writing than any other rhetorical problem. Journalists tend to think in narrow categories—feature story, hard news story, magazine piece, op-ed piece—that relate to the part of the newspaper where the article will appear. This provides some direction about purposes—op-ed pieces are more argumentative than news stories, features often aim to generate a feeling in the reader as much as to impart specific factual information. But these categories don't define an article's purpose nearly well enough to permit a writer confidently to begin writing it.

A brief news story in the metropolitan section describing

a routine burglary of a jewelry store need only recite the basic facts clearly in order to achieve its purpose. But if the store owner were a recent immigrant from China and talked about discovering in this country that freedom meant insecurity, then the bare recitation of fact will not serve. This story should aim at examining the contrasts he found, bringing in some sense of perspective to balance his understandable emotions. If the burglary were one of a record number for the year directed against Asians, the article would probably have to deal with the issue of racial animosity and would aim to discuss the causes of this kind of hostility. It would include a wide range of views—some of them hateful—and would surely show the newspaper's own disgust at hate crimes.

These variations on a hard news theme do not begin to suggest the variety of choices facing a reporter as he tries to clarify the purpose of any piece he is about to write. A profile of a movie star may mean to examine the curious circumstances that propelled him to Hollywood in order to suggest the serendipity of success. Or it may mean to lay out the emptiness of celebrity for those who achieve it. Or to show the difference between the brightly lighted and dazzling persona of the star and the dark, uncertain, confused actual person. It may simply intend to point out the ridiculousness of someone's fame or to celebrate his virtues, which—despite the value system of Hollywood—somehow still received their due reward. An article about Congress might aim to reveal the hidden machinations concerning a piece of legislation. It might mean to describe the main points and the potential effect of the proposed law. It might use the bill as a metaphor for the politics of the individual behind it. Or it might want to gauge public reaction to the proposal.

But each article must have a clear reason, and then it must be organized to achieve the end.

PRINCIPLES OF ORGANIZATION

In the nineteenth century newswriting evolved a highly stylized approach that editors and, later, journalism educators drilled into their students. One feature of this style was "tightness," that is to say, conciseness. Often editors pushed this point to the exclusion of all other aspects of style, leaving writers wondering what a copy desk would do to the "Gettysburg Address" or Macbeth's soliloquy— *"What's this 'tomorrow and tomorrow and tomorrow' business? There's only one tomorrow, isn't there? Then just say it that way."* The fixation on brevity served several purposes: It conserved newsprint and, perhaps, people's time. It provided an antidote to the prevailing floweriness that tried to pass as eloquence. It led to a simplicity of statement that fit the level of sophistication of the mass audience.

It also eliminated many useful writing techniques. I recall once writing a St. Patrick's Day parade story that began with an admittedly predictable parody of Irish lyricism: "Green ran the river, and green the marchers' clothes." The copy desk turned it into something like this: "The river ran green. The marchers wore green clothes." My lead wasn't particularly good, but the copy desk's was worse.

The emphasis on conciseness and directness also, by eliminating all redundancy, often made newswriting difficult to read.

The Supreme Court overruled an injunction yesterday that had barred the federal government from rolling back prices.

Quick, does this tell you prices are likely to go up or down?

In communications theory, redundancy increases reliability. If you want a message to get through the static, send it over and over again so the receiver can piece together a perfect text despite the garbles. Of course, too much redundancy's too much— a waste of time and an insufferable bore. But redundancy communicates. The shortest distance between two points may lose the audience. And when a piece of writing repeats a phrase— perhaps the phrase, "Brutus is an honorable man"—it may be the height of folly for a copy editor to strike the repetitions.

Another element of nineteenth-century newspaper style that to some extent comes down to the present day is the "inverted pyramid" structure. A proper news story, according to this approach, states the most important fact in the first paragraph. The second paragraph states the second most important fact. The third, the third most important. And so on. In its extreme form, this yields articles that read like this:

The Senate yesterday passed a comprehensive income tax reform bill that increases rates on the middle class by 10 percent over three years.

Senate Democrats said the bill would reduce the federal deficit by $100 billion a year over the next five years. Republicans say people will simply find ways to avoid the tax.

The bill also tightens up deductions for moving expenses and entertainment while adding tax credits for business expansions that create jobs.

Thursday a tax reform bill is scheduled to reach the floor of the House of Representatives. It increases middle-class income tax rates by an average of 12 percent. But it narrows the brackets so that some people at the low end will actually have reduced taxes.

The White House praised the Senate action as "a genuine step toward fiscal responsibility."

Before the House of Representatives can vote on its bill, a series of killer amendments must be disposed of. Some of these have strong liberal support.

The Taxpayer Coalition, a public interest lobby group, attacked the Senate vote as "another shortsighted congressional money-grab."

The Senate bill would increase the tax burden of an average married couple filing jointly with an income of $38,000 a year by about $600, according to the Congressional Budget Office. At the high end, it would cost a married couple filing jointly with an income of $150,000 an extra $5,000. Brackets would be frozen in the first year, but indexing for inflation would resume in the second.

You've come across inverted pyramid style so often that you might not even notice its peculiarities anymore. But think about the way my made-up example jumped around—from the Senate to the House, from one bill to another, from cost to taxpayer to benefit to the government's treasury.

If you were trying to describe this event in a letter to a friend living abroad, you would not organize it this way. You would probably start by saying the Senate passed a tax increase bill, but it isn't final because a House tax bill takes a different approach and has not yet come to a vote. Then you would describe all the important features of the Senate bill: what it does to tax rates in each bracket first, what it does to deductions, what kind of tax credits it adds and eliminates. Then you might talk about the dispute over how much the bill would reduce the deficit, noting the peculiarity that opponents of the bill complain that it will cost taxpayers but also say it won't reduce the deficit. You probably would say nothing about the White House comment, unless there was some real doubt about the administration's position. Finally you would move on to the House version and analyze the differences, then talk about the political situation it faces.

Like the inverted pyramid approach, this alternative is only one of many possible organizational structures. You would choose among them based on what you knew about your friend's principal interests (whether it is financial or political, for example). But whatever version you chose, it would lead him smoothly from point to point, informing him of the salient facts and a few of the more important arguments about them.

According to the usual account in journalism histories, the inverted pyramid approach emerged during the days when many stories were sent by telegraph, which was notoriously unreliable. By putting the most important fact first, the second most important second and so on, the story would be usable no matter at what point the communication line failed.

We're a long way past the telegraph. Still, aspects of the inverted pyramid style persist. Readers and journalists have gotten used to it; familiarity helps it convey a sense of straightforwardness, lack of bias. But in an information environment in which newspapers' principal competitors all move at the speed of light while the newspapers hum along at the speed of trucks in traffic, the traditional approach, with its emphasis on facts and de-emphasis of the connections between them, has gone way out of date. Newspapers today need writers and editors who do not think in the old forms or the old categories but are able to discover the proper approach to each particular piece.

Choosing the Audience and Finding a Voice

In the example above, I contrasted traditional newspaper writing with the organization of a letter to a friend. I did that to make it easy to answer what should be the writer's first question. A letter is probably the only writing in which defining the audience is easy. If you were to ask journalists who their audience is, most would probably give you the general demographic characteristics of the newspaper readership as a whole. There is more to it than that.

A newspaper appeals to many audiences, and only a few stories aim at all of them at once. When a plane crashes at the hometown airport or there is a natural disaster or a war is imminent, the newspaper accounts have the kind of sweeping appeal that should lead writers assigned to them to assume readership by the paper's whole audience. Mind you, that does not include the whole population of a community or even a representative cross section of it. It has demographic and geographic centers of gravity that help the writer narrow his focus.

On less far-reaching stories—the takeover of one Fortune 500 company by another, an election in Japan, the trade of a power forward from the local professional basketball team—the writer can assume the audience will be smaller and better defined. He can, in fact, help define the audience by his approach. He may choose to satisfy the needs of those especially interested in a subject by aiming over the heads of the general audience, which may not understand the first thing about the free agency rule in baseball or international monetary policy. By using technical words and phrases without explaining them, he can sharply limit his readership. When people ask what grade level the newspaper is written to, the only good answer is that it depends on the writer and what he's writing about.

Some sections—kids' sections are an excellent example—need to give the impression of being written for one particular group alone. No grown-ups allowed (though our experience with kids' features is that when they're done well, adults read them, too, sometimes surreptitiously, just to see what their children are thinking about). Sports sections often have something of this quality of exclusivity, arts sections do, too, a snob appeal that is created by the writers' taking it for granted that the readers have a fair amount of background knowledge.

In a newspaper of general circulation, of course, too much of this sort of focusing can be fatal. Writers should generally seek to attract the widest audience possible, given the purpose of the piece. They cannot write for experts only, as they might in learned journals or trade publications. And they certainly should not write only for each other, which is as much an occupational hazard in journalism as it is in academia.

This leaves the matter that Booth calls "voice, the implied character of the speaker." To many newspaper writers, this may seem pertinent only to columnists. But every piece of writing has a voice, even the most plain-style report. In fact, a loose synonym for voice might be "style." As with organizational structure, the question is whether it suits the purpose and the audience.

Voice defines a columnist. With it, he hopes to engage people in a regular encounter over the back fence. If he lacks distinctiveness, the sound will grow tedious, no matter how reasonable what he actually says may be.

Think of Mike Royko's mixture of toughness and mischief-making. Or George Will's bookish bemusement. Or Molly Ivins's Calamity Jane wisecracking. Or William Safire's wicked wordplay. These all reveal the character traits of the implied author—implied because they do not necessarily represent the real character of the writer himself.

The columnist has a persona. It has to fit him comfortably in order for him to carry off the act, especially in this era in which newspaper commentators seem to make their names on television. But there is a distance, too, which permits the columnist to hide certain feelings—moments of pure unreasonableness, perhaps, in Will; of dread earnestness in Royko; of forgiveness in Safire; of pure sweetness in Ivins. I'm just guessing about most of those. But I did once ask Eppie Lederer, who writes under the name Ann Landers, whether she wrote in her own voice or in somebody else's. "I write," she said, "in the voice of a person as good as I would like to be." That tells you a lot about the reason she has one of the most successful newspaper columns of the second half of the twentieth century.

As newspaper writing becomes more explanatory, as it accepts more overt judgments from the reporters, the matter of voice will grow in significance. Just as a newspaper must get its community to respect its character if it is to be believed and to prosper, so too with the individual writer. He may have established his presence through the things he has attached his byline to over the years, or he may be speaking to an audience that has not really registered who he is. Either way, the approach he takes in a piece—conversational or formal, rhythmic or utterly cadenceless, wry or grave—will tell readers who he is at the same time it tells them the information the story more explicitly conveys. If he isn't careful, he will typecast himself as deadly serious and dull or too frivolous to be taken seriously on serious subjects. He probably ought to work on building a sufficient range so that his voice can handle a variety of subjects and moods. And when he has mastered this, he should take care with each piece to adopt the voice—along with the organizational structure—that fits his purpose, keeping in mind the advice of Alexander Pope: [24]

> 'Tis not enough no harshness gives offence,
> The sound must seem an Echo to the sense.

(*five*)
NEWS AND LITERARY TECHNIQUE

OVER THE YEARS SOME JOURNALISM HAS LASTED WELL beyond its normal useful life. In that sense, if in no other, I suppose it has qualified as literature. Think of Addison and Steele or the authors of the *Federalist Papers*, which began as a series of newspaper editorials. More recently the war correspondence of Ernie Pyle and the articles of A. J. Liebling have survived their creators and seem likely to outlast the paper on which they were originally printed. I expect that the reports and criticism of James Agee and the columns of Red Smith will periodically be revived and continue to have a following.

None of this raises any uniquely journalistic issues of the sort that might illuminate the practice of the news today. Sublime works that touch powerfully upon timeless themes have a chance to be read by succeeding generations, whether their authors originally presented them as epic poems or newspaper columns. One can debate at delightful length the question whether survival alone indicates quality. One might even engage in pleasant disagreements over whether journalism can ever match the grace of poetry, drama, or fiction. But this is not my purpose.

Journalism has increasingly been using techniques from fiction. Meanwhile, fiction both serious and purely entertaining has begun to attempt stories almost as immediate as the news. Less controversially, it has borrowed from journalism certain devices designed to enhance verisimilitude. All these entanglements have deepened the ambiguity about what makes fiction fiction and what makes journalism journalism.

This must at times confound the audience, which can be excused if it loses track of which TV program "based on" a recent news event is fictional, which is a supposedly journalistic "recreation" of the event, and which a traditional journalistic piece of work with the camera showing real people doing real things and the reporter telling only what he knows. It isn't only television that creates the uncertainty. In print journalism there are articles and books by reporters claiming to tell the truth about the news from the point of view of people other than themselves, just as fictionalized treatments of real events do.

The audience isn't alone in its confusion. Journalists themselves sometimes seem lost, too. The melding of the forms raises significant questions about what fictional devices are appropriate for journalism, and there is no consensus. Some highly regarded journalists use techniques that seem to be at odds with the basic truth discipline, and the profession reacts inconsistently, sometimes castigating and sometimes honoring it, without making any clear distinction between the proper and improper use of literary technique. In 1994 a Pulitzer Prize jury selected as a finalist one piece that presented a ghastly crime from the point of view of the participants, a group of young people who had not gone to trial at the time the article was published.

Meanwhile, editors of mainstream newspapers such as Shelby Coffey of the *Los Angeles Times* summon newspapers to produce more work that deserves to be called "literary journalism,"[1] and most others recognize that to fit into an information environment that offers customers vastly increasing choices and great immediacy, they must approach the task of journalism in new and unconventional ways. So we can afford to lose no more time before sorting out the proper realms of fiction and fact.

THE TRUTH OF FICTION

The question did not begin with Truman Capote. Again Aristotle had the early line:[2]

The distinction between the historian and poet is not in the one writing prose and the other verse—you might put the work of Herodotus into verse, and it would still be a species of history; it consists really in this, that the one describes the thing that has been, and the other a kind of thing that might be. Hence poetry is something more philosophic and of graver import than history, since its standards are of the nature rather of universals, whereas those of history are singulars.

Notice what Aristotle said about the claim of truth. He did not argue that it made a crucial difference that poetry can be made up and history cannot. Both have a responsibility to the truth. But they are of different orders. For Aristotle, poetry dealt in higher truths and history in lower.

Cleanth Brooks and Robert Penn Warren follow a similar line in *Understanding Fiction*, which gives a good summary of the principal distinctions between history (or journalism) and fiction:[3]

[O]ne often thinks of "fiction" as being opposed to "fact." But in one real sense, this is a false proposition. It is simply a matter of what kind of facts fiction can use and of the way in which it can use them.

They distinguish between the truth of "correspondence" to the facts, which guides history, and the truth of "coherence," or inner consistency, which guides fiction. And they elaborate this by listing the elements that go into making the truth of fiction:[4]

(1) the *consistency* and *comprehensibility* of character;
(2) the motivation and credibility of action; and
(3) the *acceptability* of the total meaning. [Emphasis in original.]

Fiction, they argue, also characteristically provides a narrative line in which something significant changes. Fiction writers embed their meaning in this movement. Of course, nonfiction also could proceed this way, as many histories, biographies, and pieces of journalism do. But in the Brooks and Warren view fiction is capable of effects that history or journalism cannot achieve. "[R]eal life," they write, "either present or past, never fully gives the fiction writer the kind of facts in which he . . . [is] most interested. For those facts concern psychological processes and human motives."[5]

I am not sure Brooks and Warren fully appreciate the potential for "coherence" in journalism. Writers of first-person accounts can produce work that has the elements Brooks and Warren identify without having to make things up. Consider, for example, "Colleagues" from Michael Herr's *Dispatches*,[6] a vivid, extended account of the life war correspondents lived in Vietnam. It represents a coherent portrait of character—Herr's. In fact, the only serious objection that can be made to Herr's remarkable war reporting is that it told more about Herr and his colleagues than about Vietnam. The hallucinatory, hard-rock vision of the experience—a vision so compelling that it has established itself as the prevailing view of the war—more adequately represented the perspective of the college-educated correspondents based in Saigon who ventured forth occasionally into the field than it did the young combat soldiers hopelessly mired there. This, however, detracts neither from the credibility of the action Herr depicts in "Colleagues" nor from the acceptability of its meaning. The way Herr's vision has taken hold proves its rhetorical power.

All that Herr's account seems to lack, by the Brooks and Warren definition of fiction, is a strong narrative line, which is a matter of writerly choice rather than a fundamental limitation imposed on Herr by the values of journalism. "Colleagues" tells many stories, but it does not really feel like a piece of fiction because Herr does not tell it principally through action. He does not permit the meaning to reside mainly in events. His stories illustrate the meaning, the way anecdotes do. They do not embody it, the way fiction does.

Here is an example. Herr sets up his point in purely expository fashion:[7]

A lot of things had to be unlearned before you could learn anything at all, and even after you knew better you couldn't avoid the ways
in which things got mixed, the war itself with those parts of the war
that were just like the movies, . . .

Then, after a half page of essayistic flourishes on that
theme he launches into an account of a moment during the Tet
offensive of 1968 in Hue when he and David Greenway, then of
Time Magazine, asked a Marine to cover them as they raced
from one location to another under the enemy's guns.

David and I ran all doubled over, taking cover every forty meters or so
behind boulder-sized chunks of smashed wall, and halfway through it
I started to laugh, looking at David and shaking my head. David was
the most urbane of correspondents, a Bostonian of good family and
impeccable education, something of a patrician even though he didn't
care anything about it. We were pretty good friends, and he was willing
to take my word for it that there was actually something funny, and he
laughed too.

"What is it?" he said.

"Oh man, do you realize that I just asked that guy back there to
cover us?"

He looked at me with one eyebrow faintly cocked. "Yes," he said.
"Yes, you did. Oh, isn't that *marvelous!*"

It is a story, but it does not work like conventional fiction.
Nor does it take full advantage of the first-person point of view's
capacity for intimate, internal observation.

This does not really distinguish between Herr's article and
other works that most everyone would agree are fictional. Great
fiction is sometimes written to read like exposition. Think of
Jorge Luis Borges's stories or certain aspects of John Dos Passos's
novels. Herr might easily have made his points purely through
a narrative of events he participated in, as Norman Mailer did
in *Armies of the Night* and *Miami and the Siege of Chicago*.
Would this have made "Colleagues" a short story?

I find it difficult in principle to distinguish first-person
accounts such as Herr's from fiction unless I use a criterion for

which the text itself does not necessarily provide the evidence. One such test would be whether the author depicts events and people in the world in a way that he has reason to believe accurately reflects their reality at all levels. Another test might be the reasonable expectations of the reader concerning the veracity of the story.

Of course, even meeting these criteria does not necessarily mean that an account lives up to all the journalistic disciplines. Herr's book decidedly *does not* live up to the Golden Rule, for example, in that it gives no generous account of any understanding of the war but his own. And it is not at all modest in the conclusions it draws.

The "New" Journalism

The two Mailer books were earlier examples than Herr's of a genre which came to be known as the New Journalism. Some earliest works in this mode came from accomplished novelists who claimed that for these books they lived by the news reporter's rules. But most New Journalism—whether written by novelists or journalists—never came close to living by the truth discipline. Lewis Lapham has called these works "the first spawn of the synthetic melodrama that leads, more or less directly, to Oprah and Geraldo and Joe McGinniss pretending to be Teddy Kennedy."[8]

The "newness" of the New Journalism has long since faded, and its claims and practices would hardly deserve mention as anything other than a passing fashion if they had not left a strong stamp on the journalism that followed. Born in the 1960s as one of that decade's many audacities, the New Journalism included figures as varied as Jean Genet and George Plimpton, Hunter Thompson and Garry Wills. It gained notice, especially when it ran in newspapers or was written by people whose names were identified with newspapers, by its fundamental violation of the old traditions of the craft, beginning with the tradition of colorlessness of expression.

In this sense all journalism owes New Journalism a debt, for its adherents recognized early that television's vivid and instantaneous reporting required written journalism to change. It could no longer count on being first with a fact, so it had to provide something more than fact. One thing it provided was the style and quality of its writing. People increasingly came to written journalism more for the pleasures of reading and less for simple facts than they once did. But now that the novelty has faded, concern about truth and the quality of the reporting arises again. In shattering the traditional conventions, New Journalism also created the conditions, with which everyone now in newspapering must live, for confusion in the audience about what is journalism and what is made up.

The most audacious practitioner of the New Journalism also became its principal theoretician, Tom Wolfe. After getting his Ph.D. in American studies from Yale in 1957 he went to work in newspapers, ending up at the *New York Herald Tribune* in 1962, then in its last years. According to Wolfe, his objective was—like that of many other journalists at the time—to write a novel.[9] With characteristic understatement, Wolfe described the general view of the novel at mid-century among writers: "The Novel was no mere literary form. It was a psychological phenomenon. It was a cortical fever. It belonged in the glossary to *A General Introduction to Psychoanalysis*, somewhere between Narcissism and Obsessional Neuroses."[10]

Then a remarkable thing happened. He discovered a way to satisfy the narcissism and keep his day job. Reading the work of older newspapermen such as Jimmy Breslin and then experimenting in his own pieces, Wolfe began to believe he could not only pay deference to the novel by picking up some of its techniques, he could deliver the equivalent of fiction in his journalism. For a sensibility like Wolfe's it is a short step between this and the notion that he and his colleagues would "dethrone the novel as the number one literary genre, starting the first new direction in literature in half a century."[11]

Wolfe's aesthetic centers on the question of social status. The "richest terrain of the novel," in Wolfe's view, is "society, the social tableau, manners and morals, the whole business of 'the way we live now,' in Trollope's phrase."[12] Lest anyone might think he means to leave much to other novelistic approaches, Wolfe goes on to argue that the only literary technique worthy of genius is realism.[13] Even simple realism will not do. Only social realism, the vivid rendering of the manifestations of social status, really makes genius hum. Not surprisingly for a social realist, Wolfe seems to think this is a matter of biological determinism. "I am fascinated," writes Wolfe, "by the fact that experimenters in the physiology of the brain . . . seem to be heading toward the theory that the human mind or psyche does not have a discrete, internal existence. . . . During every moment of consciousness it is linked directly to external clues as to one's status in a social . . . sense."[14]

Of course, the play of status can inspire interesting fiction. Wolfe's *Bonfire of the Vanities* is an amusing example of the pleasures and limitations of social realistic fiction. It was a considerable commercial success, owing both to Wolfe's vivid wit and to the crowd-pleasing ability of caricature that brings everyone down to the same base level.

But social realism isn't the only basis for interesting fiction. And it is hard to imagine anyone taking very seriously Wolfe's doctrinaire aesthetic pronouncements anymore. Still, it would be a mistake to overlook his discussion of technique, because this is where he and his contemporaries have lasting influence.

The power of novelistic writing in journalism, he writes, comes from four basic devices: (1) "scene by scene construction, telling the story by moving from scene to scene and resorting as little as possible to sheer historical narrative";[15] (2) "the recording of everyday gestures, habits, manners, customs, styles of furniture, clothing" and other details "symbolic of people's status life";[16] (3) "realistic dialogue [that] involves the reader more completely than any other single device";[17] and (4) "the technique of presenting every scene to the reader through the eyes of a particular character, giving the reader the feeling of being inside the character's mind and experiencing the emotional reality of the scene as he experiences it."[18]

The first two raise no fundamental issues for journalism. The third may, depending on how much liberty in reconstructing quotations one allows. But the fourth, which marks many supposedly nonfiction accounts by journalists today, is extremely troublesome in light of the truth discipline.

WHAT QUOTATION MARKS MEAN

You don't have to be a New Journalist to get into trouble with quotes. Janet Malcolm proved that in her *New Yorker* piece about Jeffrey Masson, former Freud archivist, which followed conventional nonfiction lines.[19] The article was typical Malcolm, with all guns blazing, and it included some seriously stupid quotations attributed to Masson himself. Masson sued for libel, saying Malcolm had made the quotations up. At the original trial, Malcolm had to acknowledge that she had reconstructed one and elided another. Three more did not appear in her interview tapes, only in typed notes she said she prepared later. The first jury ruled against her after deciding she had fabricated five quotations, though it deadlocked on how much damage this did.[20] She was exonerated in the second trial on the basis that she did not deliberately make up or recklessly misstate the quotes.[21]

When a writer is trying to do what Wolfe calls "realistic dialogue," especially when recreating conversations that took place outside his hearing, the temptation to improve the original or fill in the gaps becomes dangerous. If you have never tried to take stenographic notes, I urge you to turn on C-Span when it is featuring a panel discussion, get a tape recorder running, and start writing down everything everybody says. After ten minutes or so, type out the notes. Then run the tape and compare it with your version. If you don't have a court reporting machine or at least take shorthand, there is no chance you captured much of the original perfectly.

Now try another experiment. Put a tape recorder on during some conversations around your home or office. A few days later, ask a participant to recall what was said. Try the same thing yourself with a conversation in which you took part. Compare the recreation with the original.

If you have the makings of a reporter, your version will get the gist of what was said. But it will probably miss things and undoubtedly will be all wrong about the exact words and sequences.

Most human speech comes in fits and starts, not in sentences. Gestures punctuate it, facial expressions add missing words. Speakers double back on themselves, repeat, elide, let silence finish the thought. Only the very rare fiction writer really does "realistic dialogue," because the real thing does not suit many purposes. One exception is George V. Higgins, whose crime books proceed almost entirely by conversation in such a precise rendition that they offer a glimpse of what real speech looks like on the page. ("I don't like gloves," the fat man said. "In this weather especially, I don't like gloves. What the hell, somebody spots me, the heat comes, I'm dead anyway. Gloves ain't gonna help me. You wait like you say you're gonna, nobody's even gonna know I was in there until everybody's been around handling things and so forth."[22]) I have a hunch that Higgins learned to capture the odd cadences of real speech while reading the logs of wiretaps as an assistant United States Attorney.

Difficult as it is to do effectively, turning human speech into realistic dialogue poses no aesthetic problem for the fiction writer, whether or not he has listened to wiretaps or takes shorthand. He simply must decide what effect he wants and then tune the dialogue to produce it.

For the journalist, though, problems abound. First, he might not have the whole quotation in his notes but might think he can complete it from memory. Or he might be relying on somebody else's memory, perhaps long after the fact, and the person who recollects it might have a bias. Or he might have a perfect version, recorded from a tape of crystalline quality with no swallowed words or background noises that overwhelm the speaker, but the quotations wander all over without ever crisply making the point. Or else the speaker reveals his ignorance or shows crudeness in his language, and the writer wants to clean it up to protect the individual from looking silly (or to make him appear more credible or simply to avoid distracting readers from the main points of the article).

In all these cases judgments have to be made, and they do not always strictly honor the principle of accuracy. Few newspapers, for example, will quote a street person in perfect vernacular unless they have a strong rhetorical reason to do so. In the American press high school dropouts usually speak in diagrammable sentences. Unless, of course, there is a TV camera around, in which case the reporter knows his version might be compared with the original. Hence the increasing use by print reporters of small tape recorders to capture speech whole, just in case they need it that way.

If everybody at times fixes quotes and rebuilds quotes from memory, why did the use of dialogue in the New Journalism cause such professional controversy? "This can't be right . . . ," Wolfe imagines conventional journalists thinking. "These people must be piping it, winging it, making up the dialogue. . . . Christ, maybe they're making up whole scenes, the unscrupulous geeks (I'm telling you, Ump, those are *spit*balls they're throwing)."[23]

Some traditional journalists may have felt threatened by superior reporting and writing and wanted an umpire to get them back in the game. But many simply felt uncomfortable that the New Journalists were taking the limited traditional exceptions to the principle of accuracy and making them the rule. These traditional journalists may not have articulated the restrictions they lived by, but they did restrain themselves, because they thought the discipline of truth required it. The New Journalists did not seem to care.

The time has come to establish some clear standards in this area, because one of the legacies of the New Journalism has been to provide an excuse for practices that do not stand up to scrutiny in the light.

Let's begin with the proposition that a journalist should only use quotation marks when he has a reasonably reliable record of exactly what was said. If he makes any change in a quotation or has any reason to question the reliability of the quotation, he should let the reader know what he has done. He can do this by using brackets in quotes to indicate added or changed words, ellipses to indicate elisions. He can explicitly state what he has done. (For example, he might indicate that the following dialogue is presented as John Jones recalled it five years later.)

I would make a few exceptions to this general rule.

Several times already in this book I have used quotations recreated from my own memory, and I do not think I offended the discipline of truth. The reader could easily tell where they came from (they were embedded in personal anecdotes recalled from a considerable distance, so the reasonably attentive reader could make a judgment as to how perfect they might be). To be sure, I went beyond the ordinary call of duty and pointed out what I was doing. But even without the cue, I believe people can understand what it means to remember a conversation. They do not need a formal statement that the memory might not be perfect. If a reasonable reader[24] can easily figure it out without being told, let it go.

In ordinary circumstances cleaning up grammatical lapses in quotations does no disservice to the truth. This exception would not apply when the intelligence or education level of the speaker is important in evaluating what he said. Nor would it apply when the speaker is prominent enough that a lot turns on his words. The President provides the usual example. (Would a newspaper ever use the word "fuck?" Only, says the prudent editor, if the President said it on television.) This category may include others beyond the country's Chief Executive, but it is very narrow. Unfortunately, professionals in language probably fall inside it, if only because their usage can affect dictionaries. Live by the sword, die by the sword.

I would permit reporters to use their memories to fill in the gaps in the quotes in their notebooks as long as they took the notes recently and can remember well what was said. Here no clear-cut rule will work, but the more vivid or important the language, the more undesirable it is to depend on memory. Reporters should use tape recorders whenever possible if they are intending to use direct quotations. (In many circumstances, of course, the recorder will not do, either because the reporter must do the interview on the fly or in otherwise difficult circumstances or because the recorder would inhibit the person being interviewed.)

There may be occasions in which a reporter might properly attribute quotations to Mr. X that he obtained from Mr. Y without indicating the real origin of the information, but I cannot think of any. Perhaps if the quotation is innocuous enough or the reporter's source has compelling evidence (stenographic notes, for example), it could pass muster. But I would *always* sacrifice literary effects to the truth discipline.

When in doubt, it is best for the journalist to reveal exactly what he has done. He should forget the posture of absolute precision. He should say what he heard directly and what he got secondhand. Just as acknowledging error, candor about what one knows for sure and what one does not builds credibility.

POINT OF VIEW AND OTHER MIND-READING TRICKS

Of all the techniques Wolfe listed that blur the distinction between journalism and fiction, writing from the point of view of another person conflicts most sharply with the truth discipline. Without some intimacy with the characters, newswriting cannot create the feel of a traditional, realistic novel. But with too much intimacy, newswriting accepts a standard of truth that is far too low.

Literary point of view has many complexities, but let me give a simple sketch of the way writers use it.[25] The most basic distinction is between first-person and third-person narration. In the first person the narrator speaks directly to the audience about what he himself has thought and done. In third person the narrator can relate the perceptions and thoughts of others. In first-person fiction the narrator may not be the author himself. Marlowe in *Lord Jim* was not Joseph Conrad. Nor need the implied author who writes the narrator's part be the real person doing the writing, any more than the newspaper columnist's persona has exactly the columnist's real personality. Likewise, in the third person the narrator might refer to the author as a character (as, for example, in *The Education of Henry Adams* and Mailer's *Armies of the Night*).

The third-person narrator may be omniscient—getting inside everyone's minds—or limited in some way. The narrator may adopt an individual point of view for a single chapter or section and then change to another point of view. The writer also can adopt various levels of intimacy with his point-of-view characters. He might simply describe the passing scene from the physical point of view of a particular character. (*John Jones turned. Before him loomed a pale man with a black patch over one eye.*) He might report a few, obvious internal reactions. (*The man had a horrible countenance. And when he spoke, Jones drew back, a shudder passing through him that he struggled unsuccessfully to hide.*) Or he might get completely inside the character. (*Who is this monster? Nobody I know. No man. I am no man. What the Cyclops said, wasn't it? In English class. Scared then, too. Scared of the nuns.*) The variations are endless, because the degrees of intimacy form a continuum.

Third-person narration can be purely "objective," meaning that it reports only physical details observable by anybody. But once again, there are variations, depending on whether the narrator sees all or sees from a particular position, which turns him into one kind of a point-of-view character.

Finally, you might narrate in the second person—as you have followed this sentence in the second person. But this is awkward and rare in extended forms.

Of all point-of-view techniques, first-person narration holds the greatest untapped literary opportunities and fewest risks for newspaper journalists. Unfortunately, somewhere along the line in the push for professional objectivity, newspapers all but abandoned the first person. This was a mistake. First person can become an exercise in egotism, of course. But properly handled (and instruction in this would be welcome in the journalism schools), first-person journalism in news reports can be both compelling and candid.

The first-person journalist does not pretend omniscience. He can confess the things that restrict his viewpoint or bias his reactions. Here are two examples of the use of first-person technique. They come from the work of the consummate reporter,

Homer Bigart, and they refer to a February 26, 1943, bombing raid over Germany:[26]

AN AMERICAN BOMBER STATION, SOMEWHERE IN EN-GLAND, Feb. 26, 1943—Our target was Wilhelmshaven. We struck at Fuehrer Adolph Hitler's North Sea base from the southwest after stoogeing around over a particularly hot corner of the Third Reich for what seemed like a small eternity.

I could not quite make out our specific target for obliteration, the submarine pens, because at our altitude the installations along the Jade Busen (Jade Bay) seemed no larger than a pinhead. But the street pattern of the Prussian town stood out in perfect visibility and so did the large suburb of Rustringen, down the bay.

A few days later, Bigart filed another report about the raid for the *New York Herald Tribune*:[27]

. . . True perspective is rather hard to maintain in the hours immediately after an assignment in which your own neck was directly involved. You are apt to feel you had a ringside seat at the most crucial engagement since Waterloo or that final Yankee-Cardinal game at the Stadium.

Those pieces were excellent journalism in 1943, and they would be excellent journalism today: vivid, accurate, duly modest in their claims to truth.

First-person narration also permits the writer to produce difficult effects in the reader. An example is the Pulitzer Prize–winning series "Rosa Lee's Story," by Leon Dash of the *Washington Post*.[28] It tells the painful story of the life of a poor and troubled family—including crimes, drug use, and unconscionable behavior by Rosa herself—while still maintaining in the reader an empathy for the subjects of the piece. Use of the first person lets Dash acknowledge the effect his presence had on the action and interactions he witnessed and the effect the things he saw had on him, which helps guide the readers' reactions.

VARIETIES OF VENTRILOQUISM

Wolfe is not content with staying within his own consciousness:[29]

Only through the most searching forms of reporting is it possible, in non-fiction, to use whole scenes, extended dialogue, point-of-view, and interior monologue. Eventually I, and others, would be accused of "entering people's minds" . . . But exactly! I figured that was one more doorbell a reporter had to push.

The trouble is, the door never really opens, and the man inside is a notorious liar.

Various degrees of intimacy are possible in third-person journalistic narrative. Consider first this passage from *In Cold Blood*:[30]

[W]hile Mr. Clutter was shaving, showering, and outfitting himself in whipcord trousers, a cattleman's leather jacket, and soft stirrup boots, *he had no fear of disturbing her*; they did not share the same bedroom. For several years he had slept alone in the master bedroom, on the ground floor of the house—a two-story, fourteen room frame-and-brick structure. Though Mrs. Clutter stored her clothes in the closets of this room, and kept her few cosmetics and her myriad medicines in the blue-tile-and-glass-brick bathroom adjoining it, she had taken for serious occupancy Eveanna's former bedroom, which, like Nancy's and Kenyon's rooms, was on the second floor. [Emphasis added.]

Capote gives a taste of Clutter's point of view by describing his morning ablutions and then noting that he had no fear of waking his wife, an internal thought not necessarily manifest in his expressions or actions. How would Truman Capote know Mr. Clutter had no fear? He could not have asked the man, because Mr. Clutter was the victim of a murder and Capote did all his reporting on the crime after the fact. But he could infer it from certain other bits of information he had gathered, and he has the grace to lay the evidence out for the reader so that the "had no fear" line has support in external evidence.

Contrast this with a passage from *The Final Days* by Bob Woodward and Carl Bernstein describing an exchange between President Nixon and Henry Kissinger not long before the President's resignation:[31]

He [Kissinger] walked into the alcove. There was the President in his chair, as he had seen him so often. Kissinger really didn't like the President. Nixon had made him the most admired man in the country, yet the Secretary couldn't bring himself to feel affection for his patron. They sat for a time and reminisced about events, travels, shared decisions. The President was drinking. He said he was resigning. It would be better for everyone. They talked quietly—history, the resignation decision, foreign affairs . . . .

"Will history treat me more kindly than my contemporaries?" Nixon asked, tears flooding to his eyes.

Certainly, definitely, Kissinger said. When this was all over, the President would be remembered for the peace he had achieved. The President broke down and sobbed.

Kissinger didn't know what to do. He felt cast in a fatherly role.

How do the authors know that Kissinger could feel no affection for Nixon? Or that when Nixon wept, Kissinger felt as if he had been put in the role of a father? Few emotions are more intimate than these. The contrast between the ordinarily distant, icy presence of these world leaders and the intimacy of Kissinger's thoughts give the scene its drama (all right, melodrama). Unlike Capote, Woodward and Bernstein do not favor the reader with any evidence to support the inferences that reach into the internal thoughts of the point-of-view character. A bit later in the scene they note that Kissinger talked to other people about the incident, so it is impossible even to feel confident that Kissinger himself told them. It could have come to the writers second- or third-hand, making the inference even more tenuous. But even if Kissinger had given the writers his account himself, how much credence should they or their readers put in it? The nature of affection and of paternal feelings is complex and changeable under the best of circumstances. And here the person with the feelings is one of the more subtle figures in recent American history, a genius at manipulating public images. It would take a psychologist cleverer than Kissinger to infer with any confidence the truth of the person behind his door.

Now consider a passage from Wolfe: [32]

All these raindrops are *high* or something. . . . The plane is taxiing out toward the runway to take off, and this stupid infarcted water wobbles, sideways, across the window. Phil Spector, 23 years old, the rock and roll magnate, producer of Philles records, America's first teen-age tycoon, watches . . . this watery pathology . . . it is *sick, fatal.* He tightens his seat belt over his bowels. . . . A hum rises inside the plane, a shot of air comes shooting though the vent over somebody's seat, some ass turns on a cone of light, there is a sign stuck out by the run-way, a mad, cryptic, insane instruction to the pilot—Runway 4, Are Cylinder Laps Mainside DOWN? . . . Schizoid raindrops. The plane breaks in two on takeoff and everybody in the front half comes rushing toward Phil Spector in a gush of bodies in a thick orange—*napalm!* No, it happens aloft; there is a long rip in the side of the plane, it just rips, he can see the top ripping, folding back in sick curds, like a sick Dali egg, and Phil Spector goes sailing through the rip, dark freezing. [Emphasis in original.]

Now *that* is intimate. It is very close to stream-of-consciousness. The moment-to-moment sense perceptions, the precise and unintelligible words on a particular runway sign, the vivid, detailed nightmare fantasy. Did it really rush through Phil Spector's head at just that instant? The thick orange of na-palm flames? The sick curds like a Dali egg? All of it? Tom Wolfe provides absolutely no evidence on which to judge the veracity of the passage except the verisimilitude (or lack of it) of the text itself. I have reasons to doubt. But that may just be because my fears upon takeoff do not generally assume the form of a Robin Williams monologue. They tend to be more prosaic, a tension in the muscles, a thought of my wife and children, that sort of thing. In his essay on the New Jour-nalism, Wolfe claims that Spector said that he found the passage quoted to be accurate. "This should have come as no surprise," wrote Wolfe, "since every detail in the passage was taken from a long interview with Spector about exactly how he had felt at the time."[33] But that does not quite end the matter, because a person's description—in this case his gleeful description—after the fact does not necessarily represent or even come close to representing the emotions of the moment. Another way of put-ting it: this description lets us infer more about Spector's way of talking about himself than about what he was actually feel-ing the moment the plane took off. The man on the other side of the door often lies about his inner state. He may even lie to himself.

Finally, let's turn to a book that touched off a controversy, Joe McGinniss's treatment of Senator Edward Kennedy, *The Last Brother:*[34]

> He glanced again at the clock. Not quite 1:40. If only, right now, this very minute, he could scoop up all the papers on his desk, stuff them into the briefcase by his feet, and get up and walk out of the Senate, leaving Prouty right there in midsentence, and go home and take a shower and hook up with Claude and go out for a few drinks. . . .
>
> Having to listen to Winston Prouty, on a Friday afternoon the week before Thanksgiving, preaching about the evils of using taxpayers' money for library books, was about as deep in the morass as Teddy had yet found himself.

This passage takes place in an account of the moments just before Kennedy learned that his brother Robert had been shot. It is not quite as intimate as Wolfe's passage, but it does include a fantasy (the Senator dreamed of just getting up and walking out) and a self-pitying internal judgment (a trivial moment of boredom seemed to the Senator the deepest morass he'd ever been in, even deeper, McGinniss leads one to assume, than the muddy bottom at Chappaquiddick). And the remarkable thing is that McGinniss admitted that he made it up. Or at least that is a reasonable inference.

In an "Author's Note," McGinniss reported that the Kennedy family had resisted his research, so he apparently never talked to the Senator about what his feelings were in this moment of tedium before the horror. But he did have "many dozens of interviews" with Kennedy acquaintances and "immersed" himself in "vast amounts" of published material about the Senator. "From this base of existing knowledge and verifiable source," he wrote, "I have tried to convey to a reader what it *might* have been like to be Teddy Kennedy [emphasis added]."[35]

Respected journalists attacked the very idea of this. Veteran political writer Jon Margolis in the *Chicago Tribune* wrote:[36]

This book should immediately be studied by all Americans, not because of its intrinsic values—for it has none, none whatsoever—but as an illustration of just how corrupt and decadent our cultural, intellectual and political life has become.

Francis X. Clines in the *New York Times* called McGinniss "shameless" and declared his literary devices "licentious."[37] Neither of those reporters nor their newspapers have gone in for the "novelistic" approach. But even the *Washington Post*'s book critic, Jonathan Yardley, proclaimed *The Last Brother* "a textbook example of shoddy journalistic and publishing ethics" and went on to say it represents "a mockery of even the most minimal standards by which biography is written."[38]

Of course, there is a distinction to be made between *Final Days* and *The Last Brother* in that Woodward and Bernstein claim that *somebody* told them everything they reported in the book and McGinniss admits that he made the leap of imagination himself. But that distinction cuts the truth discipline too thin, especially since Woodward and Bernstein don't reveal who said what. Except in cases in which the assertion itself is news (because of who said it), the issue for journalists is not whether somebody says something but rather whether there is reason to believe it is true. And as the Kissinger example suggests, Woodward and Bernstein are as vulnerable as McGinniss on that score.

The intensity of the reaction to McGinniss's book was peculiar, since McGinniss was just a little more candid about his method than most. And the book was much less harsh in its inferences about Kennedy's inner life than many others on the subject. When Joyce Carol Oates published *Black Water*, an unveiled *roman à clef* devoted entirely to the moments during which a young girl drowns in a car sent hurtling into the water by a prominent politician, it met no similar cries of outrage, though it was far more severe about the real life subject than McGinniss's book.

It would be encouraging if the outcry against McGinniss were the beginning of a reconsideration of the whole genre, a step toward the development of some standards about what is acceptable journalistic practice and what is lying. But I am afraid that the controversy over *The Last Brother* had more to do with McGinniss's vulnerability after his clash with Janet Malcolm than with any fundamental and sustained concern about this element of our craft.

THE REACH OF INFERENCE

The truth discipline does not prevent journalists from making inferences. Reporters do so whenever they sort out facts and arguments, even on the most routine matters. (*Three homes in the Main Street neighborhood were burglarized in a similar fashion last night. The police refuse to say the crimes are related.*) Nor should journalists be forbidden from inferring some things about the internal states of the people they write about. (*Fresh from Officer Candidate School, 2d Lt. Ron Jackson stood in the jungle clearing turning the plastic-covered grid map around and around, trying in vain to orient it to the treelines and paddies that stretched flat to the horizon. His men looked at him warily. If he was going to have a hope of getting them to follow him, he would have to start now. "Sergeant," he shouted. "Where the hell are we?"*)

How far should journalists feel free to go in making these judgments? And how much do they need to let their readers in on the basis for what they have done? One factor must be the degree of uncertainty one properly has concerning a statement. If I had spoken neither to Mr. Clutter or Senator Kennedy, I would be a lot more confident saying that Mr. Clutter did not fear (or, more precisely, did not have reason to fear) that he would wake up his wife than I would be in saying that on the day his second brother was murdered, Senator Edward Kennedy fantasized about walking away from presiding over a dull Senate session and going drinking with Claude. The degree of confidence depends on all the circumstances, not just whether a person told you so.

By simply keeping his eyes open, a reporter traveling with an infantry unit would learn enough about the lieutenant to understand that he was trying to get the men's confidence by deferring to their superior knowledge. Of course, there might be other explanations for the lieutenant's actions. He might have panicked and yet had the wherewithal to hide his fear. But without any indication that the most obvious inference is flawed, it is usually safe to choose it. On the other hand, if somebody a reporter thinks is a liar or is not in a position to know the things he is asserting tells the reporter something, this does not create the basis for publishing it as fact. If the Senator was in the habit of hiding his drinking habits, an admission that he was thinking about going out for a pop with Claude might have a fair amount of force. But if he were a self-abusing depressive, I might be concerned that he had concocted a maudlin, humiliating tale. And if Claude or a Senate page told the story of what was going on in the Senator's mind, I'd be very dubious.

Uncertainty increases as the narration's intimacy with the point-of-view character grows closer. The writer can choose where on the continuum he plans to locate his narration. At a certain distance, there is little reason for concern about the inferences because their reach is small. (*Jim O'Leary could barely whistle for his grinning as he walked down Park Street after the letter came. It said his boy had been accepted to Harvard. Harvard. Though it was only a few miles from his South Boston neighborhood, until Jim Junior began turning in a spectacular performance at school, the university on the other side of the Charles River was to the people in O'Leary's community another country, with a border that his kind was not allowed to pass.*) Although in one sense novelistic, this example builds on some simple and determinable facts—the expression on O'Leary's face, his behavior, the arrival of the letter, the way people in his community looked upon Harvard.

Move the point of view a little deeper into the character, and the inferences become more problematic. (*The smell of boiling cabbage came sharp to O'Leary's nostrils, as familiar as his mother's kitchen. Wouldn't she be proud, though? Her very own grandson going where the Kennedys had gone. Though he grinned as he whistled a little jig, too there was a twinge. She would have lorded it over everybody in the neighborhood, imposed it on them like the smells from her window in the*

summer, whether they bloody well liked cabbage or not.) Here
the writer puts precise sense impressions and memories into
the specific moment and gives them vivid expression, even
trying to use distinctive rhythms and vernaculars suggesting
the point-of-view character's patterns of speech. Unless Jim
O'Leary told it all to the writer just this way, the inferences are
pretty audacious.

But they are nothing compared to what is done in the most
intimate approach, stream of consciousness. (*O'Leary trium-
phant! O'Leary a king! Did the Kennedys themselves have
anything on him today? Hell, didn't their boys all get into one
kind of trouble or another? But Jim Junior, now there was a lad.
Could've been a priest, so dutiful. Not one to go fooling with
every Colleen showed him a little leg.*) Only generosity would
describe this kind of report as an inference from the evidence. It
comes as close to making it up as a writer can with characters
who have a real life off the page. Such an approach has no business in news reporting.

Other factors in deciding how far to take an inference
should be the nature of the stakes and the consequences of getting it wrong. Any misjudgment has the potential for inflicting
pain upon the person whose internal thoughts the reporter mis-
characterizes. But it is one thing to infer certain feelings in a
warm and flattering account of a father's pride at watching his
son pitch his first professional baseball game and another to attempt to guess at what went through a policeman's mind as he
fired a shot that killed an innocent boy. This is why it is so utterly inappropriate to attempt to do a piece from the point of
view of people awaiting trial for a crime. Their state of mind is
the very essence of the legal question, and no newspaper should
pretend to know it. Likewise, I have problems with most efforts
to do intimate, internal portraits of powerful political figures,
especially when their internal states (of knowledge or motivation) bear heavily on public choices. This was certainly the political situation when *The Final Days* was published. Nixon
had resigned, but other figures in the book were either trying to
get beyond those days or were already planning comebacks.

That raises another factor, the passage of time. McGinniss,

defending himself against the criticism that greeted his Kennedy book, used three examples of well-regarded history and biography in which the writers had described the internal life of
their subjects. One was a book about Mozart, another about the
French Revolution, and a third about Samuel Johnson. Without
getting into any of the historiographical issues those books
might raise, I would note that even recognizing the importance
of the lessons of history, the individual damage these accounts
could cause was small because the events depicted were so remote in time that everyone depicted in them was dead.

Unfortunately, the greater the uncertainty and the greater
the contemporary stakes, the greater the temptation to write
an internalized account. This approach has become popular
simply because in such circumstances curiosity runs high. But
if the truth discipline means anything, it means journalists
should resist the temptation.

THE MARSHALING OF PROOF

Even when a journalist has confidence in more modest inferences he has made about what was going on in his subject's
mind, he still has a duty to the reader to disclose the basis for
his judgment and deal with all legitimate counterarguments.
Going back to the elements of the basic truth discipline, intellectual honesty demands at a minimum that when a writer
makes a judgment, he should set forth the evidence tending to
support and to refute it. And when the matter is controversial
(a sense of the true nature of the relationship between Kissinger
and Nixon, for example, might have colored the public's perception of Kissinger sufficiently that he would not have survived
into the Ford Administration), then it might be better for the
writer to withhold judgment.

Curiously, the novelist Truman Capote seemed to understand the need for these restraints better than many journalists.
Again and again in *In Cold Blood* Capote finds clever and subtle
ways to marshall the evidence and make his assertions about
the characters' internal states credible to the reader, just as he
marshalled the evidence in the passage I quoted earlier to show
why Mr. Clutter wasn't afraid of waking his wife. For example,

early in the book he quotes at length a letter sent to Perry, one of the murderers, by a jailhouse friend. It makes a series of significant observations:[39]

"You are strong, but there is a flaw in your strength, and unless you learn to control it the flaw will prove stronger than your strength and defeat you. The flaw? *Explosive emotional reaction out of all proportion to the occasion.* Why? Why this unreasonable anger at the sight of others who are happy or content, this growing contempt for people and the desire to hurt them? All right, you think they're fools, you despise them because their morals, their happiness is the source of *your* frustration and resentment. But these are dreadful enemies you carry within yourself—in time as destructive as bullets." [Emphasis in original]

This introduces an element of the murderer's motivation that Capote develops throughout the rest of the book. But the fact that someone who knew the murderer well believed this about him is not enough to support the weight Capote put on this analysis, so he makes a point of establishing a close link with the murderer's own assessment of himself. "Perry," he reports, "flattered to be the subject of this sermon, had let Dick read it."[40] In other words, a close observer of Perry made conclusions about his emotional makeup, and Perry had accepted the judgment. This does not, of course, mean that the reader must accept the account of Perry's state of mind, nor does Capote insist that he do so. The evidence provides the reader a means for evaluation.

Even the architecture of *In Cold Blood* seems carefully designed to permit Capote to marshall persuasively the evidence of his characters' motives and emotional lives. The first section ends with the discovery of the murder of the four members of the Clutter family. But exactly what happened remains a mystery. Though Capote early on shows certain aspects of the two murderers' characters that help explain how they could have done such a cold-blooded deed, he never suggests in the first half of the book precisely why, not even why they selected the Clutters. This sets the stage for a careful development of the evidence.

First Capote slowly lays out the physical details—where the bodies lay, how the victims were killed, various small things such as a missing portable radio. Then he follows the false starts of the police investigation until a tip from an informant provides both the first link to the murderers and the first suggestion of why they picked out the Clutters to attack. All the while, Capote periodically cuts to the two killers as they make their way to Mexico and back, then to Florida, but he only teases the reader at the edges of the mystery. At first, he keeps a great enough distance from their internal states that the reader learns nothing about what they might be thinking about the terrible thing they had done. Then slowly he permits them to speak briefly to one another about it, hiding as much as they reveal. Only when police capture and interrogate them does Capote dare suggest what was really going on in their heads as they contemplated and executed the murders.

Perhaps a novelist naturally takes a cautious approach to what his readers will believe. Since he ordinarily makes it all up, he knows he has to get the audience to suspend its disbelief. Unlike journalists, who often take it for granted that the reader will accept the basic truth of what they report, the novelist has to use all his tricks to get them to this point. And so when he wants to persuade them, not that the story is as good as true, but that it in fact *is* true, we shouldn't be surprised that he keeps his claims modest and marshalls his evidence carefully. For this he earned some gentle criticism from Wolfe, by the way, who chided him for not using point of view in as "sophisticated" a way as he did in his novels.[41] In fact, Capote's approach is very sophisticated, moving in and out of intimacy as the level of uncertainty changes during the course of the story and the audience's willingness to accept his inferences grows.

Journalists have a lot to learn about rhetorical techniques from novelists. They would do well to begin by studying the clever, restrained approach of *In Cold Blood*. Capote understands rhetoric well, and the need to persuade skeptical readers shapes every aspect of his piece, from its basic structure to the details of individual sentences. Journalists who want to use literary techniques need to recognize that this kind of extraordinary care is how people make literary fiction.

WHO TOLD THE WRITER?

Capote's approach is instructive, but his work is an imperfect example for journalists in one glaring respect. He rarely attributes information to the sources from whom he got it. This is not surprising. The journalistic discipline of attribution often comes into conflict with a writer's use of sophisticated literary techniques.

In traditional newswriting the reader does not have to deal with much ambiguity about who and what the writer want him to believe. The newspaper reporter simply tells the story in as straightforward and accessible a manner as he knows how. The voice of the piece is the writer's, and he intends it to be taken as sincere and knowledgeable. Not that the newspaper reader accepts everything he is told. Nor should he. But the simplicity of the reader's general understanding of newswriting—or for that matter of most essay forms—contrasts sharply with the complexity that fiction presents.

When journalism adopts storytelling techniques from fiction it takes on some ambiguities, too, which may make it difficult to fulfill the basic requirements of journalistic discipline. How, for example, is a newswriter to fulfill his obligation to tell the source of his information when he is writing from somebody else's perspective? A fiction writer has no such duty, and the ambiguity in the narrator's relationship with the implied author, not to mention the delightful ambiguity between the implied and real author, provides part of the pleasure of the enterprise to writer and sophisticated reader alike. The fiction writer only needs to keep the thing plausible, so that when a character is shown to know something, the reader finds it believable that he does.

A writer who does not follow journalism's disciplines has a lot of latitude in this. How did the murderers know about the Clutters? An informant comes forward to say that he had told one of them about the family. The writer can also hint how he

got certain details without giving a leaden recitation of his
sources. Capote does this masterfully. Take, for example, the
simple passage describing a moment in the last day of the Clutter daughter's life to which nobody was a witness: "Barefoot,
pajama-clad, Nancy scampered down the stairs."[42] At first this
reference is as mysterious as the killers' motivation. The skeptical reader wonders how Capote expects him to believe that he
did not simply make this up. Then, two pages later, Nancy
walks into her father's office where another person sees her.
Aha! That's how Capote knew what she was wearing. And as to
the scampering, it might have been an embellishment or a description he had heard of her general behavior and then applied
to this specific instance through a small inferential step. The
trouble is, Capote never says that the man in Nancy's father's
office told him how Nancy was dressed that morning, nor does
he reveal who described the girl's way of scampering down the
stairs. He cannot do so without inserting himself into the story
too early, violating the basic chronology he has established.

A journalist doing the same story would have to use another approach that permitted him to identify at significant
points of the narrative who told him what. This is especially
true when he reports details that are disparaging to an identifiable individual, because in these circumstances fairness makes
the need for attribution compelling.

There are several ways a writer might accomplish this,
and most of them prick the illusion that the reader is getting
the story from the point of view of someone other than the
writer. This may cause anguish to the writer who wants to
show off his novelistic purity. But I think the serious journalist
ought to see this as an advantage. Attribution not only provides
the factual basis that readers deserve to find in newspaper writing, it also helps reestablish a simple relationship between the
reader, the narrator, and the writer. With the reporter present in
the story through his attribution of significant information, the
narrative voice clarifies. The reader no longer has to wonder
whom he is meant to believe. He is meant to believe the reporter, who is always there.

There may still be ambiguities between the implied author and the real person doing the writing. He may not register all his sincere observations about the story because of journalistic self-restraint or because he writes through a persona that does not display all the emotions he himself does. But even these complexities decline in importance when the writer establishes his presence clearly throughout the narrative.

For this reason regular attribution is better than using notes to the reader at the end of stories to set forth in a general way the places information came from. (*The Herald reconstructed the burglary at the National Herald Bank of Centerton after interviews with the following people:. . .*) Since such general statements do not really provide detailed attribution of specific facts (who said what about what?), I think they are inadvisable.

THE LITERARY VISION

For most of my adult life, I have made my living in journalism. Meanwhile, I have published five novels,[43] and I continue to write fiction to this day. At various times people have suggested there was something odd, even conflicted, about this double life. More than once I have heard Hemingway's warning to the effect that a little journalism is good for a writer, so long as he abandons it before it ruins him. I have also heard that a journalist writing fiction risks not being taken seriously in either mode. The warnings may have had some validity, but I have disregarded them. And I have found that the two kinds of writing, far from coming into conflict, support one another in large and small ways.

Sheer practice is one of them. For most of us, learning to write takes more than a lifetime, and the learning mostly takes place in the act. You write and rewrite. You try out things. You fail. You try them another way. Something works. You try to remember it so you can use it again. The fancy term for this is finding one's voice. I'd call it five-finger exercises, getting the notes properly under the hands. And in the process of doing them, you often find in one mode little tricks and writerly discoveries that prove to be useful in the other.

While cruising the Internet one day I came upon a quotation from Robertson Davies, a wonderful Canadian storyteller who also has worked as reporter, editor, and businessman. "All this," he wrote, "I consider necessary to my life as a writer. It has kept me from too great a degree of that fruitless self-preoccupation which is one of the worst diseases of the literary life."[44] The other side of Davies's point is that the writing also helps sort out what is important in the other work. Though I have often been asked how I can keep writing while doing other challenging things, the real question is how I could stop and still retain my balance.

In more purely aesthetic terms, the practice of journalism—its discipline of fact and the encounters with reality that reporting entails—confers some immunity against the fashionable tendency to see the creating of literature as the only proper subject of literature. In the right hands, reflexive work can be beautiful. But lately there has been too much of it, and not enough of it good. It has shown us the dark side of the old advice to writers that they should write only what they know.

Most people who write fiction have to do something else to support themselves and their families. At one time, this forced most writers into situations—sometimes exotic or raw—in which they also happened to find material. (I am reminded of a cartoon that showed a pilgrim going through a miserable wasteland labeled "Slough of Despond." He says to a bent, wizened companion, "I'm only gathering material for a novel.") Writers today have marvelous new opportunities to support themselves by teaching their craft, but I am afraid this has led to a narrowness in our literature. The limitations of academic fiction are well known. The university community rewards the conceptual and the abstract. Its concerns can become remote from the common life of the society and the interests of the general, literate audience. This may be the reason we have so much literary fiction today whose principal interest seems to be in formal invention rather than the expression of a fundamental human vision.

Of course, a great many fine writers have brilliantly avoided the academic dangers. As Henry James said, a writer should try to be a person upon whom nothing is lost.[45] But for someone like myself upon whom too many things are lost, journalism has provided close contact with an extraordinary range of human behavior that has helped feed my fiction. It was my means of experiencing the most overwhelming moments of my life, covering the Vietnam War. As a writer I am still living off the capital I accumulated during my years as a police reporter. Even in the more rarefied business of the editorial page it was not uncommon to see people at the moment of crisis—the political candidate caught in a lie, the public official on the verge of indictment, the leader locked in a struggle for the survival of his cause.

As Graham Greene has said, there is a splinter of ice in the heart of every writer.[46] I am reminded of a moment during the invasion of Cambodia. I was with a reconnaissance unit, and suddenly an explosion sent a jagged piece of metal into the man standing next to me. He fell. A medic rushed up. My first instinct was to turn and shoot a photograph. I still have a print of that picture, to remind myself of both the physical and spiritual dangers our correspondents run.

For better or worse, fiction is like that photograph. It feeds on moments of intensity, when basic things about human character show themselves.

Working on fiction has deepened and strengthened the journalism, too, because fiction is—like journalism—a way of discovering truth. What, the journalists might ask, can anybody learn about the real world by making up a story about a world that exists in the writer's head?

Of course, the novelist might reply that journalism also involves the projection of the writer's vision on his material. It cannot help but do so. Seeing the world is an active engagement, not just the passive reception of sensory data. Every waking moment we impose order on the flux of experience by an act of the brain that could be described as imagination. So it is not surprising that imaginative ordering turns out to be common to the writing both of fact and of fiction, or that one can inform the other in fundamental ways. Fiction's need to establish plausibility makes the relationship between depiction and reality in a novel different but no less important than it is in journalism, even when the writer is attempting to create a whole alternative reality. No matter how radically different the fictional world is from the earthly situation in which we are rooted, its only claim on our attention is that it somehow illuminates our situation.

When I sit down to write a novel or short story, it becomes a kind of thought experiment. I begin with a few characters and an initial idea of how to complicate their lives. Then I set them loose to work the situation out. In that process, they tell me something. More often than I would like to admit, I have worked with characters who begin to expire on the page even as I try to breathe life into them. They become like ventriloquists' dummies. They say what I make them say, but my lips are moving for everyone to see.

When this happens, it means I have gotten something seriously wrong. It might be as small an error as misunderstanding the immediate relationship between the characters. This happened to me as I was writing the novel *Mass*. I had set up two estranged people for hundreds of pages to have a confrontation, and when they finally met, they kept trying to renew their bond. I had to grant them their wishes in the end, which was the making of the scene.

This kind of problem is easier to solve than one that goes to the essence of the story. More than once I have written my way well into the draft of a novel only to discover that I had the wrong person telling the tale or made some other fundamental structural error. And when I finally discovered the error, I saw that it violated the truth of the thing I had set into motion when I put the characters in their fix to begin with.

When a story falls into error, I become stuck. And until I discover what exactly is wrong and come up with another way, I am not somebody anybody would want to be around very much. But once the alternative opens out before me, the effect is exhilarating. The words go down on the page effortlessly. The characters speak through me rather than vice versa. And in the end, I do not believe it is too much to say that I have learned something about the nature of things.

What I have learned is a new way of seeing. This can transfer into journalism. One of the editorials that won the Pulitzer Prize in 1986, an essay on the anniversary of Hiroshima, represented a straightforward statement of some of the things that were revealed to me in the writing of *Mass*. I have done pieces on intelligence policy that probably would have been impossible if I hadn't tried through the novels *Convergence* and *Legends' End* to give some coherence to what I had seen while working in the Justice Department. The ideas about radical skepticism I worked through in *Convergence* helped me write pieces on subjects as diverse as moral relativism and the jurisprudence of original intent, not to mention earlier parts of this book. In *Fragments* I worked on questions of freedom and responsibility in extreme situations. The things I learned about ambiguity in dealing with the raw material of war helped me think about determinism, criminal punishment, and the basis for the open society.

Ambiguity may seem to have nothing to do with journalism, especially its polemical forms such as editorial writing. The purpose of an editorial, as a rule, is to persuade readers to accept the public policy position the editorial espouses. The arguments are supposed to march to a bright conclusion, not wallow in the gray. Decisions must be made in this world, and editorials mean to influence them.

Fiction, of course, has a different purpose. What is a virtue in an editorial is a terrible vice in a novel. A polemical novel is usually worse than melodrama, which is bad enough. Occasionally such a piece is so well done that, like a political cartoon, it has its own kind of artistic validity. *Candide* and *1984* come to mind. But usually the polemical novel's characters are flat. It does not render life with the sort of fullness that inspires great fiction, and this fullness—along with the encouragement of the free play of language—provides the best excuse for freeing fiction from the discipline of fact.

Most of the fiction I admire shares what psychologist Roy Shafer describes as the "tragic vision":[47]

The tragic vision is expressed in a keen responsiveness to the great dilemmas, paradoxes, ambiguities, and uncertainties pervading human action and subjective experience. It manifests itself in alertness to the inescapable dangers, terrors, mysteries, and absurdities of existence. It requires one to recognize the elements of defeat in victory and of victory in defeat; the pain in pleasure and the pleasure of pain; the guilt in apparently justified action; the loss of opportunities entailed by every choice and by growth in any direction; the reversal of fortune that hovers over those who are proud or happy or worthy owing to its being in the nature of people to be inclined to reverse their own fortunes as well as to be vulnerable to accident and unforeseen consequences of their acts and the acts of others.

This tragic sense also informs journalism at its richest. It links news reporting with a vision of human nature that underlies the open society and its system of free expression. It helps journalism be intellectually honest by providing an antidote to *hubris.* And it provides a powerful reason for respecting other points of view.

But still journalism must do its own work. It must take events serially and attempt to reach some resolution regarding their meaning. It must recognize that the tragic vision can lead to paralysis and that in the world of affairs one has to act. Where fiction wants to put people to impossible moral choices, journalism needs to help people know about the events that affect them and to decide what, under all the circumstances, is the best that can be done. Fiction savors the richness of ambiguity. Journalism seeks to resolve it, at least tentatively, and then move on.

Ultimately, the worlds of fiction and journalism can enrich one another through the sharing of techniques, experiences, and fundamental visions. But they must remain separate, even in the soul of a single writer who cannot seem to help himself but to do both.

(PART THREE)

THE FUTURE OF NEWSPAPERING

(*six*)
THE CHALLENGE OF COMPLEXITY

THERE'S NOTHING NEW ABOUT COMPLEXITY. IT'S JUST that what seems complicated keeps changing. At one time newspapers found it challenging to understand and communicate the way bacteria cause disease or how a telephone works. (In 1906 Henry Adams professed astonishment at the complexities of the Daimler motor.[1]) Now those things have become familiar. But human retrovirology and cold fusion are something else again.

Knowledge is fragmenting, intellectual disciplines becoming more insular and specialized. Each involves daunting antes to get into the game—opaque jargon, methodological quirks, deep strata of background information that academic discussion assumes all participants share. A lot of this is probably unnecessary. In my experience, the more formidable the intellect, the more likely the person blessed with it will put his arguments clearly. Of course, in mathematics, the physical sciences, and the empirical branches of the social sciences, the models need first to be expressed in quantitative and possibly abstract ways. But translation can soon follow, if there is the will and the brightness to do it. The principle of elegance, after all, assumes that the truth has a simple beauty, which ought to be communicable.

Unfortunately, not all scholars, even English professors,

see the importance of writing so one can be understood.[2] Yet it has never been more important that nonspecialists understand what scholars and researchers have to say. Public decisions increasingly ride on the outcome of debates among experts. And the vast fiscal commitments made to pursue scientific theories or turn abstractions into real instruments of peace and war are only the beginning. Whole new areas of the law—environmental, occupational health and safety, even constitutional definitions of individual liberties (such as the right to have an abortion)—build directly and specifically on hypotheses still under scientific debate. The management of the government's role in the economy has the qualities of a clash of intellectual theories. Leading-edge technology and thought now shape governmental action as surely as they shape commercial activity. And as rapid communications and fierce competition shorten the time between the formulation of an idea and its use by decision makers, the public can easily find itself left in the dark.

Meantime, the stakes of the intellectual game—not only glory, but also cash—have increased. The mechanism by which basic professional values pass from generation to generation has faltered. And as a result, some important members of the very groups society counts on for truth-telling have fallen into habits of intellectual dishonesty. Every new medical and environmental hazard seems to have its academic advocates ready to terrify us—the depletion of the ozone layer, global warming, global cooling, not to mention asbestos, toxic chemicals on apples, and the risk of pediatric AIDS. Behind them stand strong interests with broader political and economic agendas. The same goes for nostrums, whether oat bran, supply-side economics, or managed competition in the health care industry. And journalism is all too willing to pass technical misinformation along.

This is not the place to go deeply into the nature and causes of this change in the intellectual environment. But if specialization and complexity have proliferated, and if members of the truth-telling professions (including academics, research scientists, and journalists) have lost their sense of clarity about the obligation of intellectual honesty, then the role of newspapers has become crucial. They must umpire a debate that has fewer and fewer ground rules, and they must help people parse the complex technical matters that shape our lives.

These are challenging tasks. Far easier to make the sage observation that perception is reality and then deal with perception than to wrestle with the formidable barriers to understanding and communicating the complicated realities about which misperception readily forms. But in some of the most complicated fields misperception can mean errors in social policy that have mortal consequences. And in all of them misperception leads to misallocation of scarce resources and misuse of taxpayers' money.

A TEXTBOOK EXAMPLE

In 1989 the *Tribune* published a sixteen-page section, without advertising, devoted to a story by John Crewdson detailing the history and mystery of the discovery of the virus that causes AIDS and the development of a blood test to detect the virus.[3] Had it been a conventional history, the article could have been much shorter and more accessible. But the accounts the principal scientists gave of their work did not square with the facts, and that made the story both extremely important and extremely difficult to tell.

Parts of the story had been made public when a group of French scientists from the Pasteur Institute in Paris filed suit to dispute the American patent on a blood test made possible by the isolation of the AIDS virus. When the suit was settled by diplomatic intervention from both sides of the Atlantic, the contending scientists wrote an official history. It bore little relation to what had actually happened, both because of what it said and what it did not say. Crewdson's article laid out in detail the discrepancies between what the American team of scientists from the National Institutes of Health (NIH) reported in scholarly articles and public statements and what records from their lab and other documents showed. This was not a story in which the participants gladly sat down with the reporter to help him through the nuances. The key scientists in the NIH lab refused to cooperate and devoted their energies instead to keeping Crewdson from completing his reporting and the *Tribune* from publishing it.

To understand the cryptic lab notes, documents, and memoranda, Crewdson had to become thoroughly familiar with the leading-edge field of retrovirology (the study of a particular kind of virus that has been shown in humans to cause a form of leukemia and AIDS). Once he mastered this, he did the detective work of organizing thousands and thousands of pages of material and then pursuing further inquiries to fill in the gaps so he could reconstruct the history. Finally he had to pull himself back from the obscure world of retrovirology and find a way to tell the tale to those of us whose knowledge of viruses begins and ends with a case of the flu.

He and his editors, of whom I was one, did not succeed in meeting the challenge of creating a rhetoric suitable to the task. The article made too many demands on the audience. Science is hard enough to communicate when the information is clear and unambiguous. (Quickly, explain the basics of quantum mechanics.) But when the evidence is scattered, missing, and obfuscated, this creates another thick layer of difficulty. Outright lies make telling the story even harder. It is often challenging enough to follow an investigative report of a conventional financial fraud, and everybody knows how money works. Investigative stories' difficulty arises from the need to deal with conflicting evidence and arguments and to explain the basis for the key inferences. Often the reporter does not know everything he would like to know. After all, he doesn't have the subpoena power and cannot force anyone to swear under penalty of perjury. So to do an honest job in the writing, he has to recognize the gaps in his information and deal with them openly. This often prevents him from making a straight-line presentation.

In the investigation of the discovery of the AIDS virus, there was a further complicating factor. We knew that we had to reach and persuade not only our basic audience but also the scientific community. If scientists failed to take us seriously, Crewdson's work would have come to nothing. And the scientific community was not exactly eager to accept the idea that they might learn something from the *Chicago Tribune* that they could not learn from *Nature* and *Science* (leading scholarly publications in the field). We knew that the scientific community's first line of defense against accepting Crewdson's work would be that the journalistic account was simpleminded, that as a layman Crewdson just did not begin to comprehend the nuances. Had we simplified the story too much, we would have fallen prey to science's immune reaction to outside criticism. So we made compromises between audiences—the general audience and the narrow specialty audience—which left the piece far more challenging to read than anything else we publish in the *Tribune*.

Meantime, the reporter and editors had to make sure every assertion had documentation, that the researchers had an opportunity to state their views (an opportunity they rarely took), and that significant counterarguments were responsibly dealt with. In this respect the article succeeded. Every major accusation in Crewdson's article has been confirmed.

The article reported that we could not conclude whether an act of theft or contamination had occurred in the American scientist's lab, and the evidence on this point is still indeterminate. But most scientists who pay close attention to these things now accept the fundamental facts of the discovery of AIDS as Crewdson laid them out and have rejected the many misstatements by NIH scientists involved. Those main elements are as follows: Despite Dr. Gallo's many statements to the contrary over the years, the virus samples sent to his lab at NIH by the Pasteur scientists were genetically virtually identical to the virus he claimed to discover and used in the blood test he patented. (Because the AIDS virus mutates rapidly, this is what led Crewdson to conclude that there had to have been either an accidental contamination in Dr. Gallo's lab or a theft.) Despite Dr. Gallo's many statements to the contrary, his laboratory was growing the French virus in quantities sufficient to do a great number of experiments with it. And the cell line in which he got the AIDS virus to grow continuously was not a creation of his lab, as originally implied by the articles and statements coming out of his lab, but rather one previously developed by another scientist. So the Americans did not create the medium in which the virus could grow, nor did they discover the virus that causes AIDS. They "discovered" a virus the French had already determined to be the cause of AIDS. And either by accident or design, they appropriated it as their own.

Several of these issues have much more than historical importance. Acknowledgement by Dr. Gallo's lab of the real identity of the cell line alone would have permitted research outside his lab to move more quickly, since that cell line was readily available. According to the panel of scientists from the National Academy of Sciences who reviewed the NIH investigation, Dr. Gallo was "essentially immoral" in his reluctance to share samples of the cell line he used.[4]

Again and again, Crewdson proved right on the science and the history and Dr. Gallo proved wrong. But despite this record of journalism helping to correct significant scientific misstatements, I do not know whether most scientists to this day accept the idea that newspapers have a proper role in investigating such matters. I am not sure most newspaper reporters and editors think so either.

Should Newspapers Investigate Science?

What can newspapers presume to add to the open exchange and competition among scientists that is supposed to advance knowledge and correct important errors? We can never constitute ourselves as research institutes in all or any of the myriad specialties into which science has fragmented. We will always be generalists caught in a labyrinth devised by experts. We will always be amateurs, outsiders looking in, dabblers in things that are above our heads.

And yet if you put the question the other way, the appropriateness of the newspapers' role in examining science critically becomes clear. Journalism is supposed to illuminate matters of public concern, and this includes the job of discovering significant information that otherwise might be hidden. So journalism *must* approach science (and other specialized disciplines that command large amounts of public money and deal with grave public issues) with the same disciplined skepticism with which it approaches the activities of a city council or a governor.

Open communication and competition among scientists clearly provide the most powerful mechanism for perfecting the state of knowledge through discovery. But science does not necessarily correct itself quickly enough to prevent misdirection of public money or the abuse of the public trust. It does not necessarily correct scientists in time to keep them from adversely influencing public decisions, even on subjects as pressing as a deadly human plague. And AIDS research is not an isolated example of this. After Crewdson revealed that some of the data in an important breast cancer research project had been systematically falsified, an editorial in the *Journal of the American Medical Association* stated, "What is astonishing, indeed completely inexplicable, is that we had to learn all this from the *Chicago Tribune*, rather than from a scientific journal, and that we have had to wait so long to do so."[5]

Scientists, particularly those working on the leading edge of discovery, may not be particularly interested in going back to review the details of another's work unless there is something odd about it that under critical examination might prove useful to their own. A scientist with sufficient influence can, if he is ruthless enough, use that power to frighten off colleagues who might otherwise suggest imperfections in his work. Other scientists' interest is not, and probably should not be, to protect the integrity of the process of issuing government research grants or the quality of information going into government decision-making. These are closer to newspapers' traditional concerns.

SCIENCE AND DUE PROCESS

The scientific community itself has recently established formal mechanisms to supplement the informal, imperfect, free play of scientific exchange. Private and public research institutions have elaborate procedures for handling allegations that scientists have engaged in misconduct of one sort or another. But these procedures have themselves become terribly cumbersome as they merge with and adopt the standards of an adversarial legal proceeding.

The discovery of the cause of AIDS provides a vivid example. Dr. Gallo and his lab chief, Dr. Mikulas Popovic, were found guilty of scientific misconduct by Department of Health and Human Services (HHS) officials charged with examining issues of research integrity. The panel of outside scientists from the National Academy of Sciences asked by NIH to review its investigation sharply criticized Dr. Gallo. They reported that they had found in the matter "a pattern of behavior on Dr. Gallo's part that repeatedly misrepresents, suppresses and distorts data and their interpretation." And they accused Dr. Gallo of "intellectual recklessness of a high degree" and the "intellectual appropriation of the French viral isolate."[6]

Both accused scientists appealed the official findings of misconduct (the report by distinguished fellow scientists was advisory and thus not appealable). An appeals board of lawyers (not scientists) convened by the Department of Health and Human Services reversed the scientific misconduct charge against Dr. Popovic, saying it found that the record of its hearings did not support such a finding. It held that unless statements in scientific publications are capable of no reasonable interpretation that squares with the truth, there can be no finding of misconduct. The appeals board also significantly narrowed the case concerning Dr. Gallo offered by investigators. In both cases the panel excluded all evidence of the larger context that shed light on what the scientists did and what they meant people to believe by what they wrote and said. This was done on the ground of "fundamental fairness."[7] After these appeals board rulings the HHS integrity office withdrew its case against Dr. Gallo, though it stated publicly that it had not changed its mind about Dr. Gallo's conduct.

Crewdson had from the beginning been under fire from science writers from the *Washington Post, Science* and *Nature* magazines, and others. So it was not surprising when in the aftermath of the appeals board rulings and HHS withdrawal of charges *Time* Magazine said Dr. Gallo had been vindicated despite the fact that the *Tribune* had "crucified" him.[8] *New York*

Times science editor Nicholas Wade in the *Times Sunday Magazine* concluded that critics of Dr. Gallo, including Crewdson, "were far too slow to correct their misjudgment of the one scientific hero who has yet emerged in the fight against AIDS."[9] Meantime, a compendious congressional committee staff report supports Crewdson's assertions. And Frederic M. Richards, a Yale University professor emeritus who served as a scientific consultant to the NIH Director in the Gallo inquiry, called for the reopening of the investigation.[10]

History will have to pick up where government procedures left off. But the progress of the matter through the bureaucracy suggests something about the nature of official mechanisms for dealing with allegations of scientific misconduct, including fraud.

By the time the case reached its conclusion, it had narrowed down to a few very specific points concerning the scientists' behavior. This was in part the consequence of the legalistic approach that often focuses on individual, isolated actions rather than reflecting on a course of behavior as a whole.

Approaching the matter from the legal point of view, one can see some strained basis for the lawyers on the HHS appeals panel ruling as they did. Fairness and due process are maddeningly elastic concepts that provide lawyers with a lot of discretion. There were also other values in play. The rule that reads all ambiguous statements in scientific articles in favor of a truthful interpretation has the effect of permitting scientists considerable leeway in expression, not unlike the leeway journalists have under the rule in *New York Times v. Sullivan*[11] (and standards like the "innocent construction rule" in Illinois[12]) to write about issues of public interest without undue fear of libel judgments. Under *Times v. Sullivan*, American courts may not hold a newspaper liable unless it is shown to have intentionally lied or acted in reckless disregard of the truth. (The standard of truth for scientists is considerably lower than this. The HHS appeals board indicated that it believed federal guidelines do not sanction scientists for anything short of intentional falsehoods, so even reckless misstatements would not be misconduct.[13])

If one believes that in science, as in politics, a free and open system of expression has the greatest opportunity of approaching truth, one has to respect the appeals board decision to read ambiguity in favor of the author, even though it had to strain the English language to the breaking point to find ambiguity in the challenged statements. This does not necessarily reflect any lack of scorn for violations of the moral duty to tell the truth. It simply recognizes that a strict legal duty might inhibit the open communication on which the system depends. The trouble is that the legal rule can get confused with the moral rule so that people who should be driven by the exacting ethical discipline get confused. In science as in journalism, practitioners may see their right to get away with misstatement as a license to lie.

The difference between moral and legal duty helps explain why the members of the National Academy of Sciences panel saw clarity where the nonscientist members of the appeals board saw ambiguity. The scientists were measuring against a sterner obligation.

Unfortunately, the legalistic approach is gaining ground on the purely scientific. Government labs, where the impact of misconduct on the spending of public money and on public policy discussions is the greatest, lean strongly toward the legal model. This is because government may take action that affects individuals adversely (even high government officials such as doctors who run major publicly supported labs) only after following procedures that afford the individual due process of law. But even in private institutions, where less legalistic methods would be more appropriate, the adversarial model has been adopted more and more. "This," wrote Charles Maechling, Jr., a law professor and former deputy general counsel of the National Science Foundation, "is distorting the delicate task of investigating questionable research practices and could do lasting damage to the health of U.S. science."[14]

Maechling is not alone in his concern. The following is a statement approved by the Council of the National Academy of Sciences and several other groups:[15]

Recent decisions by the Department of Health and Human Services in specific cases have been interpreted by some scientists as limiting the activities that are defined as misconduct in science. These decisions must not be taken to mean that the scientific community can reduce its efforts on ethical issues. In addition, other problems, such as questionable research practices, require our constant attention. *As members of the professional research community, we should strive to develop and uphold standards that are broader than those addressed by the governmental regulatory and legal framework for dealing with misconduct in science.* [Emphasis in original]

If the trend toward the legalistic, due process model for the consideration of accusations of scientific misconduct— especially lying about research—continues, it will leave us with the following situation: The informal method of scientific self-correction will operate slowly, if at all. The formal mechanism will tolerate many violations of the discipline of truth-telling so as not to inhibit the free expression that in the long run offers the best way to advance knowledge. So unless the press, which also has legal latitude, or other private institutions give scientific matters close and independent scrutiny, the community's interest in speedy correction of misrepresentations by scientists engaged in projects of immediate and significant public importance will often not be satisfied.

This is why the newspaper must begin paying more critical attention to the work of science and other complex specialties that so powerfully affect people's lives. It is probably more important that newspapers exercise vigilance for fraud in these areas than in the more traditional places they like to look (such as the letting of government contracts, selection of people for jobs, and so forth), just because the job is so hard that few others will undertake it.

Crewdson wrote of this in an article entitled "'Perky Cheerleaders,'" in *Nieman Reports*, in which he took science writers to task for credulousness about science, medicine, health, technology, and the environment, which he calls the "technoplex":[16]

The failing of American journalism is about more than failing to have kept science honest. It's about failing to have become as sophisticated about what goes on inside the technoplex as about finance or politics or world affairs. Ultimately, the technoplex isn't about science anyway. It's about vital questions of public policy, about how enormous sums of public money are spent, about how lives are saved and lost and how those lives are lived. The technoplex is too important to be left to reporters who like science, reporters who are more interested in why volcanoes explode and how bumblebees mate.

There is a place for explaining why volcanoes explode, of course. It is part of what newspapers do for their readers. But Crewdson is right that science writing must also advance into this other realm. That leaves the question how newspapers can hope to do this, when the issues involved are often so obscure and difficult.

The Kind of Journalists Newspapers Need

The answer lies in the education of journalists and the expectations newspapers have of them. At one time newspaper reporters only needed a gift for words and enough chutzpah to get in the door. After that, they learned on the job. They learned how to write hard news and features. On some papers they might even have gotten a taste of magazine work. They learned the techniques for getting information over the phone and face to face. They also learned about the world, usually starting with the police department.

They got an anecdotal education about institutions, often over a few drinks in the local hangout after hours. (*"You hear what that goofy superintendent said today, kid? He said he was going to put all beat patrols in one-man cars. Well, hell, you might as well give the bad guys a set of master keys."*) In effect, learning began at the end rather than at the beginning. It built upon current matters of debate rather than from a foundation of general knowledge and analytic skills.

This did have the salutary effect of preparing newspaper reporters to be comfortable dealing with matters that were new to them. Since they often had little formal education, almost everything was new to them. And when it wasn't new, as often as not their insight reflected the received wisdom of the institution they covered. No wonder it took such a long time for newspapers to deal boldly with issues like police brutality and racial and sexual discrimination. By the time a reporter had gained the stature to go after stories like that, he may well have stopped seeing them as stories at all. Sometimes it took journalistic malcontents or obsessive outsiders finally to break through the conventional view.

Education in the skills and values of the news trade worked the same way. Reporters and copy editors learned by doing. (*"What do you call this, chum? Poetry? Leave it to the eggheads. A newspaper gives it to them straight and simple. Bing. Bang. Boom."*) They learned from peers and news sources where the lines were, whom it was safe to bully and who could fight back. They watched some reporters embellish the facts and get good play. They watched others lie on the telephone and get results. Nobody gave them a rulebook. And nobody wanted to debate ethics very much. One night when I was working at the *Chicago Daily News* the night city editor sat shaking his head at a syndicated column he was reading off the wire. "Look at this. He's got George Romney pausing to take a sip of Scotch. Romney's Mormon. There's a lesson in that, kid. When the wind blows, make the curtains move." On the job ethical training in those days was ruthlessly practical.

Journalism schools provided some counterbalance. They were instrumental in professionalizing news reporting, writing, and editing. They often included required classes covering the history of journalism, the social role of the press, and the legal and moral issues confronting the business. They emboldened graduates to insist on the independence to publish things that might conflict with the interests of advertisers, to question practices such as deception and embellishment that had gone on for years. Usually the undergraduate curriculum required students to take courses concentrating on a social science discipline such as political science, history, or economics to provide a base of knowledge of the institutions newspapers write about. At the graduate level, the curriculum might tailor these lessons to the specific needs of journalists. (When I taught a graduate journalism seminar in law, one of the greatest pedagogical challenges I faced was to make the students understand that it was not a particularly high use of their valuable time for me to teach them how to cover a trial.) And at all levels there was practical, "laboratory" training in writing and editing, lots of it.

These elements of journalism education—practical instruction in newswriting and editing skills, introduction to the social and moral dimensions of the work, and general grounding in a traditional academic discipline—need to be rethought in order for journalism education to help transform the practices of the business tomorrow as effectively as they professionalized it in the past.

The importance of providing a firm grounding in the social and moral imperatives of a free press remains undiminished, though from reading professional publications it seems that too many people are fighting the last war. The need for independence from advertisers in making news judgments has been well established, as has the need to view significant institutions in the community from a critical distance. But the right relationship between the news and marketing functions needs careful examination, as does the issue of how the news should handle the reporting of perceptions when the news has such an instrumental role in shaping them. We need the schools to push students to think about such central questions as how newspapers can have a unique voice and roughly coherent sense of the world and stay true to their truth discipline. I would like to see more searching discussions that link the issues in journalism with the main currents of general moral thought. We don't lack ethical debate, God knows. Sometimes it seems as if we like nothing better. But we lack the kind of discussion that advances understanding beyond the passionate reliance on cliches. Journalism schools need to refresh the discussion in the news business both through what their professors publish and through the students they send into the newsroom.

Practical skills in news reporting and editing need not be taught at the university level. Students' time is limited, and the other pedagogical needs are vast. The old, on-the-job model for learning the rudiments of reporting and writing conventional news stories and mastering other basic techniques works quite well. The best a university can do anyway is to try to simulate real newsroom experience, either through laboratories or by actually putting out a newspaper or magazine. On the other hand, since the nature of newswriting is changing, with the old forms falling away leaving only the more classic elements, the basic writing component of journalism education needs strengthening.

We need writers on newspapers today who can think their way to the right approach to each story rather than simply fit their notes into the closest existing newspaper category—hard news, news feature, human interest. And we need editors willing to publish the results. In this demanding art, a lifetime is not long enough for all the learning a writer needs. And as the message becomes more complicated, the challenge becomes greater. We need journalists who will be able to tell a story like the tale of the discovery of AIDS in a way that will reach and persuade both the scientists and the general audience. English faculties have by and large surrendered the task of teaching this kind of writing. In too many instances they also have given up on doing this kind of writing, as a casual stroll through most of the academic journals of literary criticism and scholarship will demonstrate. Young journalists may find it difficult to learn on the job a kind of writing that newspapers are only beginning to discover they need. So intensive work in college or graduate school on the classic elements of good writing should be the center of every journalism curriculum—even at the expense of general, practical training in newswriting, editing, and page design.

But how to prepare journalists to deal with complex technical issues? The old reliance on the lessons of history or political science—useful as those disciplines are in helping students form a coherent understanding of the way the society as a whole functions—will not necessarily prepare them to scrutinize the technical areas of inquiry. Newspapers cannot subdivide beats in these fields the way universities have subdivided academic areas; narrow beats would not be productive enough over the long term. In fact, too long on a single beat runs the risk of capture by the worldview of the institution covered as well as by the issues that were most current during the years the reporter started in the field. Whether or not journalists rotate through specialized assignments, they must be more generalists than technical experts, and yet they also must be capable of dealing with the experts from a position of strength.

I have a few suggestions.

First, journalists are going to have to become more comfortable with technology. The science component of a journalism education, if it exists at all, usually involves no more than a single year's study. It needs to grow. If nothing else, a journalist today must be thoroughly grounded in computers and what they can do if he is going to have a chance of understanding our world, or for that matter of helping news organizations navigate the changes that technology drives. This is true for all journalists, not just those who intend to do science or business reporting and editing, to which those interested in technology typically gravitate. A movie critic cannot understand what goes on the screen without understanding modern computerized film technique. A sportswriter cannot understand the making of an athletic team—or the making of athletic profit—without paying mind to medical and other machines. In writing about food, fashion, you name it, ignorance of technology is as appalling in journalism today as ignorance of history was a hundred years ago.

Second, we probably need more journalists who have had a rigorous education in a specialized discipline. It is no longer uncommon to find lawyers working as reporters and editors. Some newspapers have physicians on their reporting staffs. Academic training in literature, music, or art often prepares young journalists for careers as critics. Intensive, graduate level work gives an individual the vocabulary, the analytic skills, and the confidence to deal with complex issues. It should prepare him to deal with complex issues outside the specific field in which he trains. The reporter with a strong economics background should find that, having immersed himself in this difficult discipline, he can move more quickly to understand an area of the physical sciences than if he had never before had to work with complicated masses of data and high-level mathematical abstractions.

In this regard, we need to make journalism education more intellectually challenging in its own right. Instead of having students read work written for generalists or specifically for journalists, they should read original texts in philosophy, science, law, and other disciplines that are as difficult as what they will have to deal with on the job. Since most journalists are never taught to read an article in a scientific journal critically, is it any wonder that they report flawed research as definitive and narrow conclusions as sweeping?

We may have to use mid-career education more frequently to prepare journalists for specific assignments. The editorial departments of newspapers are notoriously poor in offering training. They have begun to awaken to the need to give new editors some exposure to modern management techniques through programs such as Northwestern's Newspaper Management Center. And some have sent staff members for foreign-language training before overseas posting. Programs like Yale Law School's one-year course of study for journalists have promise—though I remember a comment by the late Fred Rodell, an eccentric member of the Yale Law School faculty, to the effect that one year of law school makes a person feel too well-disposed toward the law while three years' stay creates a more fitting distaste. Shorter programs—such as those put on by the Foundation for American Communications—to give journalists a grounding in specific areas such as economics, law, or environmental science provide a valuable antidote to some of the prevailing ignorance about these subjects. But they are simply too modest to get someone ready to investigate science or other technical fields in the depth and with the independence we need today.

Finally, we need to let reporters know that we expect them to produce work in complex fields that holds up against sophisticated examination. We cannot accept the kind of ignorance of basic statistical methods that so often lead to preposterous reporting of scientific claims.[17] The simple, anti-intellectual pose that is so common in newsrooms is no longer acceptable, and every reporter on our editorial staff must understand that. Dismissiveness is as unprofessional as credulousness, and failure to look critically is as unacceptable in technical fields as it would be in reporting the letting of highway construction contracts.

OTHERS' DUTY TO THE TRUTH

No matter how vigorous newspapers become in reporting on the complexities of science, medicine, and technology, they will be no substitute for a reexamination by those institutions of their own commitment to the discipline of truth. The cause of intellectual honesty, lately a losing battle, needs to be revived in all areas of society. The confusion between what the law requires and what decency and self-respect demand must be cleared up. Legal analysis is vital, but it must be kept in its proper place. Learned societies should become more active in these matters. Their publications and others serving specialized fields should take on some of the burden of doing what newspapers do in examining critically the conduct of those engaged in important research and publishing their conclusions when they find something amiss. The competition might motivate the newspapers to expand their coverage, and the need for careful, searching reporting in these areas is so great that there will surely be enough story opportunities to go around. Meantime, the leaders of science, medicine, and technology should learn to welcome the scrutiny from the outside as well as create the means for greater scrutiny from within. It is time to recognize that these disciplines could use some help in living up to their ethical obligations.

If newspapers do not give science, medicine, and technology the kind of attention they have gotten used to giving presidents, governors, mayors, and legislatures, journalists will deserve ridicule when they talk high-mindedly about their essential social purpose, because the leaders of science and technology today may make more of a difference in people's lives than heads of state. For reasons I will discuss in the next chapter, people may be more interested in them, too.

(*seven*)
HELPING PEOPLE
MASTER THEIR WORLD

NEWSPAPER PEOPLE TAKE SATISFACTION IN NOTING that the future of newspapers and the future of self-government have a vital linkage. I suppose this means to them that all right-minded citizens should commit themselves to helping newspapers thrive in the interest of the republic. Unfortunately, the relationship between newspapers and the health of a community's political life cuts both ways.

Newspaper readership depends in large part on the level of public interest in the institutions of democratic choice. Show me somebody who has a deep involvement in the twists and turns of public decision-making, and I will show you an addicted newspaper reader. Show me somebody who does not care about government, politics, and public affairs, who feels that he has no control over the way governmental and other important social decisions are made, and I will show you someone we're at risk of losing as a reader, if we have not lost him already.

Unfortunately, there is a lot of evidence suggesting that more and more people would just as soon not pay attention to the social and political debate. The general trend in participation in federal elections has been downward since the 1960s.[1] People just seem to be losing interest. When I give speeches on this subject I often ask the audience how many of them can immediately name the state legislators from their district. Few, even among journalists, can readily do so. Why? They simply don't care. Meanwhile, people have also grown more cynical. This is reflected in data from the Yankelovich national opinion survey. In 1990 36 percent of respondents reported they were angry about campaign promises not being carried out. By 1994 45 percent reported being mad about it.[2]

Time is a big factor in the audience's growing distance from government and politics. Is there anyone who has not felt everything speed up and become more stressful in the last decade or two? Where is the time for reflection? For putting the feet up on the porch rail and contemplating the curious social behavior of birds and higher animals? Is it any wonder that people don't get interested in politics the way they used to? But I am afraid that isn't all of it. People find the time to indulge their curiosity about other things—sports, entertainment, self-help. Why has concern for the commonweal been edged out?

As mobility and the scale of society increases, personal relationship with politics becomes more attenuated, more mediated. It is harder to feel engaged with a politician on television than it is to feel a personal bond with one you have seen in person. The experience of TV watching is passive. The viewer is not fully engaged. This, too, has taken a toll on the spirit of participation. The decline of political parties and the big city political machines has eliminated a powerful element of personal contact from community life. Nobody from the Organization comes to the door anymore to help you get a tree cut down or a summer job for your teenager and to ask your help on election day in return. Television, not precinct workers, has become the way to get the Boss's message into people's living rooms.

A conversation I had in 1990 drove home to me the degree of the change. The political organization built by the late Mayor Richard J. Daley of Chicago was having difficulty finding someone willing to take over the party chairmanship. I asked Daley's son, Mayor Richard M. Daley, what he thought of that remarkable turn of events. He grinned and said, "Do you want the job?"

Repeated scandals and the reforms they provoked, including the federal judiciary's attack on political patronage, did away with whatever remnant of the political machine might have survived in the era of television. In addition, scandal has created a deep well of public doubt about whether anyone in government is playing it on the square.

Journalists, of course, have long embraced the lesson of Original Sin as it was expressed by Willie Stark to a reporter he hired to get the dirt on one of his enemies in Robert Penn Warren's political novel, *All the King's Men*: "Man is conceived in sin and born in corruption and he passeth from the stink of the didie to the stench of the shroud. There is always something."[3] Journalists' experience usually demonstrates that if they expect the worst, they will not be disappointed. But this view has grave consequences. When they write this assumption into their news reports, they suggest the extremely simpleminded view that all social problems could be solved if only the people wrestling with them were honest. Worse, to the potential voter, if all politicians are the same, then why bother knowing their names, let alone keeping up with them in the paper?

Beyond the changes in the way we live, major changes in the way we think have alienated people from the institutions of the commonweal and distanced them from the community debate. Some of the unifying ideas that made it easier to keep things in perspective have collapsed, making it more difficult to keep a grip on the events that shape our world. The Cold War, for example, and the belief that science means progress used to offer steady reassurance that we understood—or at least were capable of understanding—why things happened and what they portended. Even when the news was bad, it did not seem as gratuitous. Old prejudices also had an anchoring effect, which helps explain the intractability of certain forms of bigotry. The mind seems to have a tropism for the all-encompassing explanation. And when rich systems of understanding break down, poor ones take their place.

In other words, people need mental moorings. Alfred North Whitehead once remarked to his fellow philosopher Bertrand Russell, "You, Bertie, are simpleminded; I am muddleheaded." William Barrett explains the distinction in his book *The Illusion of Technique: A Search for Meaning in a Technological Civilization*:[4]

The "simpleminded" fasten upon the clear fragments of fact that lie in the foreground to the neglect of the complex background of reality against which those facts emerge. The "muddleheaded," on the other hand, are so engrossed in this complexity of background that enters into every atom of fact that clarity of expression emerges dimly if at all.

Most people find muddleheadedness too uncomfortable to bear for very long. The usual metaphor is walking around in a fog. Worse, occasionally a lightning bolt strikes at random out of the gloom, without warning, without reason. This is what it feels like when facts overwhelm a person. Is it any wonder that such people tune out?

Information overload manifests itself emotionally as a profound sense of loss of control. Of course, even in much simpler times people did not feel in control of everything that affected their lives. Disease, war, the forces of nature humbled mankind. But in the days when people had recourse to prayer rather than engineering, they had access to a kind of control that today we have all but lost. Neil Postman described this, somewhat romantically, in his book *Technopoly: The Surrender of Culture to Technology*:[5]

Ordinary men and women [in pre-technological societies] might not clearly grasp how the harsh realities of their lives fit into the grand and benevolent design of the universe, but they have no doubt that there is such a design, and their priest and shamans are well able, by deduction from a handful of principles, to make it, if not wholly rational, at least coherent.

Even when one cannot change something, he can still get a measure of control over it by establishing it firmly in a system of belief. We cannot stop death, but we can control its influence on our lives through wise understanding and various forms of faith. When international events pose frightening prospects, no one of us can make the situation otherwise, and yet we all look for knowledge about the situation so that we can gain control over our intellectual and emotional—if not our physical—environment.

In his odd way, Henry Adams was onto the phenomenon and its largest implications before anybody else, seeing them in a technological device that today seems simple (though it is actually still quite mysterious):[6]

The magnet in its new relation [to the dynamo] staggered his new education by its evidence of growing complexity, and multiplicity, and even contradiction, in life. He could not escape it; politics or science, the lesson was the same, and at every step it blocked his path whichever way he turned. He found it in politics; he ran against it in science; he struck it in everyday life, as though he were still Adam in the Garden of Eden between God who was unity, and Satan who was complexity, with no means of deciding which was truth.

Today the issues that shape our future have become so complex that they sometimes seem simply too hard to understand even at the most basic level, let alone to locate them in a context that lets us exercise control over them. Think of nuclear power, international monetary policy, the irruption of violent tribalism, the AIDS epidemic. Think of the succession of news stories warning that this or that factor in your diet is deadly, only later to be followed by another report suggesting the opposite.

When knowledge shatters, this invites the kind of adversarial contest that is rapidly supplanting all other forms of discourse. Dueling experts for hire wield sharp fragments at one another while the crowd looks for blood. Without a way of relating the competing assertions to any system of thought that would help explain or evaluate them, people are ready for the journalist's vision of Original Sin. They are ready to think the worst of everyone, including the journalist himself. Complexity invites cynicism, and cynicism eventually leads people to tune out.

Unity and multiplicity, coherence and complexity, clarity and ambiguity, simplemindedness and muddleheadedness, belief in perfectability and cynicism, control and chaos, the idea of progress and the fear of the future. These opposites frame the rhetorical landscape today.

Overcoming Malaise

During his troubled presidency Jimmy Carter made a memorable speech on the spirit of the times. Journalists said he was talking about "malaise," and suddenly public disaffection had a name. The speech was a terrible gaffe. (A gaffe has been defined as revealing a secret that everybody knows.) This exemplifies one of the troubles with social malaise: it is very difficult for anybody involved in political affairs (including newspapers) to talk about. It was no coincidence that the man who defeated Carter was simpleminded. People wanted somebody to give them an old, sentimental, confident homily, even if they did not really quite believe it anymore.

But no matter how difficult it is to deal candidly with malaise or whatever one wants to call the contemporary condition, newspapers have a profound interest in attacking it and reviving the public's belief in the efficacy of public participation as a means by which a community can control most of the determinants of its happiness. It is one of the points at which newspapers' public interest and the larger interests of society join.

I can't pretend to offer a comprehensive approach, but I can suggest a few elements.

Technology isn't the whole answer, but it is part: The modern spirit is shaped by technology, even when it rises up in Luddite opposition. It is all but impossible to escape the encompassing effects of electronic media today, or even to control them—as any parent attempting to limit the movies his children see will attest.

Postman isn't alone in seeing advances in communications technology as a central reason for people's sense that things have gone out of kilter. Many journalists would probably share his view:[7]

Technology increases the available supply of information. As the supply is increased, control mechanisms are strained. Additional control mechanisms are needed to cope with new information. When additional control mechanisms are themselves technical, they in turn further increase the supply of information. When the supply of information is no longer controllable, a general breakdown in psychic tranquillity and social purpose occurs. Without defenses, people have no way of finding meaning in their experiences, lose their capacity to remember, and have difficulty imagining reasonable futures.

He is part right. Technical control mechanisms cannot by themselves manage the information glut, and in fact they can make it worse. (Think of the fax and then of junk fax.) But when technology drives a phenomenon, we cannot afford to overlook the technical means of channeling it. Technology is nothing but knowledge in action. When it comes into being, in an open society at least, it changes the situation inalterably. Simple rejection does not work; it has never worked.

For journalists, the new information technologies will offer vast possibilities. They will also impose their own constraints and have their own significant social effects regardless of how they are deployed. The only way to get them to serve the cause of informing a sovereign people and helping restore interest in the institutions of public choice is for journalists to master them.

In simpleminded terms it comes down to this: Who is going to control the new media? If newspaper reporters and editors back away, they can count on others to be there, willing to shape the future to their own ends, which will not necessarily have anything to do with enhancing the institutions of self-government and free choice.

If we truly believe as journalists that we have an obligation to provide the daily information and education that the public needs in order for the open society to function properly, neglecting this new means of reaching people would be malfeasance, especially as increasing numbers of people begin to use the new media to inform themselves. On the other hand, journalists must recognize that the new technical means of controlling information—whether interactive systems that provide people more choices or software that filters e-mail—cannot themselves create meaning. That is still the job of rhetoric, which always begins with a sense of purpose.

We must resist the cynical impulse: News organizations must begin to exercise more self-control over their own darkest habits of thought. Watergate may have damaged journalism more than it did the presidency. Some journalists made their reputations simply by showing hostility to the President and his men. Those who mistakenly doubted that the White House would do such a thing found themselves discredited. The lesson was this: There are great benefits to be found in assuming the worst—often quite cheaply through assuming a posture—and there are great risks in bringing cynicism under proper journalistic discipline.

Since Watergate, political and policy disputes routinely have been transformed into criminal inquiries. A new mechanism, the statutory special prosecutor, has been created which invites this to happen, then turns it into a spectacle. The accusatory congressional investigation—with all its limitations and its capacity for unfairness—has become standard fare for gavel-to-gavel coverage, which only encourages more investigations. Good old disagreements over the way to build or defend the good society seem colorless by comparison to these battles to the death. And the implication is clear: unless something is criminal or unconstitutional, it is not wrong.

Through all this, journalism has become the means by which, like people of primitive myth, we anoint and then kill our kings. It isn't only presidents who receive this treatment. Very nearly anybody whom journalists help to raise high, they can be counted on to try to bring down.

This has taken a toll, not least in the decline in interest in newspapers. But it is easy to miss the connection, because when the story is hot enough, it will actually sell newspapers. So, one might think, if people want that kind of story, let's give them more. By this reasoning, though, the *Tribune* might start running pictures of naked models on the front page. I guarantee you, it would sell newspapers. And then it would kill the franchise. It attracts attention by selling off credibility, which is like eating grain that should be put away for seed. The reductive view of government and politics may provoke knowing nods in the readership, but only until they stop reading because they've become convinced that it's all a game rigged against them.

I don't suggest that news organizations abandon their role as critics and investigators. Quite the contrary, they need to expand the areas in which they accept this challenge. But I do think they need to pause before assuming the worst, hold back when allegations are made until they develop some credible evidence supporting the charges. This takes courage, because competitors who do not recognize or accept the need for such discipline will accuse the careful newspaper of timorousness or, worse, of having some venal interest in protecting the subject of the allegation. And at times it will mean that a malefactor will go unmasked for a time. But it is worth the risk. Until all the better news organizations realize what they are doing to the community and to themselves by leaping instinctively to the malign conclusion, they will continue to be both the cause and the victim of their actions.

We need to help recreate public discussion: Newspapers should begin taking creative steps to revive the kind of public discussion that invites the alienated back into the conversation. A consulting firm in Bethesda, Maryland, called the Harwood Group has done a series of thought-provoking reports for the Kettering Foundation and others along these lines. After extensive discussions in small focus groups with Americans from various backgrounds, the Harwood Group concluded that Americans have not turned away from politics, they are "abstaining from politics," because the public debate today does not engage or even show any particular interest in them.[8] The intimacy has vanished, and people cannot see themselves in the political system's eyes anymore.[9]

Some newspapers, such as the *Charlotte (N.C.) Observer* have experimented with new ways of inviting people into a broader and more satisfying public discussion, using the newspaper as the center of the conversation, with as yet unclear results.[10] Other papers have looked for ways to involve people at least in the paper's own decision-making. The *Ft. Lauderdale (Fla.) Sun-Sentinel*, for example, has a "reader awareness" program that invites people into the newsroom regularly to discuss with reporters and editors their thoughts and reactions to the paper. In at least one instance the *Sun-Sentinel* went so far as to consult with readers about how a story should be told before the story ran in the newspaper.

The emerging interactive electronic information medium has demonstrated the power to provoke and facilitate conversations, discussion, debate. The new medium may offer newspapers powerful new ways of connecting with people by connecting them with each other. It may be a means of helping to rekindle public discussion and putting newspapers back into the middle of it.

We need to write and edit for coherence: One of the most interesting things the Harwood Group discovered in its research was the strong appetite for "coherence" in the presentation of information about public affairs. A 1993 report described it this way:[11]

> Sometimes it seems that more attention is paid to the quantity and newness of information than to its quality; indeed, people are bombarded daily with bits of facts and figures, revelations about old news, conflicting or unconnected statements about a public concern. People often cannot make sense of all this information—it lacks coherence.

In short, people want knowledge, not just facts or data. Regardless of what the radical skeptics argue, people still passionately believe in meaning. They want the whole picture, not just a part of it. They are wary of polemics, which are everywhere. They are tired of polarized discussion, the "McLaughlin Group" model of public discourse. They want to listen, speak, and be heard, but they also want to be challenged to think.

This takes us back to some of the ideas discussed in earlier chapters. The acceptance of modest opinion in news accounts provides context and coherence and communicates meaning. The discipline of intellectual honesty resists polemical treatment of public issues and serves as an antidote to polarization.

At the *Chicago Tribune* we have struggled to find a simple way to describe our fundamental purpose. The phrase we have come up with is: "helping people master their world through knowledge." In some ways those words hearken back to a kind of old-time newspaper religion, one that believes that knowledge gives people power. But even as we reaffirm this old truth, we also have to recognize that dramatic change is newspapers' future and there is no going back. We must not surrender to technology, but rather we must shape it to our purposes— which must conform to the sound, decent, underlying interests of the free and sovereign audience.

Still, there are many journalists today who doubt that newspapers in a commercial context and corporate form can hope to do this. This sense has become so pervasive that it deserves a thorough examination, because it goes to the heart of the question of the future of newspapering.

(*eight*)
MAKING MONEY
MAKING NEWSPAPERS

AS THE LAST CENTURY ENDED, AMERICAN NEWS-papers had invented the comics, the sensational headline, extra editions, and yellow journalism. They sold for a penny or two, reaching for as big an audience as they could get. A few press barons such as Joseph Pulitzer and William Randolph Hearst had empires that stretched across the continent and exerted strong and unified political power. In the big cities, daily news-papers proliferated—both in English and in the languages of immigrants' native lands. Many households bought more than one paper a day, just to keep occupied or to triangulate on the truth, since few papers felt the tug of intellectual honesty. They were partisan, in that their publishers found their greatest influ-ence within one of the major political organizations. But mostly they expressed the unashamed preferences of the individuals who owned them. Meantime, editors rose and fell on newsstand sales. So they worried incessantly about what the editor across the street was going to play on the front page of the next edition.

As the twentieth century ends, American newspapers have created the op-ed piece, the news graphic, briefing pages, and the "news analysis." Papers sell for anything from a quarter to seventy-five cents during the week. Most households don't buy a newspaper every day. The number of cities with competing dailies has dwindled to a perilous few. Meantime, beyond the city limits, papers catering to the local news appetites of sub-urbanites have eaten away at the metro papers' market share. And editors worry about whether corporate ownership is inimical to the seriousness and independence of the press.

Odd as it seems to some of us who can still remember what it was like to work for privately owned newspapers, there are journalists who pine away for that institutional form. They appear to have forgotten some of its worst qualities: the authoritarian management system in which editors were like children before the powerful father; the use of the papers' coverage for owners' personal needs (my father used to tell a hilarious story about having to find somebody to give him daily rabbit price quotes after the paper's owner with a taste for Hasenpfeffer went shopping for hare and felt he'd been clipped); the way editorial positions were established at the flagship paper and printed in all the others in a chain regardless of how this might fit with local conditions; the commingling of resources so that a photographer might find himself detailed to shoot the picture for the owner's Christmas card; the shameless willingness to give advertisers (and personal favorites of the owner) privileged access to the paper's news columns.

But beyond the nostalgia, what really gives rise to the supposed contrast between the past glories of private ownership and the depredations of the corporate form has to do with something much more basic: corporate newspapers not only make money but talk about it regularly. The old press barons made money, too, but talked about other things.

The basic argument critical journalists make against the corporate form is that corporations have taken money out of newspapers at a rate far higher than private owners did.[1] I do not have the historical data from other papers, but in the 1920s during the *Tribune*'s heyday under the proprietorship of Colonel Robert R. McCormick, when the newspaper's reach became global with correspondents around the world and a separate edition in Paris, the company turned out more profit per dollar of revenue than at any time during the high-flying, cost-cutting, corporate 1980s. The operating margin reached almost 29.8 percent in 1929, compared with 24.6 percent at its highest afterwards. Even during the Great Depression, the newspaper's margins never dropped into single digits.

Journalists have traditionally been wary of business because they have seen themselves as speaking up for the powerless (which, by the way, is an effective way to get on the good side of large numbers of readers, who can be counted on to feel aggrieved). But whether rooted in the drive for circulation or a more deeply felt kind of populism, newspapers have attracted to their editorial staffs a lot of people who feel that journalism is different from other businesses in that it has a soul. So naturally it has been uncomfortable for them to hear their publishers speak openly and unashamedly about their cost and profit goals.

Most reporters and editors see it the other way around. Profit is not the goal; social benefit is. They would probably agree with this statement by Bill Kovach, curator of the Nieman Foundation and a former editor of the *Atlanta Journal and Constitution* and Washington editor of the *New York Times*: "Inherent in the First Amendment freedom provided to the owners of a newspaper is an obligation to provide the kind of public-service information a self-governing people need." The business of a newspaper, he adds, is to provide the funds to meet this social purpose.[2]

Of course, some of this is hyperbole. The First Amendment imposes no obligation of any sort. That is its point. But if newspapers' social purpose is to provide the information people need to make their sovereign choices, they must be independent of government and other interests on which they report. And to be independent they must be financially strong. Colonel McCormick used to shock students at Medill School of Journalism at Northwestern University by telling them that the first duty of a free press is to make a profit. McCormick, of all people, understood that newspapering was richer than money.[3] He relished the business because it gave him a means of forcefully speaking his mind, of making a difference. But he understood that to have the wherewithal to succeed in the marketplace of ideas, a newspaper has to succeed in the economic marketplace.

Beyond that, the market provides some measure of whether a newspaper is successful in communicating. A newspaper that reaches people with information they want and need will attract advertising and, unless otherwise mismanaged, will turn a nice profit. A newspaper that pleases its writers and editors but is not a vital part of the community's life will be a commercial failure because it is a rhetorical failure.

So whether because independence requires financial strength or because commercial success is one measure of whether a newspaper is getting its message through, the question is not whether a newspaper should serve the public interest or the financial interests of its owners. The question is how it can best square the two.

EDITORIAL INDEPENDENCE

Time Magazine, rarely given to understatement, usually gets credit for originating the metaphor of church and state to describe the proper relationship between the editorial and business functions of a news organization. Business shall make no law establishing editorial policy or abridging the free exercise of news judgment. The inflated terms of comparison suggest the depth of journalists' feelings on the matter. Editorial independence from business intrusion is a fighting faith.

And it should be, at least in the terms in which the creed arose. The separation of church and state in news organizations began as a doctrine to keep advertisers from getting control of the news columns. The reasons for this have proved themselves many times over. In the first place, editorial independence from advertiser control follows directly from journalism's truth discipline, which is inconsistent with reporting fact to suit the highest bidder. Even in terms of pure self-interest, news organizations cannot afford to turn their news judgments over to anybody, especially not to individuals or organizations with whom they have business relationships. Newspapers face a skeptical, even cynical audience that has watched the lines between news and entertainment willfully blurred, an audience that has grown increasingly distrustful under the assault of incidents as large as the Watergate scandal and as petty as celebrity singers lip-syncing their concerts. Such an audience always stands on the lookout for examples of advertisers (and others such as politicians who are in a position to help newspapers be more profitable) getting favored news treatment. Nothing erodes trust more effectively than the suspicion of venality.

Holding the line can be difficult. Angry advertisers have been known to pull millions of dollars of business out of a newspaper to punish it for printing something they believe inimical to their interests. Smaller publications have the greatest problem because their base of economic support can be narrow, making any withdrawal of business proportionately more painful. (Imagine the trouble a trade publication for the cosmetic industry might have if it began crusading against cruelty in the use of animals for testing.) But even at the larger papers, painful issues do come up, making it important to preserve and reinforce the original meaning of the church and state separation.

Unfortunately, the metaphor's grandiosity and imprecision have led to confusion. The establishment of journalists as a kind of priesthood has introduced an element of insufferable self-righteousness in newsrooms that has aggravated the journalists' natural inclination to see themselves as living in a world apart from ordinary, mercenary concerns. The notion of church and state also drives toward a separation of function and purpose in newspapers that is much too cavernous for journalists' own good. And they feel discomfort whenever they have to contemplate what is good for the economic vitality of the publication—even when it involves no suggestion of letting money interests influence the editing of the news. This sometimes leads to irrational results.

Take, for example, the question of what regular and onetime feature sections a paper should publish. Typically, the advertising department will come up with an idea. Say, ad salesmen think they can get home entertainment companies to place ads in a special tabloid section devoted to the topic. Some journalists have trouble with this kind of arrangement because on the surface it seems to permit advertisers to select the news content of the newspaper. There has even been debate whether it is appropriate for newspapers to build regular sections covering food or home decorating or real estate or fashion, since these are clearly designed to bring together audiences especially interested in what particular advertisers want to sell. But the newspaper does not violate the truth discipline in these situations unless the advertiser is promised a certain kind of news report in the section (favorable to the sound or price of compact discs, for example, or disapproving of efforts to censor video games). The editorial department may exercise its independent judgment in deciding what to say on the topic, and the advertisers have to take their chances—as they do everywhere else in the paper—knowing full well that journalism is drawn to controversy.

True, advertisers might suggest some subjects for sections that should not be included in the paper, even if independently reported and edited. Most papers would probably not do a section built on the market for sex aids. Nor would they probably consider, these days, a section solely devoted to alcoholic beverages. But the conflict here is self-limiting so long as advertisers know they must expect editorial independence. There is not much chance that a tobacco company will want to be in a newspaper section devoted to journalists' reports on smoking.

That raises the next issue, which is whether advertisers should be allowed to do their own sections, clearly labeled as advertisements and wholly paid for by them, for insertion into the newspaper. Here it is difficult to come up with a perfectly clear rule. Newspapers encourage advertisers to use their pages to put their messages out to the public. They insert large numbers of separate printed supplements—advertising a grocery store's specials, for example—every week. The problem arises only when the design of the supplement mimics the look of a newspaper or Sunday magazine. So even with proper labeling, there are several reasons to say no to an advertiser's section. The sex aid supplement would not be any more appropriate as an "advertorial" than it would be as an editorial section, maybe even less appropriate. On the other hand, permitting charitable organizations to do special supplements for the paper can serve a social purpose. Judgment needs to be exercised in each instance, based on what the reader is likely to think when coming upon the advertising section, whether he may confuse it with the voice of the newspaper or otherwise think less of the paper's integrity when he finds it there.

Other issues also come up. In designing regular as well as special sections, a newspaper must understand clearly its fundamental character and never do anything that conflicts with it. No newspaper needs to be deadly serious throughout, but most have to worry about being too frivolous or appearing to pander to crude tastes. Newspapers also need to draw a fortification around work meant to inform people of the facts and arguments they need to understand to function effectively as citizens of a self-governing community. If most advertisers don't want to be in a section devoted to election coverage, then that section will have to be run with mostly editorial content. If advertisers have grown tired of reports of nationalistic discontent in Europe and the former Soviet Union, a newspaper should listen politely and continue to cover this story, which surely shapes its readers' future.

Finally a newspaper must decide how much of its editorial resources to devote to sections designed to meet the curiosity of particular segments of the audience that advertisers want to reach. If a newspaper devotes too much of its efforts to these projects, it can come up short on its other coverage. On the other hand, if it does this job effectively, it should produce the income to support the basic news report. The trick is to find the right tone and balance, and doing so will mark the excellent papers from the rest.

THE CORPORATE FORM

When critics of contemporary newspaper firms condemn the corporate form, they are really talking about public ownership. The corporate form in itself simply has certain tax and liability consequences and some formal requirements concerning governance. Even sole proprietorships can be corporations, and earlier in this century many newspapers were closely held corporations whose shares were owned by a single individual or members of one family.

Public ownership introduces other, more significant elements. First, it separates management from ownership. Owners have very little direct say in what the business does. A board of directors, whose membership is ratified by shareholders, has a duty to see to it that management serves shareholder interests. As a consequence, managers exercise their duty to the shareholders impersonally. Typically, management consults the owners directly only once a year at annual meeting time, when it seeks—and generally easily obtains—shareholders' proxies ratifying certain basic corporate decisions. In contrast, in sole proprietorships management and ownership usually reside in a single person. In closely held corporations with a small enough group of owners, each could be individually consulted about major decisions.

Shareholder activists have complained that the management of the modern publicly held corporation operates without effective accountability to shareholders. These arguments have grown in importance with the increasing economic power of institutional investors. Outside directors in a number of large and visible firms have stepped up to oppose management in dramatic ways, and this has made the management of other companies more attentive to the expectations of the owners. Meanwhile, in takeover battles the courts have reversed board decisions supporting management's plans to resist when the judges felt this did not adequately protect shareholder interests. Still, public ownership does not and cannot have the same potential for direct, immediate owner impact on management decisions that proprietorship or closely held ownership affords.

Unlike most closely held companies, publicly traded corporations must report their financial results openly and regularly. Beyond the legal requirement, public companies promote the interest of their shareholders by discussing their business in a variety of forums, hoping to stimulate interest in their shares on the market and lift the price. The process of courting investors gives great influence to elements of the business media, stock analysts who follow a particular field, and large institutional investors such as pension funds, whose investment decisions can by themselves cause swings in the price of a stock.

A public relationship with investors, of course, increases the potential supply of funds and reduces the cost of capital. Closely held corporations face daunting legal restrictions on sale of equity and thus usually find themselves in the debt market when they need to make investments that outstrip their cash reserves. At the same time, public ownership can also lead to pressures for short-term results at the expense of long-term performance, in newspaper companies as in all others. Finally, a public company has a duty to maximize shareholders' economic value, while a proprietor may choose to take less of a return in dollars in order to satisfy a nonfinancial appetite—for power or glory or the satisfaction of serving the public interest.

Other features distinguish public companies. But the separation of ownership and management, the requirement of public reporting of financial information, the need to market openly the company's stock, the ready access to equity capital, and the need of public companies to maximize shareholders' economic value are the most pertinent in assessing whether critics of public ownership of newspapers can point to any irreconcilable conflict between a publicly traded corporation's market values and news values.

The separation of ownership and management does not make public corporations ill-suited to run newspapers. If anything, it protects journalists from direct pressure to substitute the owners' personal preferences or individual financial interests for editorial judgments in accordance with the truth discipline. Just as it is easier to deal with advertiser pressure when a newspaper has a broad ad revenue base, it is also easier to deal with owner interests when ownership is vast and various. This is not to say that closely held companies cannot produce professional journalism. Many family newspapers have been committed to excellence and the truth discipline. It is only to say that public ownership has promoted the independence of journalistic judgment by dividing owner power.

Jay Rosen, an associate professor of journalism at New York University, gave this description of the history of the change from private to public ownership of newspapers:[4]

One of the simplest ways of understanding objectivity is simply to say that it is a contract between journalists on the one hand and their employers on the other. The contract says this: Publishers, you give us the right to report the news independently and leave us alone and in exchange we won't make too much trouble for you by introducing our politics into the news pages. Objectivity is a kind of contract between [a] group of professionals we call journalists and the people who provide the plant and equipment for them to do their jobs. This contract arose in the 1920s and 1930s as the ownership base of journalism was transformed. Editor/proprietors were out and corporations were in. So there arose a negotiated peace between journalists and corporate employers. The name of that negotiated peace is objectivity.

Now this tale of a bargain bears about as much relationship to real history as John Locke's story of the social contract. But it does make the accurate point that the separation of church and state occurred at roughly the same time as the rise of public ownership and mirrored the separation between ownership and operational control. This may have been little more than a division of labor as people trained in business moved in, recognizing that they had no particular experience or interest in the evaluation and presentation of news. But whatever the reason, the separation has become a common feature of modern American newspapers.

Management's concern for investor opinion—because of its fiduciary duty, its fear of legal or board intervention, and its efforts to increase the demand for (and price of) shares—has probably touched off more criticism from within the ranks of journalists than any other factor. The need to communicate with the market means that leaders of news companies speak publicly with great regularity about financial issues. They are concerned about costs, and they say so again and again. So are the investors, who compare companies on the basis of how well they manage this variable. Corporate officials talk insistently about profit margins, which has led to the belief among journalists that public ownership has driven them to all-time highs. And they do not talk very much about news values.

Public ownership does mean tight cost control. But closely held ownership does not necessarily mean the opposite. You only need to examine newsroom salaries in the earlier part of the century to see that proprietors watched the expenses, too. And there were plenty of privately owned newspapers that did not spend as large a proportion of their revenues on news gathering as any number of publicly held papers do today. Of course some publicly held newspaper corporations have ruined papers by cutting budgets so severely that they cannot do their work properly. The tug of short-term thinking has to be carefully managed, in part by having a persuasive story to tell about prospects for the future, otherwise the pressures for immediate returns will cause newspapers to grind away on the cost side until they suffer malnutrition that will starve the news values that keep papers strong and vital. This is not inevitable, but the risk is great unless the corporations that own newspapers have clear plans for the future of newspapering and the confidence to carry them out.

The story of public ownership of newspapers has been varied. In some places papers have improved. In some they have been cheapened. On the whole, I see improvement. But whether publicly or closely held, a well-managed company must strike a balance. It must be attentive to costs, but it must not hesitate to spend what it makes financial sense to spend to get the job done successfully.

The ease of using equity markets to raise capital becomes an important factor to news companies in several ways. It helps them diversify, which can balance the down cycles in advertising-driven newspaper profits during economic slowdowns. This may diminish the proportion of the assets of the company that newspapers represent, which is all to the good as long as the newspapers continue to understand the importance of the news values, both to the community and to the commercial success. But if the broader company becomes too distant from the peculiar ways of journalism, trouble can ensue and business can suffer.

The ability to engage in capital-intensive activities—through acquisition or internal growth—may become important to news organizations as they head into a period that promises significant change in the way people get their information. Many newspaper companies have diversified into television and other electronic interests as well as into businesses even further afield from putting ink on paper. And even the traditional ink on paper business involves substantial capital requirements in the way of production systems, presses, and packaging equipment. As metropolitan communities spread over wider and wider geographic areas, more newspapers may want to decentralize their press capacity the way the *Los Angeles Times* has. This is an expensive proposition, as is increasing the color capacity of presses to keep up with advertisers' need for color. In addition, advertisers and readers are demanding a more targeted newspaper. Right now the *Tribune, Los Angeles Times, Philadelphia Inquirer, Newsday,* and other papers offer several versions of the newspaper daily, each aimed at a specific geographic area in order to provide the local news most relevant to the readers there. This segmented delivery also offers advertisers the means of targeting readers in zones as small as a single zip code. In the future newspapers may have to deliver newspapers tailored to specific readers, giving each reader the specialized sections that interest him the most or that advertisers are most interested in making sure he has. All these developments would require substantial investments.

One of the strongest arguments against ownership of newspapers by public corporations is that the demands of the market force public companies to forgo investments that build the franchise for the future. This should not be the case, unless investors are pessimistic about newspapers' prospects in the long run. And it does not distinguish the public and privately held corporation from one another. Unless the reason for an investment makes economic sense, owners of closely held companies should balk at it, too, if they don't look upon the enterprise as a form of philanthropy.

This leads to the final distinction. A proprietor might be willing to take less of a return than he otherwise might in order to promote the public interest. A manager of a public company has a duty to maximize shareholder value and so cannot accept less. But in order for a proprietorship to be better at serving public values, the owner must not only be charitable with his money, he has to be willing to use it selflessly rather than simply to promote his own causes. He must himself adopt the news values, even when adherence to them does damage to his own interests. There have been such people, of course. And there may be a few such people today. But the future of the newspaper, as vital as it is to the future of society, cannot be allowed to depend on charity.

The Spending Decision

Here is another way of putting the point: The future of news-papers is most secure if the decisions concerning it make financial sense. This is an absolute requirement in public companies, where the fiduciary duty to shareholders makes this approach a matter of law. But it is also true of proprietorships, because un-economic decisions can only go on for so long before they begin to sap the viability of the firm. Colonel McCormick was right. The first objective of a newspaper is to make a profit. The real questions are how much return to take out in any given year and how much to reinvest.

This is no place for a thorough discussion of how such de-cisions should be made. It is always a struggle and not always rational. The best guides are prudence and a sense of balance, and the analysis at a newspaper of how much is enough is fun-damentally no different from the analysis at any other firm.

An investment should be made if its rate of return is greater than what is available through other investment alter-natives. But the choice of a comparable rate of return depends on the level of risk thought to be involved in the investment, and that reflects a judgment about the future competitive strength of the enterprise. If one thinks that newspapers are slowly but inevitably dying, that people's tastes have shifted irretrievably against them, then one would only make very modest investments to keep the enterprise running as it winds down, drawing as much cash as possible from it in order to grow in other areas. On the other hand, if one thinks that newspapers are poised for renewal, that the road ahead seems built for them, then the projected return on investments would be higher than under the pessimistic assumption, the risk would be lower, and it would make excellent sense to put money into the enterprise to position it for takeoff. Far from simply using newspapers as a generator of cash for other projects, one would even consider accepting lower returns today to accomplish the things that would create substantially increased profits later.

Several factors have recently come together to produce uncertainty about the future of newspapers: the recession of the early 1990s, trouble in segments of the retail business that had traditionally been a key to newspapers advertising revenues, the fragmentation of the media through the growth of cable TV, and the prospect of even greater fragmentation with the potential widespread rollout of interactive systems for consumer uses. From both inside and outside the newspaper industry came talk of "secular decline." Even if the economy came back, it was said, newspapers never would. Not long before, of course, at the height of the Roaring '80s, the talk was pretty much the opposite. Newspapers were licenses to print money—and would be for as long as anyone could imagine.

This volatility in the conventional wisdom is odd. The recession in the early 1990s came to be known as the worst newspaper depression in memory, and yet most newspapers' profits remained at levels that would be the envy of other industries. There has been trouble in some of our advertisers' businesses, but other advertisers have emerged in their place. Competitors for the advertising dollar have come on strong, but there is reason to believe that most of our customers would like to use newspapers to reach their customers, if only the papers would take steps to provide the kind of service these advertisers require. Though newspapers surely have weaknesses they must work to eliminate, the 1994 performance of newspapers made the "secular decline" of newspapers seem like the report of a death that has been greatly exaggerated.

The long-term success of newspapers depends on how they will fit into the new, fragmented information environment whose features are even now dimly apparent. This is the subject of the last chapter. Suffice it here to say that success will not be possible without a measure of confidence inside and outside the newspaper industry that newspapers can master the new environment. If good journalists look on this medium with hostility or treat it as suited only for vapid entertainment, then it will be no wonder if investors decide that papers have no future. But if journalists put their minds to the task of translating news values and moving customers into the new modes of reaching the audience, they will make investment in what they do much more attractive.

To accomplish any of the things that might be required to preserve or enhance the position of newspapers in the future, papers will have to become both very adaptive and very sure about what they are at the core. The division of church and state, important as it is in enforcing the values of journalism, also makes it difficult for newspapers to be supple enough for the coming challenges.

The Two Cultures

For executives who haven't grown up with it, a corporation running a newspaper might seem like an unnatural act. In what other kind of company would one subsidiary attack the products of another? Or publicize embarrassing information about itself? Or praise a competitor? Yet these are things that newspapers that are part of diversified companies may be led to do to fulfill their obligation to the truth discipline. Think of A. H. Raskin's report of the strike at the *New York Times*.[5] Or the decision by the editor of the St. Petersburg, Florida, newspaper to put the story of his arrest on drunk-driving charges on the front page of the newspaper.[6] At the *Tribune* we have a lot of experience in these matters, since Tribune Company owns the Chicago Cubs. Feelings get hurt when the newspaper criticizes the Cubs or WGN-TV publicizes embarrassing information about the newspaper. But in a company that understands the importance of news values, the tensions are accepted as part of doing business.

That is only the beginning of the peculiarity of management of news enterprises. Newspapers are complicated businesses that must be tightly run in all areas, especially editorial, where the most vital judgments arc subjective and the results often not easy to quantify. At the same time, they must attract and hold people who have a gift for questioning authority, whose first loyalty is to the truth, and who thrive on controversy.

One consequence of these selection criteria is that too few journalists have thought through the relationship between commercial success and their independence to do their work, and this often yields an antagonistic reflex between the newsroom and other parts of the newspaper. The relentless pressure to control costs only deepens journalists' hostility. It would be very unusual to hear anybody in a budgeting or spending discussion in an editorial department refer, even obliquely, to the duty to the shareholder. It would be much, much more rare, in fact, than a discussion among members of the finance or advertising staffs about the newspaper's need to take business risks in order to be courageous and honest in reporting. When I first became editor, I was invited to give a talk to the advertising department. I spoke about cooperation between the two sides of the business, but I also made it clear that editorial was not interested in protecting advertisers when making news judgments. After the talk I asked an old friend in the department how she thought that message had gone down. "They may gripe about it," she said, "but nobody here wants to work for a shopper."

The separation of church and state has unfortunately meant in practice that journalists feel commerce would sully them. Though the situation on the business side is not as antagonistic, it is easy for professionals there to develop hostility to what they come to think of as the impractical, knee-jerk self-righteousness of the editorial department. As a result, neither side may fully accept the goals and values of the other, even though both sides' values are essential to the enterprise's success.

Employee ownership—through stock purchase programs or stock-based retirement plans—should move everyone's interests closer together. But still in large companies most ordinary, individual decisions appear to have such a scant effect on the performance of the company's shares that stock ownership still has only a subtle effect on behavior. (If it had too great an effect, I suppose, we would have to worry about a creeping, short-term orientation as everyone tried by every decision to nudge the stock price upward, day by day. The danger, which I have heard some journalists raise, that editors might balk at playing a story big because they would worry that the market might react badly to it, is laughably remote.)

Newspaper organizations have a lot of work to do to bridge the two cultures without threatening the independence of judgment that is necessary for the newspaper to live up to the truth discipline. Editors and ad salesmen, reporters and financial analysts, photographers and engineers, graphic designers and circulators all need to take responsibility for reconciling the interests of shareholders with the rigorous adherence to news values, because news values are fundamental to a newspaper's business success, and business success is fundamental to the vitality of the news values. As a first step, a news organization must identify what it believes its fundamental values really *are*. At the *Tribune*, this process has been quite satisfying, though it has been very difficult to move it past the top management level and make it into something that reaches everyone in the organization. Discussions of values can also be painful because they can reveal the lack of a deep, shared sense of what those values are, and disagreement over them can take on an almost religious intensity.[7]

The exercise requires an organization to come to some conclusion about what makes up the essence of the enterprise. On the business side, this involves a consideration of strengths and weaknesses, competitive opportunities and threats typical of strategic planning methods in most organizations. The more challenging part is for the journalists, who are not generally trained in strategic planning and are often oriented toward the preservation of what exists without much discrimination between what is vital and what is superficial.

In the early 1990s the *Chicago Tribune* began working out the details of its informal partnership with Tribune Broadcasting Company to produce an all-news, twenty-four-hour-a-day cable television channel. The idea was to give the cable channel access to all the news the newspaper was developing, in real time, and to put *Chicago Tribune* journalists on the air as part of the cable channel's reporting team. The initial response to this in the newsroom was not unanimously supportive. To help think through our involvement, the top editors of the paper went through an exercise in which we tried to imagine looking back on the *Tribune* from retirement. As we oriented ourselves to look from such a vantage at what the *Tribune* had become, we asked ourselves what would make us feel satisfied that we had brought the enterprise through the changes intact? What would the *Tribune* of the twenty-first century have to be doing in order for us to feel we had left it better than we found it?

We came up with a short list. It would have to provide information as authoritative, serious-minded, and comprehensive as the community needed to govern itself. It would have to offer the courageous community leadership that newspapers traditionally have aspired to provide. And it would have to include excellent writing to build and satisfy the appetite for reading, which we associated with the capacity for independent thinking that a self-governing republic needs to thrive.

We did not think it was vital that the newspaper continue to be embodied in ink on paper. Nor did we think that all aspects of the newspaper had to be written (any more than they are in the traditional paper, which features graphic and photographic elements).

Doing this exercise made it a good bit easier to understand what the all-news cable channel needed to be to become a useful extension of the newspaper. And I think it began a process that made us more comfortable about experimenting with other nontraditional means of delivering the news.

I am not sure it is possible to go through the changes that loom up before newspapers today without coming to some fundamental agreement about what they are and what they value. It will be much easier for us to have the confidence to change if we are sure we all agree on what should abide. In fact, it is dangerous to go into the process of change without attention to the core of our beliefs. Dangerous not only because, without a moral compass, we can easily get turned around. Dangerous, too, because as media merge, it may be easy to overlook the aspects of a newspaper that have held people's interest for years. Overlooked, they may be discarded. And if we discard them, we may be throwing away the very things that give newspapers their greatest competitive advantages in the new environment.

Nobody knows for sure how the new interactive media will develop or how they might shape the messages they deliver. We must make guesses about that today, experiment with the new technology, and try to understand how people will relate to it. But as we do, we have to be very sure about our purposes. The medium may affect the message, but the message comes first. Just as with the use of marketing techniques, we have to know what we want to say before deciding upon the best means of getting the message through to the people we want to move by it.

(*nine*)
WILL ANYONE STILL BE UNDER THAT WINDOW?

LATE IN COLONEL ROBERT R. MCCORMICK'S CAREER AS publisher of the *Chicago Tribune*, the story goes, a young reporter from out of town interviewed him in his grand office on the twenty-fourth floor of Tribune Tower. "You have a newspaper, radio and television stations in New York City," the reporter said. "You have had newspapers in Washington, D.C., and Paris. Why in the world have you stayed in Chicago?"

The colonel rose up to his full, magisterial height behind his great marble desk, pointed to the grand view of the Wrigley Building, Michigan Avenue bridge, and the Chicago River below.

"Every day I sit on that windowsill and look down," he said, "with a dozen roses in one hand and a handful of night soil in the other. And eventually *everyone* passes under that window."

I must confess that I cannot prove that this story is true. Perhaps it is only part of the legend. I did repeat it once in a talk attended by the Colonel's widow, and she smiled. That is the best evidence I have.

In any case, the anecdote is surely true to the attitude the Colonel shared with other newspaper publishers of his time. These press barons had confidence that the world would pass in review before them because the press was the principal gateway to people's minds.

But even then they worried that technological change might move them away from the center. Most newspaper publishers were so frightened of these changes that they tried to use their political and economic power to resist the growth of the new technologies. They might as well have tried to stop the change of the seasons.

Although politically Colonel McCormick was very conservative, he was also a shrewd businessman and a fancier of technology who often boasted of his inventions. Twice he split with his fellow publishers, refused to resist the development of electronic media, and pioneered radio and television stations in Chicago, giving both the call letters WGN, which modestly stood for World's Greatest Newspaper, the enterprise from which they were born.

Today again people are worrying about whether newspapers—or for that matter any popular form of writing—will survive the onslaught of new electronic media. Several factors have converged to make that question particularly uncomfortable. Newspaper readership has not kept up with the growth of the population. But almost 70 percent of the adult population reads at least the Sunday newspaper.[1] And the economically successful are the most literate and most likely to read a paper every day. Well over three-quarters of the most literate 20 percent of the population are regular newspaper readers.[2] Baby Boomers have not become habitual newspaper readers as readily as did members of their parents' generation, and this is usually attributed to their having been born in the glow of the television set. The video game-immersed, computer-savvy generations that follow the Boomers cause even more concern. Their elders wonder whether their *only* literacy will be computer literacy. These factors, along with the decline of the American educational system, the growth of an urban underclass, and the proliferation of visual and aural media, raise the specter of a new Dark Age in which most people will give up on reading altogether and return to an oral culture.

Meanwhile, a powerful new information delivery system is emerging that might become as radically different from television as television was from newspapers. And it threatens to change everything. The television networks have already watched their audiences decline as the visual media become fragmented with the growth of cable and video-cassette recordings. Some say that on the "information superhighway" traditional television channels will cease to exist because there will be so many choices that people will be able to pick whatever show they want whenever they want it rather than having to choose from what is available on the daily TV grid. In such an environment the program will be the draw, not the channel it is on. The widespread use of TV remote controls has already started that process by making it much easier to overcome inertia and navigate the TV spectrum.

As cable channels cut into network audiences by going after specific segments (rather than trying for the mass), network affiliated stations have often responded by going downmarket. Local TV news on most stations reached such a level that the *Tribune*'s TV critic described it as a "loosely assembled collage of sex, death and dancing bears."[3] Meanwhile, metropolitan stations face increasing difficulty trying to cover an expanding geographic market in which the growth and affluence take place at the edges. This creates the conditions for further segmentation of the market by competitors. Cable news could be programmed specifically for various geographic segments. This was how suburban daily newspapers chipped away at the market share of the metropolitan dailies. The technology exists today to do this on cable, and the new delivery systems will just make it easier.

In response to these changes, some newspapers seem intent on trying to compete with television by becoming just like it. *USA Today* has been the most interesting experiment of this sort. But others, too, have tried emphasizing short text, more lists, replacement of textual narrative by graphics, and so on. Many of these innovations have been intriguing and useful. But putting them all together in a traditional, ink-on-paper newspaper and sending it forth against television is like a turn of the century oil company trying to compete with electric light by getting petroleum to burn brighter with less smoke.

Every medium has strengths and weaknesses, which it imposes upon the messages it carries. New media do not usually eliminate old media, they just push them into areas in which they have comparative advantages. The printed newspaper will be around for a long time, and not only because people's habits change slowly. The new media are showing us advantages of communication on paper that we never thought about before we began to see the alternatives—portability, disposability, ease of browsing, and so forth. There is a reason why the paperless office did not immediately follow the spread of computers through the workplace. But it would be a mistake to underestimate how much the new communications technology will affect the way we live and learn or to overestimate our ability to predict its ultimate consequences.

THE NEW MEDIUM AND ITS MESSAGE

When metal workers of the fifteenth century tinkered with new ways of extracting metal from ore, they did not have in mind revolutionizing the way people thought of themselves. They did not give a moment of their busy days to consideration of the future of poetry or the possibility of the novel, let alone to the breakdown of authority and the rise of individualism. When Johannes Gutenberg borrowed money to begin using the metal workers' discoveries to experiment with moveable type, he did not think of helping Martin Luther shake the foundation of the Roman Catholic Church. He was preparing to print a Latin Bible, and those who followed him in the trade made a good business out of mass-producing letters of indulgence. In the nineteenth century when James Clerk Maxwell theorized about the transmission of electromagnetic waves, he was not thinking about reducing the attention-span of the average twelve-year-old or forcing political leaders to speak in sound bites. Guglielmo Marconi had no idea that he was about to force statesmen to make decisions faster or change forever the quality of family conversation.

Today inventions in a number of disciplines have begun to reduce communications costs as dramatically as microchip technology has cut the cost of computing power over the past couple of decades. This is only the beginning. To get a sense of the possible scale of what might happen in the next few years, just think of what the fall in the cost of computation has meant. I have on my desk at home an original IBM personal computer, which I have used to write most of my novels. A friend from college who went into the computer programming business astonished me one day by telling me that this ancient instrument had as much computing power as the entire Northwestern University computing center had when we were in school. And the laptop computer upon which I am writing these words in an airplane is exponentially more powerful than that big old IBM PC.

The cost of transmitting data will decline because bandwidth will increase, bandwidth being a measure of the amount of information a channel can carry. This means that tomorrow it may be cheaper, much cheaper, to send a full-length, color feature film to someone's home than today it is to send a signal to someone's beeper. And nobody can predict with any certainty the implications, any more than Gutenberg or Maxwell or Marconi could.

Most people in the field expect that radically cheaper communications will allow consumers to take more control of the messages they receive. When the cheap videotape machine replaced the expensive and cumbersome home movie projector, it meant that people could see whatever film they wanted whenever they wanted rather than having to settle for what the theaters happened to be showing or television happened to have on. Likewise, as transmission costs decline, the customer will be able cheaply to summon up what he wants, and the information supplier will be able to make money without having to mass-distribute his wares.

Beyond this, many people who have tried to predict the course of the new medium believe that it will involve active participation by the customer in other ways. Interactivity not only means consumer control, it also means conversation. As the cost of communicating drops, you can expect people to do more of it: sending pictures as well as text and sound, engaging in remote conversation much more extensively than they ever have before—with their bank, their grocery store, their politicians, their church.

One consequence of this will be to accelerate the decline of mass marketing. Cheap communications means that messages will be individualized and targeted, because basic rhetoric and marketing teach that an appeal directed at a person's individual needs and tastes is usually more effective than one that treats him as one in a crowd.

Targeting also may make it more difficult for this large, diverse country to find elements of commonality. Radio and television helped eliminate the Bible as a text everyone knew. Cable television has steadily reduced the importance of the network evening news as the day's common chapter and verse. Interactive multimedia—the awkward phrase for the new way of communicating—may put further pressure on the social bond.

As I write this, much of the speculation concerning the new interactive medium involves the delivery of such things as movies on demand or home shopping. It is natural that the first things that come to mind are extensions of the products and services that were successful in the older technologies. Television once was radio with pictures. Computers once mainly did mathematics the way an adding machine did. The new interactive medium will surely surprise us as much as earlier inventions did.

It does seem likely, though, that the new medium will eliminate the distinctions among the older media—which specialized in the delivery of text or high quality sound or moving images. On the new medium, everything will be sent and received at once. Customers will be able to choose the mix they want: the completeness and mental engagement afforded by text, the concentrated imagery of video, the evocative qualities of sound.

It should not be surprising in an era of radical skepticism that some people are gleefully predicting that the new medium will overthrow the authority of all texts, finally establishing the audience as the true creator of the message. The idea seems to be that people have been yearning for a way to break free of the tyranny of linear arguments and conventional narratives embodied in traditional written texts. The new medium, so the prediction goes, will permit them to get their way and thereby shatter the author's authority and take the inquiry any direction they please.

But as we have seen, the basic premise is fundamentally askew. People are looking for more coherence, not less. They want guidance about the meaning of things, and the linear argument and straightforward narrative are the best way to communicate such meanings. Part of the challenge of those who pioneer the new medium will be to devise ways in which it can meet the audience's yearning for a sense of meaning. This will require journalists to embrace and master the lessons of rhetoric, because their task is nothing less than to create a whole new mode of expression and persuasion.

Complicating this task is the fact that the audience is a moving target. Young people and pioneers in computer use have been the first to adopt this new medium, and, of course, youth and pioneers are restless. Through television and the video game, youngsters have developed attention spans that it would be charity to describe as flickering. But it would be wrong to read too much into this without critical inquiry. It is always tempting to look at young people's behavior and project it out in a straight line through their advancing age. Using that methodology you would have said that the Baby Boomers would still be playing with drugs and radical politics. To predict whether anybody will still be reading texts in the future, you have to look to matters deeper than the generations.

THE FUTURE OF THE WRITTEN WORD

Every once in a while literary fashion seizes upon the idea that civilization has reached a point at which old forms have become obsolete, the way epic poetry fell to the written word. How often have we heard that the novel is dead? That story has become an anachronism in a random, violent, and meaningless world? The *New Yorker*'s 1994 fiction issue carried a cartoon showing an updated version of the familiar bearded prophet of the apocalypse walking down New York's streets. But instead of carrying a sign, he had on his shoulder a television set whose screen bore the words, "The End of Printed Matter Is Near!"[4] With somewhat more seriousness in 1967 the novelist John Barth published an essay called "The Literature of Exhaustion," in which he sighed wearily about the end of prose fiction.[5]

If Barth were a newspaperman, he might be writing an essay called "the journalism of exhaustion," describing a postmodern environment in which television parodies old, abandoned newspaper genres while newspapers either flirt with devices that have sizzle on TV or pump themselves into an academic self-importance that takes the audience's lack of interest as a sign of moral decay. Some news people even suggest that serious journalism had better start looking upon itself as filling a "niche" market, even though that would mean abandoning the ideal of providing the common body of daily knowledge a free people needs in order to make its sovereign choices.

Will reading about reality become an acquired taste, like Wagnerian opera or anchovies?

Despite the signs of deterioration in the reading habit, there are reasons to be optimistic about the long-term future of written journalism. This is not to suggest that newspapers can afford to disregard the message that declining readership is sending them. Nor is it to overlook the growth of illiteracy—both on a national and a global scale—or the impact on educated people of electronic audio-video alternatives to the work of reading. But it would be an abdication of our social purpose in an open society to embrace a vision of the future in which barbarian ignorance triumphs among all but a tiny elite, the centuries of progress brought to us by the discovery of the written language comes to an end, and we prepare to slip back into an oral culture.

THE DURABILITY OF READING

Consider for a moment the history of reading. Written language first appeared in China, Egypt, and Mesopotamia about five thousand years ago. According to Henri-Jean Martin, the invention of writing "appears every time that a revolution in communications and exchanges prompts a fusion into a larger whole."[6] The rise of writing coincides with the rise of what we call civilization, and each language takes its form from the individual shape of the culture that occasions it. The decline of reading in the Dark Ages did not come about as the result of a change in taste or the development of a new means of communicating. It came about because illiterate tribes conquered the literate, which is an entirely different kind of risk. And the risk increases when the literate begin to doubt the enduring value of their culture, when they lose their nerve.

One way of looking at language—written or spoken—is to consider it a technology, like fiber optics. Compared with other technologies that emerged at about the same time as writing, language is so incredibly subtle and complicated that its independent development in so many different places suggests that it was not discovered at all. It suggests that language's basic components—including the development of the written word—were hardwired by evolution into the human brain. The mind has a craving for reading which, though it can be distracted or undernourished, will reassert itself until the brain radically evolves again.

We should be grateful for this, because reading facilitates the development of humans as free, individual beings. The relationship between the reader and the written word is different from the relationship he has with the words emanating from a television set or a loved one. No speaker invites the mind's independence the way the act of reading does. Watching television is such an intellectually passive act that it is not uncommon to sit there waiting for a particular moment—the weather segment of the news, for example—and then have it pass without ever registering.

Shortly after he lost his election campaign to become president of Peru, the novelist Mario Vargas Llosa gave a talk called "Literature and Freedom." It was an eloquent statement of the connection between the intimate realm of reading and the public life of the community:[7]

Because of the solitude in which it is born, the speed at which it can be reproduced and circulated, the secrecy with which it conveys its message and the lasting mark on people's conscience of literary images, the written word has revealed a stubborn resistance against being enslaved.

. . . Unlike books, the audio-visual product tends to limit imagination, to dull sensibility and create passive minds. I am not retrograde, allergic to audio-visual culture. On the contrary, after literature I love nothing more than the cinema and I deeply enjoy a good TV program. But the impact of the audio-visual never matches the effect of books on the spirit: it is ephemeral and the participation of the listener's or the spectator's intellect and fantasy is minimal compared with that of the reader's.

In other words, reading not only will survive, it must survive. The basic characteristics of the new medium are encouraging in this respect. It requires engagement on the part of the audience. After all, interactivity is one of the qualities that distinguish it. The participant is invited to take imaginative control. Like reading, it encourages independence of mind. As one pioneer of the new medium put it, it has "the soul of print."[8]

The written instruments of general information must also survive, for they are the means by which tomorrow's society will understand events of moment. Having a common basis of information for discussion and action becomes more vital the more a society becomes segmented. Newspapers are one of the few strong, unifying institutions that have a chance of thriving in such an environment. Others are already falling. The cities, which used to provide steady centers of attention upon which to organize a region's transportation, communication, and thought, now have lost their singularity. The metropolitan area, whose central city used to be thought of as a nucleus holding its suburbs like electrons in orbit, now begins to resemble a molecule made up of several cities, loosely bonded at the edges. The mass approach in marketing and communicating has suffered deep fractures. We are learning to celebrate the diversity of people's cultures and in the process may miss what is common among them. We know how to increase exponentially the number of signals that can reach an individual so that his choices will be effectively boundless.

The segmentation of society will not soon run its course. Nor will the double-edged process of multiculturalism, which enhances the American ideal of embracing the many but increases the difficulty of making them one. Nonetheless, history suggests that against these centrifugal forces a powerful centripetal force still draws us together.

American history has been marked by an interplay between the diverse and the shared, fission and fusion; this is inherent in the paradoxical notion of united states. The authors of the Constitution understood the tension when they came up with the compromises that established the federal system, an elaborate set of interconnected balances between center and extremities. Tocqueville recognized that segmentation could be a source of strength, as did Frederick Jackson Turner. As the contemporary historian Robert Wiebe has written, "What has held Americans together is their capacity for living apart."[9]

Though the social dynamic currently seems to favor fragmentation, the dynamic of history suggests that the unifying principle will find a way to reassert itself. This is one reason I see a great opportunity for newspapers as other information media become so split up that they no longer interlink us. If newspapers use their ability to provide specific audiences access to work of special interest to them while continuing to provide a common core of knowledge and harnessing the community-creating power of the new interactive medium, they will secure themselves a lasting role.

THE DAILY WHO?

Not everyone shares this view. At the MIT Media Lab, for example, they think the future of newspapers is something they call *The Daily Me*, an electronically delivered collection of articles that fit the individual reader's interests and that are selected by computerized "intelligent agents" that take material from all sorts of sources (newspapers, official documents, individual comments, anything at all that flows digitally down the electromagnetic pipeline).[10]

Is this the future? Would the *Daily Me* satisfy the appetite that newspapers fill? Or would something be missing?

It is tempting to think about news as if it consisted only of facts, bits, and bytes of information. And the contemporary newspaper does include a lot of stuff of that sort—the stock tables and sports box scores, for example, or entertainment listings. Delivering this material could be tailored to an individual's interest without much loss. No reason to give a person a report on every stock on every market every day if he's only interested in a half dozen (or none at all); no reason to give hockey box scores to people who find the sport too violent to be worthy of notice. But as we have seen, readers expect newspapers to deliver more than useful bits and bytes, and we'd better be careful not to lose sight of this as we try to navigate the changes ahead.

Newspapers have a human character. The first problem with the *Daily Me* is that it does not. On the most basic level, it does not offer any serendipity. Because a human being as unique and complex as the reader chooses what a traditional newspaper includes, the reader always stands the chance of finding in it things that satisfy an interest he did not know he had. One of the most intriguing articles the *Tribune* published recently explained in painstaking detail the physics of how ice forms on Lake Michigan. Now this is not something I sit up nights thinking about. Nor would I check it off on a list of things I'd like to read about. But a reporter with an engaging mind wrote that piece and an editor with an engaging mind put it in the *Tribune*. They answered a question I would never have asked, and I am grateful now that they did.

I used to have a secretary who went through dozens of newspapers and magazines every week and clipped out pieces that she thought would interest me. She knew I liked jazz music and novels. She knew which writers I knew and liked, which I despised. She knew I was interested in the U.S. Supreme Court. And so on. This was a very handy service. I got a kick out of glancing through the clips every day. On subjects of intense or immediate interest, I was happy to be able to read as much as she could find. It was also fun to see what she thought would interest me. But I also needed to read a newspaper. The clipping service was too much like looking in a mirror when what I needed was a window onto the world.

So why not just program serendipity into the computers that edit the *Daily Me*? We could introduce elements of chance into their selection criteria to include pieces from outside the reader's usual areas of interest. Wouldn't that do the trick? I don't think so.

People come to a newspaper craving a unifying human presence: the narrator in a piece of fiction, the guide who knows the way, or the colleague whose views one values. They want a synthesizer who can pull a world together from the fragments.

When people become immersed in the new technology, it is easy for them to forget that interactivity is just a fancy word for conversation. And conversation includes elements that go way beyond the words. There is voice, for example, the quality that helps identify a speaker so we can evaluate what he says. The words themselves usually mean more than they say, too, because together they project emotion, personality, and even character. A newspaper communicates all of this. And people expect it to.

As we have seen, readers don't just want random snatches of information flying at them from out of the ether. They want information that hangs together, makes sense, has some degree of order to it. They want knowledge rather than just facts, perhaps even a little wisdom.

They expect personality, too. I don't mean celebrity. Big-name columnists have something to do with the personality of a paper, but they're only one part of it. A newspaper's voice isn't a solo. It is more like a chorus, but still unmistakable. Like Sir Georg Solti's Chicago Symphony Orchestra or Miles Davis's great quintet.

They want to get a sense of character. They want their newspaper to stand for something. This begins with honesty and the related news values. But it also may include such qualities as compassion, tough-mindedness, moral courage, and even perhaps a bit of stubbornness. A little civility would be welcome these days, too. Character is vital to the future of newspapers, no matter how we deliver them, because it is the truest and most durable source of credibility.

And people want leadership. The *Daily Me* can't provide it, because it does not reach any community. It is private. Inward-looking. Lonely.

The advocates of the *Daily Me* recognize that this is a problem. Their answer is to let readers tell their electronic agents to give them some stories that are picked for other readers. Thus I might ask to see all or some of the *Daily You*. Or I might ask for a selection of stories selected for people on my block or in my town or my company.

Ultimately, readers will probably want the choices of people who make interesting choices. Those we will call editors. At this point we are so close to the old model that it would be a good bit simpler for the electronic reader just to ask for the *Chicago Tribune* or *Washington Post* or *Atlanta Constitution* or *Los Angeles Times*, knowing that it will include a mix of pieces and will engage other people I know or would like to know.

Newspapers not only serve but also create their communities. And then they lead them. I do not know how the solipsistic *Daily Me* could hope to do that. And yet the new interactive medium can be a powerful tool in this regard. If there is one thing that is already apparent about the new online services it is the strong public yearning for community. Product of a fragmented age, this new medium seems to appeal to its audience in large part because of the way it pulls people together. On it you can find communities of folks who could probably not find one another through any other means. Cruise the Internet and you will come across an awful lot of chatter over the back fence—though the parties to the discussion may be thousands of miles apart and may not have even known the other participants existed until they showed up in the same virtual space.

Newspapers grow out of the soil of community. They have always been a kind of *Daily We*. They should capitalize upon this communal element as they attempt to harness the power of the interactive medium. The fragmentation of society makes people uncomfortable. They need to have new ways of finding one another and connecting. They need something to build conversations on. That is what the common, traditional newspaper has always provided.

Whether delivered on paper or electronically, the newspaper must have human editors. It must continue to embody the complexities of human personality, to demonstrate judgment and character, to have a distinctive voice that relates well to the community it serves. All these elements come together in what the marketers like to call brand identity, which in a fragmented, targeted environment will be vital to differentiating one source of information from another.

THE ELECTRONIC NEWSPAPER

What might a tightly targeted, electronic newspaper be like? It would consist of text, full-motion color video, and sound. It would permit readers both to skim the surface and to go deeply into the subjects they are most interested in—by calling up the full text of a speech, for example, or a video of it being delivered, background information about a murder case or detailed maps and demographic statistics about a country in crisis. The electronic newspaper would eliminate television's competitive advantages of speed and vividness. Some students of the emerging interactive medium argue that it will usher in a newspaper renaissance.[11] I am encouraged that it might, but this will only happen if newspapers today start building the skills in video and audio news gathering and presentation that the new medium will require them to master.

If I am right about what people expect from newspapers, any electronic newspaper must begin with a general news report that gives the editors' best judgment of what basic information a member of the community should know each day plus some items that are just plain intriguing. This core newspaper could be edited a lot more tightly than it is today, something akin to the basic report in one of the British national papers perhaps. Then there would be add-ons edited specifically to satisfy a certain set of interests. The sports fan would get much more sports than an arts aficionado. The business reader would get much more complete financial tables than the entertain-

ment junkie. There would be regular segments for people with
kids or who want to see the world through kids' eyes. There
would be health and fitness reports for those so inclined; food
reports to fill up those who are not. All sorts of things.

But each would include information selected by editors
whose job it is to present a coherent report of the particular subject matter. And all would be coherent with the core report in
their tone and approach.

Then, too, there would be an automatic clipping service
like the *Daily Me*, not to replace the general, edited paper, but
to supplement it. The people at MIT are not wrong. In fact what
they are working on will surely be part of our information future. The point is, they are only part right.

The profusion of choices presented to people will make
the function of those who help make those choices more secure, not less. When people can get any information available
anywhere, they will need ways to simplify the selection process. They will need to establish time-saving habits. And they
will need ways to create meaning from the muddle.

This is one reason brand names have power. Out of the
welter of products on a supermarket shelf, a few stand out because of their comfortable familiarity. In the new supermarket
of news the same will be true. Organizations with the most
powerful brand loyalty—earned by staying close to their communities and by adhering strictly to proper news values—will
be the ones that thrive.

Again, a newspaper that wants to survive the changes in
the way information gets delivered will have to hold steadfastly
to the need to provide a comprehensive and coherent daily report of the things people need to know in order to live in an
increasingly complicated world. I do not think this is likely
to become a society modeled on the specialty magazine rack, a
narcissistic place where we are willing to learn only about that
which we already know, be it straight-ahead jazz, not so straight
sex, or skiing in the Rockies. Human nature drives people to
take an interest in that which they do not know. Whether in
hope, despair, or jealousy, their eyes are attracted to that which
is beyond them. As e. e. cummings described this deep instinct

in human nature: "listen: there's a hell of a good universe next door; let's go."[12]

The new interactive medium both threatens the status quo and promises an exciting new way of learning about the world. I understand the fears of those who worry that it may do damage to the way we think and govern ourselves, but this is no time to retreat to the monastery and pine away for the past. It is better to look for a renaissance.

The newspaper business is more thrilling today than it has ever been, because the challenge is so great and so much is at stake. If we are clever enough and quick enough, we will find a way to use the new medium to attract an audience by giving it information that matters. If we keep our news values straight, we can continue to make a profit helping society remain open and strong.

NOTES

INTRODUCTION

1. See "Timeless Values: Staying True to Journalistic Principles in the Age of New Media," prepared for the American Society of Newspaper Editors by the Harwood Group (1995).

CHAPTER ONE

1. Carl von Clausewitz, *On War*, ed. and trans. Michael Howard and Peter Paret (Princeton: Princeton University Press, 1976), 108.

2. James Agee (with photographs by Walker Evans), *Let Us Now Praise Famous Men* (Boston: Houghton Mifflin Co., 1941), 234–35.

3. Walter Lippmann, *Public Opinion* (1922; reprint, New York: The Free Press, 1965), 229.

4. *National Lampoon Sunday Newspaper Parody*, conceived and edited by P. J. O'Rourke (1978).

5. Edwin Emery, *The Press in America*, 2nd Edition (Englewood Cliffs, N.J.: Prentice-Hall, Inc., 1962), 374.

6. Michael Crichton, "The Mediasaurus: Today's Mass Media Is Tomorrow's Fossil Fuel," *Wired* (September/October 1993), 57–58.

7. Unpublished "Report of July 1992 *Chicago Tribune* Staff Review Group on Improving Accuracy Through Better Writing."

8. For a useful discussion of the problems inherent in the idea of journalistic objectivity, see Theodore L. Glasser, "Objectivity and News Bias," in *Philosophical Issues in Journalism*, ed. Elliot D. Cohen (New York: Oxford University Press, 1992), 176.

9. Gay Talese, *The Kingdom and the Power* (New York: World Publishing Co., New American Library, 1969), 314–16, 330.

10. C. D. B. Bryan, *Friendly Fire* (New York: G. P. Putnam's Sons, 1976).

11. *Ibid.*, 118.

12. Janet Malcolm, "The Silent Woman–III," *New Yorker*, 23 & 30 August 1993, 138, republished as *The Silent Woman: Sylvia Plath and Ted Hughes* (New York: Alfred A. Knopf, 1994).

13. Daniel J. Boorstin, *The Image: A Guide to Pseudo-Events in America* (1961; reprint, New York: Harper Colophon Books, 1964).

14. Michael Kelly, "The Game," *The New York Times Magazine*, 31 October 1993, 65.

15. This useful analytic tool is set forth in Stephen Klaidman and Tom L. Beauchamp, *The Virtuous Journalist* (New York: Oxford University Press, 1987), 32–34.

16. John Rawls, *A Theory of Justice* (Cambridge: Harvard University Press, Belknap Press, 1971).

17. Donald L. Barlett and James B. Steele, *America: What Went Wrong?* (Kansas City: Andrews and McMeel, 1992).

18. *Ibid.*, xvi.

19. *Ibid.*, 108.

20. Clifford Winston, "Economic Deregulation: Days of Reckoning for Microeconomists," *Journal of Economic Literature* 31 (September 1993), 1263.

21. See Klaidman and Beauchamp, *The Virtuous Journalist*, 103ff., for examples of the danger of reporting that does not follow the discipline of intellectual honesty.

CHAPTER TWO

1. Peter Kihss, "Debate on Exposé Held Up a Pulitzer," *New York Times*, 8 April 1979, Section 2.

2. Sissela Bok, *Lying: Moral Choice in Public and Private Life* (New York: Pantheon, 1978), 105. I am indebted to Bok's very useful book for many of the insights in this chapter beyond those specifically noted.

3. Bok, *Lying*, 92 (citing Ludwig Wittgenstein, *Philosophical Investigations*, ed. G. E. M. Anscombe (New York: Macmillan Co., 1953), par. 265 (p. 93e).

4. Carl Bernstein and Bob Woodward, *All the President's Men* (New York: Simon and Schuster, 1974), 173.

5. Bok, *Lying*, 121.

6. Janet Malcolm, *The Journalist and the Murderer* (1990; reprint, New York: Vintage Books, 1990).

7. See chapter 5, p. 139.

8. *Near v. Minnesota*, 238 U.S. 697 (1931).

9. *New York Times Company v. United States*, 403 U.S. 713 (1971).

10. Alexander Bickel, *The Morality of Consent* (New Haven: Yale University Press, 1975), 57–88.

11. *Ibid.*, 82.

CHAPTER THREE

1. Karl R. Popper, *The Open Society and Its Enemies*, vol. 1: *Plato*, 5th Edition (rev.) (1966; reprint, Princeton: Princeton University Press, 1971).

2. *The Republic*, trans. Paul Shorey, in Plato, *The Collected Dialogues*, ed. Edith Hamilton and Huntington Cairns (Princeton: Princeton University Press, Bollingen Series, 1961), 575–844.

3. Alexander Solzhenitsyn, "A World Split Apart," in *Solzhenitsyn at Harvard* (Washington, D.C.: Ethics and Public Policy Center, 1980), 8.

4. *Ibid.*, 17.

5. *Ibid.*, 8.

6. *Ibid.*, 13.

7. Neil Postman, *Amusing Ourselves to Death: Public Discourse in the Age of Show Business* (1985; reprint, New York: Penguin, 1986), 27–28.

8. Popper, *The Open Society and Its Enemies*, vol. 1: *Plato*.

9. *Ibid.*, 121.

10. Quoted in Gordon S. Wood, *The Creation of the American Republic, 1776–1787* (1969; reprint, New York: W. W. Norton & Co., 1972), 472.

11. *Debate on the Constitution, Part Two*, ed. Bernard Bailyn (New York: Library of America, 1993), 164.

12. Bickel, *The Morality of Consent*, 79–88.

13. Wayne C. Booth, "Speech, Bought and Sold, and the 1st Amendment," *Chicago Tribune*, 1 December 1993, Section 1. See also Sunstein, Cass, *Democracy and the Problem of Free Speech* (New York: The Free Press, 1993).

14. Mike Moore, "Divided Loyalties," *The Quill* (February 1989), 18–19.

15. Unpublished tape of Military-Media Conference, 20 September 1993 at Cantigny Park, Wheaton, Ill., sponsored by McCormick Tribune Foundation.

16. Simone de Beauvoir, *The Second Sex*, ed. and trans. H. M. Parshley (1952; reprint, New York: Modern Library, 1968), 182ff.

17. Michael Herr, *Dispatches* (New York: Alfred A. Knopf, 1977), 67.

CHAPTER FOUR

1. Cleanth Brooks and Robert Penn Warren, *Modern Rhetoric*, 3rd Edition (New York: Harcourt Brace & World, 1970), 6.

2. *Oxford English Dictionary,* Compact Edition (New York: Oxford University Press, 1971), 2535.

3. Wayne C. Booth, "The Revival of Rhetoric," in *Now Don't Try to Reason with Me* (Chicago: University of Chicago Press, 1970), 35.

4. Wayne C. Booth, *A Rhetoric of Irony* (Chicago: University of Chicago Press, 1974).

5. Stanley Fish, "Short People Got No Reason to Live: Reading Irony," and Wayne C. Booth, "A New Strategy for Establishing a Truly Democratic Criticism," *Daedalus* (Winter 1983), 175ff.

6. Fish, "Short People Got No Reason to Live," 178, quoting Booth, *Rhetoric of Irony,* 267.

7. Fish, "Short People Got No Reason to Live," 180.

8. Booth, "New Strategy," *op. cit.,* 197.

9. Karl R. Popper, *The Open Society and Its Enemies,* vol. 2: *Hegel and Marx,* 374.

10. Quoted in J. M. Ziman, *Public Knowledge* (London: Cambridge University Press, 1968), epigraph at frontispiece.

11. *Chicago Tribune,* 17 May 1990.

12. "Kick the Canon, Part II," *Downbeat* (January 1994), 6.

13. Hume, David, *An Inquiry Concerning Human Understanding* (1748; reprint, Indianapolis: The Liberal Arts Press, Bobbs-Merrill, The Liberal Arts Press, 1955), 159.

14. *Rhetoric,* trans. R. Hackforth, in *The Complete Works of Aristotle,* vol. 2, rev. Oxford trans., ed. Jonathan Barnes (Princeton: Princeton University Press, Bollingen Series, 1984), 2159.

15. *Ibid.,* 2262.

16. Rebecca Ross Albers, "The Best and the Brightest: Burnt Out?" *Presstime* (October 1993), 25. *See also* Alison Carper, "Paint-By-Numbers Journalism: How Reader Surveys and Focus Groups Subvert a Democratic Press," Discussion Paper D–19, The Joan Shorenstein Center, John F. Kennedy School of Government, Harvard University (Cambridge, April 1995).

17. Michael Janeway, "On the Duality of Newspapers," unpublished address to Advanced Executive Program, Newspaper Management Center, Northwestern University, 20 September 1993, 7.

18. *Phaedrus,* in Plato, *The Collected Dialogues,* ed. Edith Hamilton and Huntington Cairns (Princeton: Princeton University Press, 1961), 508.

19. Janeway, "On the Duality of Newspapers," 10.

20. *Ibid.,* 11.

21. Wayne C. Booth, "The Rhetorical Stance," *op. cit.,* 32.

22. See Frank Denton, "Old Newspapers and New Realities: The Promise of the Marketing of Journalism," in *Reinventing the Newspaper* (New York: Twentieth Century Fund, 1993), 40.

23. Wayne C. Booth, "The Rhetorical Stance," *op. cit.*, 27.

24. Alexander Pope, "Essay on Criticism," II.364, in *Selected Poetry and Prose* (New York: Holt, Rinehart and Winston, York, 1964), 73.

CHAPTER FIVE

1. Shelby Coffey, "Newspapers in the 90s," Lecture 28 in the (Riverside, Calif.) *Press-Enterprise* Lecture Series, delivered 3 February 1993 at University of California, Riverside.

2. *Poetics*, in *The Complete Works of Aristotle*, *op. cit.*, 2323.

3. Cleanth Brooks and Robert Penn Warren, *Understanding Fiction*, 2nd Edition (New York: Appleton-Century-Crofts, 1971), 26.

4. *Ibid.*, 27.

5. *Ibid.*, 25.

6. Michael Herr, *Dispatches*, 187.

7. *Ibid.*, 210.

8. Lewis Lapham, "Advertisements for Themselves: A Letter from Lewis Lapham," *New York Times Book Review*, 24 October 1993, 3.

9. Tom Wolfe, "The New Journalism," in *The New Journalism by Tom Wolfe*, ed. Tom Wolfe and E. W. Johnson (New York: Harper & Row, 1973), 5.

10. *Ibid.*, 7.

11. *Ibid.*, 3.

12. *Ibid.*, 29.

13. *Ibid.*, 34.

14. *Ibid.*, 33.

15. *Ibid.*, 31.

16. *Ibid.*, 32.

17. *Ibid.*, 31.

18. *Ibid.*, 32.

19. Janet Malcolm, "Trouble in the Archives I," *New Yorker*, 5 December 1983, 59; "Trouble in the Archives II," *New Yorker*, 12 December 1983, 60; republished as *In The Freud Archives* (New York: Alfred A. Knopf, 1984).

20. Jane Gross, "Impasse over Damages in *New Yorker* Libel Case," *New York Times*, 4 June 1993.

21. "*New Yorker* Writer Cleared in New Trial" (Associated Press), *Chicago Tribune*, 11 January 1994, Section 1.

22. George V. Higgins, *The Digger's Game* (New York: Alfred A. Knopf, 1973), 3.

23. Wolfe, "The New Journalism," *op. cit.*, 25.

24. Klaidman and Beauchamp, *The Virtuous Journalist*, 32ff.

25. In my discussion of literary point of view I draw extensively

on Wayne C. Booth, *The Rhetoric of Fiction*, 2nd Edition (Chicago: University of Chicago Press, 1983).

26. Homer Bigart, "Reporter Rides Fortress in Wilhelmshaven Raid," in *Forward Positions: The War Correspondence of Homer Bigart*, ed. Betsy Wade (Fayetteville, Ark.: University of Arkansas Press, 1992), 9.

27. Homer Bigart, "Raid on Wilhelmshaven: A Lesson in Perspective," in *ibid.*, 13.

28. Leon Dash, "Rosa's Story," *Washington Post*, 18–25 September 1994, Outlook Section, 1.

29. Wolfe, "The New Journalism, *op. cit.*, 21.

30. Truman Capote, *In Cold Blood* (New York: Random House, 1965), 9.

31. Bob Woodward and Carl Bernstein, *The Final Days* (New York: Simon & Schuster, 1976), 422.

32. Tom Wolfe, "The First Tycoon of Teen," quoted in *The New Journalism, op. cit.*, 20.

33. Wolfe, "The New Journalism," *op. cit.*, 20.

34. Joe McGinniss, *The Last Brother* (New York: Simon & Schuster, 1993), 33–34.

35. *Ibid.*, 618.

36. Jon Margolis, "The Last and the Lost," *Chicago Tribune*, 1 August 1993, Books Section.

37. Francis X. Clines, "See What You've Done Now, Camelot Dweeb?" *New York Times Book Review*, 22 August 1993.

38. Jonathan Yardley, "The Rise and Fall of Teddy Kennedy," *Washington Post*, 28 July 1993, Style Section.

39. Capote, *In Cold Blood*, 43–44.

40. *Ibid.*, 44.

41. Wolfe, "The New Journalism," *op. cit.*, 116.

42. Capote, *In Cold Blood*, 17.

43. *Convergence* (New York: Doubleday & Co., 1982; Chicago: University of Chicago Press, Phoenix Fiction, 1991); *Fragments* (New York: William Morrow & Co., Inc., 1984); *Mass* (New York: William Morrow & Co., 1985); *Our Fathers' Shadows* (New York: William Morrow & Co., 1987); *Legends' End* (London: Hodder & Stoughton, Coronet Books, 1989).

44. Robertson Davies, *One Half of Robertson Davies* (New York: Viking Press, 1977), 130.

45. Henry James, "The Art of Fiction," in *Essays, American and English Writers*, ed. Leon Edel and Mark Wilson (New York: Library of America, 1984), 53.

46. Graham Greene, *A Sort of Life* (New York: Simon & Schuster, 1971), 188.

47. Roy Shafer, *A New Language for Psychoanalysis* (New Haven: Yale University Press, 1976), 35.

CHAPTER SIX

1. Henry Adams, *The Education of Henry Adams*, ed. Ernest Samuels and Jayne N. Samuels (1918; reprint, New York: Library of America, 1983), 1067.

2. See Patricia Nelson Limerick, "Dancing with Professors: The Trouble with Academic Prose," *New York Times Book Review*, 31 October 1993, 3.

3. John Crewdson, "Special Report: The Great AIDS Quest," *Chicago Tribune*, 19 November 1989, Section 5.

4. Report of Frederic M. Richards (Sterling Professor Emeritus, Department of Molecular Biology and Biochemistry, Yale University) to Bernadine Healy, director of the National Institutes of Health, 19 February 1992.

5. "Breast Cancer: How to Mishandle Misconduct," *Journal of the American Medical Association*, 20 April 1994, 1205.

6. Richards Report, *op. cit.*

7. *In the Matter of Dr. Robert Gallo*, Ruling on ORI's Offer of Proof, HHS Departmental Appeals Board, Docket No. A–93–91, p. 4.

8. Christine Gorman, "Victory at Last for a Besieged Virus Hunter," *Time* Magazine, 22 November 1993, 61.

9. Nicholas Wade, "Method and Madness: The Vindication of Robert Gallo," *New York Times Sunday Magazine*, 26 December 1993, 12.

10. "Advisor in the Gallo Case Calls for Reopening Probe," *Science & Government Report*, 15 May 1994, 1.

11. *New York Times v. Sullivan*, 376 U.S. 255 (1964).

12. *Chapski v. Copley Press*, 92 Ill. 2d 344 (1982).

13. *Decision re: Mikulas Popovic, M.D.*, HHS Departmental Appeals Board Research Integrity Adjudications Panel, 3 November 1993.

14. Charles Maechling, Jr., "The Laboratory Is Not a Courtroom," *Issues in Science and Technology* (Spring 1992), 73.

15. Statement of Councils of the National Academy of Sciences and Institute of Medicine and the Executive Council of the National Academy of Engineering, Proceedings of the National Academy of Sciences 91 (26 April 1994), 3479.

16. John Crewdson, "'Perky Cheerleaders,'" *Nieman Reports* (Winter 1993), 16.

17. See Jon Van, "Press Blew Away Secondhand Smoke Truths," *Chicago Tribune*, 19 June 1994, Perspective Section; and Max Frankel, "Innumeracy²," *The New York Times Magazine*, 5 March 1995, 24.

CHAPTER SEVEN

1. Statistical Abstract of the United States 1994, 14th ed., U.S. Department of Commerce; *America at the Polls: 1994* (Storrs, Conn.: Roper Center for Public Opinion Research, 1995), 15.

2. *The Yankelovich Monitor c. 1993: Trend Reference Book —
Volume 1* (Norwalk, Conn., 1993), 574; *The Yankelovich Monitor
c. 1994: Trend Reference Book — Volume 1* (Norwalk, Conn., 1994),
622.

3. Robert Penn Warren, *All the King's Men* (1946; reprint, New York: Random House, Modern Library Edition, 1953), 203.

4. William Barrett, *The Illusion of Technique: A Search for Meaning in a Technological Civilization* (New York: Doubleday, 1978), 14.

5. Neil Postman, *Technopoly: The Surrender of Culture to Technology* (1992; reprint, New York: Vintage Books, 1993), 59.

6. Henry Adams, *The Education of Henry Adams,* 1083.

7. Postman, *Technopoly,* 72.

8. "Citizens and Politics: A View from Main Street America," prepared for the Kettering Foundation (Dayton, Ohio) by the Harwood Group, 1991, 37.

9. The phrase is suggested by "Educating for the Public Soul," a speech by Richard C. Harwood to the American Newspaper Publishers Association Foundation Conference on Newspapers in Education, 20 May 1992.

10. Edward D. Miller, "The Charlotte Project: Helping Citizens Take Back Democracy," The Poynter Papers: No. 4 (St. Petersburg, Fla.: The Poynter Institute for Media Studies, 1994).

11. "Meaningful Chaos: How People Form Relationships with Public Concerns," a report prepared for the Kettering Foundation by the Harwood Group, 1993, 44.

CHAPTER EIGHT

1. See Jim Squires, *Read All About It! The Corporate Takeover of American Newspapers* (New York: Times Books, 1993).

2. Joshua Shenk, "A Pope of the Press," *Harvard Magazine* (November/December 1993), 62.

3. See Robert R. McCormick, *What Is a Newspaper?* (Chicago: The Chicago Tribune Public Service Bureau, 1924).

4. Jay Rosen, "Beyond Objectivity," *Nieman Reports* (Winter 1993), 49.

5. See chapter 1, note 9.

6. "Times Editor Arrested," *St Petersburg (Fla.) Times,* 6 July 1976.

7. See Ken Auletta, "Opening Up the Times," *New Yorker,* 28 June 1993, 55.

CHAPTER NINE

1. "Facts about Newspapers '94: A Statistical Summary of the Newspaper Business Published by the Newspaper Association of America" (Reston, Va., 1994), 7.

2. Irwin S. Kirsch, Ann Jungeblut, Lynn Jenkins, and Andrew Colstad, "Adult Literacy in America," National Center for Education Statistics, U.S. Department of Education, September 1993.

3. Rick Kogan, "Whatever It Is, It Isn't News," *Chicago Tribune,* 13 February 1992, Tempo Section.

4. *The New Yorker,* 27 June 1994, 182.

5. John Barth, "The Literature of Exhaustion," in *The Friday Book* (New York: G. P. Putnam's Sons, 1984), 62.

6. Henri-Jean Martin, *The History and Power of Writing,* trans. Lydia G. Cochrane (Chicago: The University of Chicago Press, 1994), 86.

7. Mario Vargas Llosa, "The Power of the Written Word," printed in *Chicago Tribune,* 24 March 1992, Section 1.

8. Gerald Levin, "Playing the Interactive Game," unpublished address to the Newspaper Association of America, New Orleans, 26 April 1995, 3.

9. Robert Wiebe, *The Segmented Society* (1975; reprint, Oxford: Oxford University Press, 1978), 46.

10. Nicholas Negroponte, *Being Digital* (New York: Alfred A. Knopf, 1995), 153.

11. George Gilder, "Digital Darkhorse—Newspapers," *Forbes ASAP,* 25 October 1993, 139; "Newspaper and Electronic Delivery of Information," *Goldman Sachs Investment Research,* 7 May 1983, 1–9.

12. "pity this busy monster, manunkind," in *Poems of e. e. cummings* (New York: Harcourt Brace Jovanovich Inc., 1972), 554.

INDEX

AUTHOR'S NOTE

IN THE FIRST IMPRESSION OF THIS BOOK I MADE AT LEAST five foolish errors of the sort I discuss in the first chapter. They are corrected in this paperback edition, but in the interest of full disclosure I acknowledge them here. I mistakenly uscd "a" rather than "an" before a vowel, used "who" when I should have used "whom," and made a typographical error in the word "extremely." I also referred to Alfred North Whitehead as Albert North Whitehead and to the *Providence Journal-Bulletin* as the *Providence Beacon-Journal*. Needless to say, I wish I hadn't made these mistakes. And I hope there aren't any more.